THE WAR AND UNCLE WALTER

THE WAR AND UNCLE WALTER

The Diary of an Eccentric

Walter Musto

COMPILED BY ART McCULLOCH

ILLUSTRATED BY DAVID ECCLES

TED SMART

TRANSWORLD PUBLISHERS
61–63 Uxbridge Road, London W5 5SA
a division of The Random House Group Ltd

RANDOM HOUSE AUSTRALIA (PTY) LTD
20 Alfred Street, Milsons Point, Sydney,
New South Wales 2061, Australia

RANDOM HOUSE NEW ZEALAND LTD
18 Poland Road, Glenfield, Auckland 10, New Zealand

RANDOM HOUSE SOUTH AFRICA (PTY) LTD
Endulini, 5a Jubilee Road, Parktown 2193, South Africa

Published 2003 by Doubleday
a division of Transworld Publishers

A catalogue record for this book is available from the British Library.
ISBN 0385 604300

Typeset in 12/15pt Garamond Ludlow by
Falcon Oast Graphic Art Ltd.

Printed in Great Britain by
Mackays of Chatham plc, Chatham, Kent

1 3 5 7 9 10 8 6 4 2

Editor's Note

THE WARM-HEARTED, AUTODIDACTIC, ECCENTRIC AND POMPOUS personality of Walter Musto is clearly evident in these diaries recently rescued from oblivion in a family attic by Chris Musto, Walter's great-nephew, and painstakingly deciphered and transcribed by Art McCulloch. This book has been culled from the eleven notebooks (from Philip & Tracey of London's 'Orient' series) Walter filled between 1939 and 1945.

In the very first diary entry, on January 1st 1939, we find Walter naked as the day he was born, bringing in the New Year in his snow-covered garden over tea and a cigarette. It is six o'clock in the morning. Walter is concerned, as he approaches his sixtieth birthday, that the worsening political situation will force him to retire early. He is married to Alice Mary, seven years his senior, and living in East Molesey in Surrey with their old dog Nell. Alice Mary (whom he nicknames Pont) is his sounding board and great love. We hear how Walter takes over the responsibility for Pont's sister Ethel, an alcoholic who is about to be committed to a mental hospital. Walter and Pont do not have children of their own, but they treat their nephew, Clifford, as a son. By VE Day in 1945, Walter will have survived the Blitz and lost not only his elderly dog, but also his beloved wife and nephew.

W. J. R. Musto was born in 1879 and died in 1952. He left school aged fourteen and travelled to New Zealand while still a teenager to work on the land. It is this experience that connects him so deeply with his New Zealand friend Frank Taylor (FHT), whose letters copied out by Walter for his diary are a joy to follow. On his return to London, some time around the turn of the century, Walter was awarded a scholarship to study Chemistry at Battersea Polytechnic while working as a lab assistant. Later he took up a post as a chemist at a textile factory before moving to Yorkshire to manage a mill. Walter served in the Army in the Great War (in what capacity it is unclear, though he mentions working in the Salvage Disposal section of the War Office at the end of the war). He then started his long career with the Crown Agency at Millbank. By 1939, he held the position of Deputy Inspector, which entailed regular trips to the mills of northern England and all around the country to check on the quality and production of cloth for uniforms, and later also paper, rope, chemicals and even foodstuffs. Though Walter was too old to fight, when the bombs started to drop he enthusiastically joined the East Molesey ARP unit, for which he helped to organize a fire patrol. This episode contains more than an echo of *Dad's Army*. Much of this diary was written on train journeys up and down the country for his work. Walter delights in the mischievous observation of his fellow passengers; his hilarious portraits are often combined with a more serious contemplation of the state of the English countryside as it rushes by.

A great believer in life's simpler pleasures, Walter was never happier than when pottering around his garden in the nude, growing vegetables for the war effort. He also took up knitting, and, with retirement looming, in 1945 he enrolled in weaving classes at the Kingston School of Art. He built a hand-loom and set up a serious domestic industry in his garage, much to the amusement of his neighbours, to whom Walter tried to donate his homespun scarves. A contemporary piece about Walter's weaving in the *Surrey Comet* highlights the following: *Mr Musto's formula for contentment is based on the theory that no man is as unhappy as the one who has nothing to do.*

Much of the appeal of this diary lies in Walter's lovable eccentricity, and yet he also appears as quintessentially average as the man in the street – but as he himself writes, 'To be average is not to be mediocre or static. It is to eschew extremes.' His account of the progress of the war, and his harrowing eye-witness reports of bomb-ravaged London, are all the more immediate and powerful for the fact that they are juxtaposed with small domestic details. His diary forms part of his intellectual life, and he reveals a self-taught love of reading, especially poetry – though the reader has been spared most of Walter's own attempts at versifying. That Walter was himself a gifted prose writer is seen in his loving descriptions of nature and the humorous observations of the people around him, though his more philosophical musings sometimes land him in a muddle, especially when trying to impress his friend Frank. Spelling and punctuation have been regularized; however, some archaic or inaccurate turns of phrase have been retained to give a flavour of the original. The occasional footnote has been added to clarify or inform.

We will never know why Walter chose the auspicious date of January 1st 1939 to take up his pen; it is almost as though he sensed the impending cataclysm. What we do know, however, is that for the duration of the war Walter's journal of events both personal and political gives an amusing, affectionate, sometimes pompous, often heart-rending account of life on the home front.

To the memory of

John Arthur Musto

[illegible]

[illegible]

[illegible]

paraphrase Ruskin, there are [illegible]

[illegible]

me a place for the [illegible]

[illegible]

IN THIS DIARY I HAVE TRIED TO RELATE THE EXPERIENCES OF THE secret, elusive, invisible life, which in every man is so far more real, so far more important than his visible activities – the real expression of life much occupied in other employment. To paraphrase Ruskin, these are the pieces of time, knowledge or sight of which my share of sunshine and earth has permitted me a slice. For the rest I ate and drank, loved and hated; my life was as like vapour and is not.

Myself I spoke to
Speaking to thee.

Walter Musto

1939

January 1st

[illegible]

[illegible] early. They [illegible] cheerful [illegible] happy anyway, I thought. [illegible] too much Christmas have [illegible] the fuchsia I kept from [illegible]

[illegible] has a fine bird [illegible] out their [illegible] coconut [illegible] and [illegible] the blackbirds [illegible] almost [illegible] of the year [illegible] last week. [illegible] mustn't forget to dig the last [illegible] ony. We nearly had a [illegible] the sun which succeeds [illegible] house tops, just [illegible]

[illegible]

January 1st

MUSICALLY METALLIC, THE STRONG, SINGING NOTE OF THE chaffinch came to me with the first light of dawn on this New Year's Day. So cheerful, so confident, so full of promise: a happy augury, I thought. The year starts well. The vapours of too much Christmas have passed. I'm feeling fit. Again the chaffinch; I leap from the snug sheets, flick aside the curtains – yes, he's a fine bird, rose-red his breast. The blue tits too try out their little song and perform acrobatics about the suspended coconut and the ashet of suet. The starlings continually cluck and whistle. A mistlethrush and a pair of slick blackbirds diligently inspect the lawn and borders. Bits of soiled snow, almost obscenities, still lying in sheltered corners of the garden to remind one of the icy spell which lingered overlong last week. Our first white Christmas for ten years. I mustn't forget to lag the hot-water pipe at the first opportunity. We nearly had a freeze-up at 'Shieling'.* Red the rim of the sun, which succeeds the glow as it appears over the distant house-tops, just as I slip downstairs to make our first cup of

* Walter's house in East Molesey, Surrey.

tea. And while waiting for the water to boil, I slip off my nightshirt and stand naked in the garden for a few lovely minutes, vigorously rubbing my body and limbs until I am aglow in the cold sweet air – delicious moments. And the sound of bells from St Mary's makes the peace of this morning even more profound. Back to tea-making – a golden cup – one each for Alice Mary and Clifford* still in their beds. And I with mine to the greenhouse with a cigarette. The temperature is 45 degrees. The maiden-hair ferns look deliciously green, yet so dainty. I see the spores are well advanced. The genista gives yellow signs of the wealth of bloom soon to veil this fine plant and the winter-flowering begonias cascade sprays of pendulous pink and white blooms, which are most attractive against the natural background of their own luscious green fringes.

Two Paul Campbells still in generous bloom look wonderfully healthy as do the rest of the geraniums and their cuttings. Thus it is with the *Campanula alba*, fuchsias, chrysanths and the rest. And so, with my dog sitting close, I enjoy the quiet morning, my tea and cigarette, my greenhouse – and my thoughts, in almost cloistered seclusion. Great possessions, truly.

January 8th

A DAY AT HOME, DOMESTIC CHORES, CHRYSANTHEMUM cuttings potted, a long walk with the dog by the river, dark, silent, still. Not even an owl to be heard. Brought my accounts up to date, paid all the outstanding bills and wrote a few letters, one of condolence. Formally starting this my personal

* Alice Mary, known as 'Pont', was Walter's wife; Clifford was his twenty-five-year-old nephew (son of Walter's deceased brother, Frank).

diary from pencilled notes made en route. I must keep it alive. Pont gone to bed and I too now depart.

January 10th

THOUGHT OF THAT LITTLE OLD HEROIC MOTHER OF MINE. ON this day I would wish her many happy returns – all 84 years of them. May her spirit know the great happiness so long denied her during her lifetime.

I like to think it is through her I inherit the God-given capacity for those inward fogs that invest me with a so generous measure of self-contentment. My catholicity of interests and actively inquiring mind must come from a long line of craftsmen of whom I have but scant knowledge. Life for me seems to have been a plant of slow growth. Perhaps because of that it has rooted well. At least its branches bear abundantly, a late breaker as FHT* remarked one sunny afternoon when we sat on a mossy knoll overlooking Tillingdowne Valley: 'You've tuned in late, old boy, but the waiting's been worth while.' I feel it is so. Took Pont to Cottage Hospital for an oxygen injection in her leg to cure her rheumatism, which has kept her on the rack for three months. A quiet hour with the dog by the fire, wrote to FHT thanking him for the loan of a delightful letter from his pen pal Pollock, from South Island, New Zealand.

* Frank Taylor, a New Zealander, and Walter's most loyal correspondent and closest friend, who also shared a great love of literature.

January 13th

CALLED AT XOPHIL AT MILLIE'S INVITATION, TO ASSESS HER affairs with Ethel.* In light of Ethel's failure to take any steps for a proper resumption of business, it seemed fair and reasonable in view of all the circumstances that Millie, who stated her willingness to accept all financial responsibility, past and present, should assume control.

January 14th

MILLIE PHONED ME AT OFFICE CONCERNING ETHEL'S presumptuous demands for money from shop takings, in view of depleted state of the 'till'. I recommended resistance.

January 16th

PONT PHONED AT THE OFFICE, ETHEL VERY ILL, POSSIBLY hospital case – what to do? At 9.25 p.m. I leave for Glasgow. FHT and I have dinner, talk in town and travel to Scotland together, continuing our talk until midnight. After an interesting discussion on Havelock Ellis and his work in psychology he read to me many pages of his account of our autumn season tramp together. Taking the form of recorded dialogue, I seem to appear in it somewhat prominently. And in his diary too, which he started this year. I found that Frank makes many utterances to things I have said and written. Still, there is nothing I would retract.

* Ethel was Pont's sister, an alcoholic; Millie was Ethel's daughter-in-law and business partner.

He's a dear man. He came with me to Caldermuir paper mill this morning. I think he was privately interested in paper manufacturing processes. After lunch together I carried on with my job, he with his, and I left by the night train for Huddersfield.

January 21st

PHIL* PHONED TO INVITE ME TO XOPHIL TO ASSESS AFFAIRS with him in relation to Ethel, who is now in St James Infirmary, Wandsworth, under observation for possible classification as a mental case. Phoned Millie to say we had decided not to attend: it was a matter between themselves and Ethel's husband, suspecting that if he was unable to put his objections on her behalf it would be common equity, as soon as the business, now in Millie's hands, could afford it, to make some compassionate allowance to Ethel rather than see her finally stranded and sunk. I suggested that as Millie herself has a private income and Phil a good job, and that their son's future is provided for, that the matter of her loans to the business was not of urgent importance. It would be a charity, seeing that she would eventually recover the money as well as have a business, to help Ethel out if her husband was unable to do the needful.

Somewhat disturbed by family events but otherwise pretty cheerful, Clifford and I sit over the fire and discuss the discoveries of Pasteur and Koch in rabies, yeast and silkworm disease. Clifford's a good lad but I sometimes wonder if, for his own material profit, he is casting his intellectual net too wide. It's a long way from paper-making to rabies! Hence he must have intellectual alleviation. He's the type that needs it but surely the early harvests are gathered from the home farm first?

* Ethel's son, Millie's husband.

11 p.m. A restful, happy day, the fire low in the grate, the dog asleep under my chair. It's time for bed. Pont's rheumatism very bad today. Tried immersing her foot in Epsom salts and after twenty minutes adding hot washing-soda solution, sufficient to precipitate the magnesium as carbonate, hoping it would be deposited in the tissues of the foot – presumably in its nascent form – to neutralize its supposed acid condition which is said to be the cause of the complaint. A particularly bad night followed, the pain being more continuous and acute than ever.

January 25th

AND THIS MORNING, THE GLOOM OF WINTER, AS IF WINTER HAD never ceased to be. A heavy fall of snow. Decent folk have to talk about the vagaries of the climate – it's writ large in the annals of our people. But, like the thrush on a wet starry morning, an inner cheer compels me to sing. My neighbours – good, naturally – tell me that I am regarded as something of a queer bird, which amuses me. Filthy sludge everywhere makes walking a thoroughly unpleasant business. These nights after work is over, before an easy fire listening to the wind outside, one appreciates the homeliness of home. Tomorrow is Bert's birthday.*

January 27th

MET BLOOMFIELD ON THE OFFICE STAIRS TODAY. TOGETHER took in the view from the second-floor landing window, which is perhaps the boldest as well as the most charismatic of

* Bert was Walter's brother.

administrative London. In the middle distance, the House of Lords and the graceful tower of St Stephen's – now a network of steel scaffolding – crowned with its large Union Jack floating lazily in the cold air. Palace Yard with its giddy circus of traffic opposite the historic Westminster Hall and, at the limit of seeing, Whitehall and the Cenotaph, a symbol, melancholy and pathetic it would almost seem, of passivity. And yet we remember the severest tribute of the silence of Armistice Day and its old far-off unhappy things. And, referring to the political situation, Bloomfield remarked that he found he rather shocked his friends when he declared war to fine effect in the usage of our natural resources. 'We want forefathers of fearless leadership in this country!' Well, I'm with him on that. We need a clear-cut policy for the effective direction and development of our natural resources, regardless of vested and personal interests, vote-catching and the lumbering sentimentality that make many of the younger generation, willy-nilly, parasite on the rest. On my journeys I see the miles and miles of grassland, and think of the wretched state of agriculture and farming generally – positively our first line of national defence, capable of supporting a vast quantity of labour, and organized and financed on the lines of any other big business. Our countryside, where a more evenly distributed population would find healthy employment and creative work for craftsmen – and on the discovery that land had a soul, men and women would find their own. The hardy populace, like the hardy perennial, is so complete and unindependent in its parts that sectional reforms cannot be made without affecting the whole organization. So now a section in some old electrical installation often discloses an unsuspected weakness in the rest. Still, the surgeon plies his trade for the benefit of the patient whole.

January 30th

THE FUTILITY BUG WAS BITING ME YESTERDAY. I SOMEHOW FELT that all the talks with Frank and others, my letters to him and my essays, were just so much lumber added to dusty piles in the national attic, already full to overflowing. I had been reading in *John O'London* a well-written and apparently authoritative article by the academic P. S. Porchovskikov on 'Who was Shakespeare?' I gathered from his article that hundreds of books about the Bard had already been written, many by eminent scholars. Well, if there is in existence any authentic document that will solve this mystery of authorship, it surely will come to light sooner or later. With all the laboured research and argument about and about, there is nothing conclusive. Which brings me to a radio discussion reported in the *Listener* of December 1938, which I have only just read, on 'Setting Farming On Its Feet'. A really profitable discussion on a vital industry, when conflict of views might hammer into people some practical and constructive policy for its revival. It got no further than talk. Still, it was information, and the better informed the general public, the better the prospect of public opinion pursuing reform – especially as the nation is spending £700,000 annually on agricultural research. And it is when I think of these things that my personal futility bug bites harder. What am I doing about it but blather?

Had lunch with FHT, who was full of his own personal futilities, very much on the same line. Still, the best of our abilities are unsparingly employed in doing the work we long since set our hands and heads to. Better a known job done well than another done badly, so we shouldn't take ourselves too seriously. Nevertheless the hankering after some bigger part is there and, as he supported, there may be a little vanity in indulging the conception. The mirror doesn't show it – and, anyway, it's in a good cause. But as Robert Lynd says, 'none of us is intelligent all through' – usually it is wisdom to acknowledge our limitations. Perhaps we set too much value on doing and too little on being.

January 31st

LEFT HOME THIS MORNING FOR THE NORTH WITH THE comforting knowledge that Pont is decidedly better. Her foot still plagues her but she is in better spirits. Phil, who with Pont visited Ethel in hospital on Sunday, told me on their return that she is to be discharged shortly and had agreed with him to voluntarily enter a home. If the transfer can be arranged without waiting it will be all to the good.

At Masboro' on the way to Leeds, night seems to be stabbed with vicious tongues of flame from various smelting furnaces now busy in armament work. Here and there the interiors, like dimly lit caverns full of grotesque shadows, slide by as my train draws away from the town. Our Prime Minister's speech in Birmingham on Saturday and Hitler's reply yesterday seem likely to clear the air a little. In Nottingham today I disown the conversation around me. Confidence is a commodity we sadly need for the restoration of trade, armaments production and all that goes with such activities, while employing labour is the least profitable form of expenditure of a nation's wealth. Well, we packed away the biggest finest chop – most deliciously grilled – I've ever sat down to at the Griffin, with grilled tomatoes, dry toast and a pint of bitter beer. I know that nothing could disturb my equanimity, and that of Frank over here, than a glass of port. One could discuss poetry and philosophy 'til our hearts' content.

February 4th

A SPATE OF BAD NEWS TODAY. ETHEL CERTIFIED AND NOW AT Banstead mental hospital. Poor soul. Made arrangements with Phil to save her home till she returns to normal life and affairs. Pauline* suddenly whisked off to Midd'x Hospital late last night for immediate operation on her duodenum, which is perforated. Went and saw Sid at the Royal Oak, Isleworth, this evening. At the best Pauline is on the danger list for three days – poor kid. This new life of theirs running a pub is a tough job. I expect it has put the finishing touch to some long-standing duodenal trouble. I hope all goes well with her. From what I saw of the place I should say the venture offers enviable prospects. With hard work and good management they should, with luck, retrieve their lost fortune in a very few years. Pleased to observe a still fuller improvement in Pont today. Read something in Francis Thompson's poem 'The Hound of Heaven' which greatly interested me. There is the majesty of truth, eternal truth, contained in it. I must read it again and again. Like Milton's stuff it will grow in me. There *is* something Miltonic about it.

February 6th

PHIL INFORMED ME THAT A COURT BAILIFF IS IN POSSESSION OF Ethel's flat for a matter of over £18 rent owing, which if together with his fees is not paid within the next two or three days her furniture will be released for removal and her tenancy terminated. Tom** having disappeared, I told Phil I would

* Pauline and Sid were close neighbours of Walter's and had recently taken over the Royal Oak pub in Isleworth.
** Tom McAward, Ethel's estranged husband.

help to the extent of one-third of the sum claimed if he could raise the rest and so save Ethel's home. This accomplished, I suggested Arding & Hobbs should remove and store the furniture until she was ready to make another home for herself. Phil agreed to arrange matters on these lines with the bailiff in the morning as Millie was willing to take care of Ethel's wearing apparel and personal effects and offered to housemind her radio set and gramophone records.

February 7th

ON LEAVE TODAY. TOOK PONT OUT TO LUNCH IN KINGSTON. Doctor paid her his last visit and incidentally checked up on my heart, which has been a little troublesome of late. Said it was nothing serious – merely a warning that I was giving it too much work, to which I should give practical heed by taking things more leisurely and reduce my consumption of tobacco, when the muscle that is deficient in blood supply would return to normal.

February 8th

PAULINE'S PERFORATED DUODENUM DOING SPLENDIDLY, AS PONT tells me today. Passport photos taken, then on to look at the looms of the Dryad School of Weaving, to get ideas about the small loom I am making. We then spent an hour looking over the Bronze Age exhibit of weapons and domestic implements at the British Museum. The best example would do credit to a craftsman of modern time. One fragment of fine pottery was inlaid with tin, this from a Swiss lake dwelling. And so home with Bert and tea with his family. Leaving them at 8.15 p.m., I was home by 9.30 p.m.

February 9th

SPENT THE MORNING WITH MILLIE CLEANING OUT ETHEL'S FLAT and superintending removal of her furniture by Arding & Hobbs to their warehouse – cost of removal £2 10*s*. Paid cheque to foreman on the job plus 4*s*. gratuity. Warehouse charges 3/6*d*., everything satisfactorily cleared by one o'clock, flat locked up, key with Millie. Pont not too well today, retired early. In the faint of evening added some lines to my poem, 'Pygmy – A River Tug Boat at Hampton Court', then out for a quick walk with the old dog before turning in.

February 10th

A FURTHER ARTICLE IN TODAY'S *JOHN O'LONDON* ON 'WHO WAS Shakespeare? The Traditional View' by Dr Barrett, Lecturer in English, London University. Having acknowledged Porchovskikov, he proceeds to demolish his arguments with a gentlemanly grace and private scorn. As he says, 'It is only Shakespeare's life which is misty not his poetry.' To me as a plain reader, it all seems 'Much Ado About Nothing'.

February 12th

THIS MIDDAY, MY POCKETS LOADED WITH ORANGES, LETTERS, A hospital pass and whatnot, I proceed on my way to Banstead to visit Ethel. It's a queer world. Years ago, when in Epsom, I sometimes watched the curiously mixed crowd on Sundays in its straggling way from the station to Horton, or some other mental hospital – asylums they were then called – to visit friends, relations. Often it came to me, queerly, that not a few of the people I beheld – if appearance was any index – were engaging in a freedom to which they had little better title than the folk within the gate. Such is the impertinence of conceit.

Today I find myself in the same sort of crowd, mainly hard-working, decent, caring folk, each supporting a share, often no doubt at great sacrifice, of some family misfortune which may encumber him the best part of a lifetime. They have my respect. Following the sequence of family events there is nothing illogical for me in today's enterprise. Yet nobody but a lunatic would have predicted it.

The midday sun shines warmly through the subway carriage window as I leave Hampton Court. Almost as warmly it bathed my garden at 9 a.m. when over my normal cup of tea and cigarette I wrote Pauline letters of good cheer. And now, after sitting for a couple of hours by Ethel's bedside in the open veranda of the hospital, I shall not easily forget the bleak, cutting wind that whistled around me to chill my very bones. However, we talked cheerfully enough. I told her that her home had been safely stored up against her return from hospital and made a list of a few simple comforts to send her. The colour of old ivory she is – a wreck of her former self – but her mind is clear and vigorous if her body is sick. She still attributes her misfortunes to anybody but herself. Still, let he who is without sin cast the first stone. We must try to make things better for her as opportunity sends. The six hours out of my Sunday I don't begrudge.

February 26th

A DAY-TO-DAY ENTRY IS NOT INTENDED NOR IS IT PRACTICABLE. Last Monday 20th, evening with Frank at Highgate. Meeting Davies of the NZ Marketing Board. A very interesting evening.

And on the 24th with Millie as deputy for Pont at Queen Mary's Garden Festival. A thoroughly happy event at which I could wish Pont were present too.

February 27th

FRED* VERY QUEER AT THE OFFICE THIS MORNING. CONSIDERable abdominal pain and general weakness. By midday I persuaded him to go home and took him in a cab to Euston Station, saw him on the home train. Later by phone Laura told me the doctor diagnosed his trouble as gastric influenza. He would be at home for a spell.

Yesterday I planted the best of last year's begonias and dahlias for greenhouse decoration and made a small sowing of blackmore and schizanthus buds for early summer blooming.

March 3rd

I GATHERED FROM SOME REFERENCE TO BIRTHDAYS THAT SOME discussion is about concerning my tenure of office. I intonated, very frankly, that I would be happy to carry on so long as my activities were profitable to the service. I felt that Fred's attitude was as sympathetic as it was wholly friendly.

* Fred Walker, an old friend from college, and a colleague at the Crown Agency. Laura was his wife.

March 5th

A WONDERFUL EARLY SPRING MORNING, SUN STREAMING through the bedroom window. A few domestic chores to relieve Pont, whose foot is still troublesome. I made a leisurely survey of the garden, then declared systematic war on greenhouse parasite life and thoroughly sprayed everything including odd corners with a 1 in 30 solution of nicotine, which quickly killed all visible bugs. Returning to the greenhouse after lunch I curled myself in a rug on the camp-bed and rested all afternoon, and enjoyed my delicious little sleep. And at dusk, flocks of seagulls in formation crossing overhead from London Town on their way to their reservoir dormitories nearby, and in the opposite direction small flocks of starlings hurrying on urgent wings to their dormitories on the high London buildings. Now and again a pair of mallards would fling themselves across the sky in a mad last-minute flight before returning for the night in the river. So low were they that I could hear the reedy whistle of their rapidly moving pinions. A pair of rooks lumbered heavily across my line of vision to the dunes by the Moleside and just as it was getting up dusk, our blackbird, now perched alone in the Norwegian apple, gave me five minutes of his lovely contralto song, intimate with cadence sweet. They were delicious moments to me – and then I must have fallen asleep again, after my Pont had brought me a cup of tea, for when I woke, it was quite dark. Gathering up my bed I locked the greenhouse and joined the others in the house, feeling very rested. A stroll with Clifford later along the dark riverbank with the dog was most enjoyable too.

We talked of my hopes for hand-loom weaving when I retire from the office, and the many things I must do in anticipation of that event. Tonight I wrote to FHT telling him of *The Analysis of Confucius*, translated by Arthur Waley and reviewed by *John O'London* referring to the picture story of *The Life of Christ* by Chinese artists, a copy of which I sent him. An altogether beautiful picture book in which conventional simplicity and beauty of line vie with the teachings of Confucius to offer, that all may understand, a way of life.

March 7th

A JOYFUL MORNING, SOFT THE SUNSHINE, AIR WITH A COOL freshness and vibrant with birdsong.

In the greenhouse the begonia blooms, which for a couple of months were pink delights, now look soiled and sorry. Their charms have faded, but a brave show of hyacinths, dahlias, primula 'Wanda', crowding their respective bowls make a floral home of one corner of the canopy and to follow bowls of daffodils are coming into bloom. Now to work. After a quick lunch with Claude Yearsley we wandered off to the RHS show of alpine plants and flowering shrubs where we found his wife. And here, too, we caught a glimpse of David Lloyd George wandering around, looking much older than when I last saw him, but still very vital and smart. I noticed also among the visitors a considerable sprinkling of choice vintage pieces, more professional as amateurs, than the professional gardener himself. Now here I am on the evening train to Leeds with the lights of Doncaster already in sight.

March 9th

WONDERFUL DAY-LONG SUNSHINE AND MOST WELCOME AFTER yesterday. Saw the film *Marie Antoinette* tonight, Norma

Shearer playing the leading role with wonderful fidelity. It is 1 a.m. I am off to bed.

March 12th

A ROUND OF SICK VISITS THIS WEEKEND, WHICH LEFT LITTLE time for the garden. Yesterday I visited Pauline at the Royal Oak pub and found her sitting up in the desolation of an unfurnished room with a bowl radiator to keep her warm. Pauline, with her flair for management, her methodical industry and capacity for facing up to things, is essential to their new enterprise of the pub. It will require all her resources. And this afternoon Phil took Pont and me to see Ethel, now a pathetic character of the original. Poor soul, she loved the birds, the bees, the flowers and the centipede.

Then from Banstead on by train to Fred Walker's at Waddon. The end of his second week at home with gastric flu. Laura and Phil were present. A great little party of four around the table with tea and talk was agreeable enough to me. I was amused to see Fred's fob with pendant trinkets dangling from his dressing-gown pocket. The showman will remain in him to the end. And so to Wimbledon Park to join Pont at Xophil and an hour of congenial talk. Phil's imitation of their budgie was very entertaining – and then some. Enough for the day.

March 13th

NOTIFIED TODAY BY THE L. L. & GLOBE INSURANCE CO. THAT MY second endowment policy has matured to the tune of £300 – a very useful sum to add to our modest reserves. Had lunch with Frank today who was calling on Dr Silver for a declaration of water content in some butters. Some remark introduced a discussion concerning Jewish ancestry. I noted that the Jew Christ was the world's greatest Christian! It was Dean Inge who stated, in one of his interesting articles, that none of us could be sure that there was no Jewish blood in his veins.*

March 14th

FRED INFORMED ME OVER THE PHONE THIS EVENING, ON MY return home from the office, that he was going into Croydon hospital tomorrow for the removal of his appendix. I wrote him tonight a cheery note of good wishes.

March 21st

DREADFUL NEGLECT OF MY DIARY THESE LAST TWO DAYS BUT nothing of special import to enter. Fred was very cheerful when I visited him in hospital. Laura was there when I arrived. The abscess in the appendix is still being drained. I gathered that if the abscess properly and completely disappears, there will be no need for the operation. Very busy at the office all day and work necessary on the garden and greenhouse at home.

* An anti-Semitic remark from William Inge (1860–1954), known as the Gloomy Dean, who was Dean of St Paul's from 1911 until 1934. He was also an established columnist and the author of several books of Christian mysticism.

March 22nd

HITLER STILL DISTURBING EUROPE WITH HIS CLAIMS UPON Latvia and Lithuania. What a mess.

March 27th

A WEEK OF CLOSE-PACKED WORK GONE BY, AND SATURDAY, direct from the office, I visited Fred in hospital. Except that he is much thinner, he looks markedly well.

There was little of Saturday left by the time I got home. Clifford joined us for the rest of the evening and we talked over the fire this bitter night of paper, sadism, and Robin Hood. And this morning, Monday, with the piping of robins, the song of chaffinch, the raucous calling of rook in the weeping birch, came from the other room Pont's cheerful greetings for my 60th birthday. I'm on the threshold of another decade – facing seventy! Well, I never felt better or more tremendously alive as when I tumbled out of bed to embrace my wife and talk with her, as I gazed from the window, about the birds, the garden and the prospects of the day. For I had noticed FHT to celebrate the event as my guest for lunch and, after a busy morning, a merry event it was. FHT was most entertaining with anecdotes of his overseas pioneering days, turnip-hoeing by contract, sheep-farming in NZ and cattle-ranging in Zululand. He talked, too, about NZ cattle and cheese marketing, his European dairy conferences and the international conference at which he is soon to represent Down Under at the request of the NZ Prime Minister.

So, back to work and then home with a bottle of Moselle under my arm to share with Pont. But 'Life is a chequerboard of nights and days, when Destiny with men for pieces plays'.

An urgent message from Banstead, that Ethel was seriously ill, had distressed Pont, who was waiting for Phil to take us back to Banstead in his car. We arrived at 10 p.m. to find her in a screened bed. Nothing could be done. We redeemed at midnight. A pitiful and tragic affair seems nearing its end. Tomorrow I leave for Yorkshire.

March 31st

ATTENDED THE CONFIRMATION OF BERT AND HIS SON JOHN AT Sutton parish church, where some 120 men, boys and girls presented themselves to the Bishop of Southwark for the ceremony. A simple address was delivered afterwards by the Bishop, which by its very homeliness must have made a lasting impression. Advancing to the Bishop in pairs for his blessing I felt deeply moved when I saw my brother and his little son kneel together before him. Here, too, I met Father Whitlock, a young priest on friendly terms with my brother's family whom I should like to meet again. I met my sister Gertie, who was thoroughly glad to see me, as I was her. She does not look her 52 years. Well, God bless them all. It was a happy evening, which I would not willingly have missed.

April 1st

FRED'S 58TH BIRTHDAY. IN HOSPITAL I FOUND HIM WITH OTHER birthday visitors. He is making good progress and expects to be out in a fortnight. I arranged with the sister to intimate to his doctor that an afternoon of convalescence would be agreeable to the office authorities. And then on to see Ethel at Banstead, more dreadfully pathetic to behold than ever, a mere travesty of her former self. Her eyes were quick dark pools reflecting the mental aberration behind them. Dispiriting, fearful and watchful. Every little noise to her some sinister import. Rambling and often incoherent, there were few lucid moments and sometimes, during my hour and a half with her, the vehemence of her energy was surprising, in so frail and weak a body. Recognizing me instantly, 'Thank God you've come, old sport,' she said, when I appeared to her within the screen. 'Get a cab and take me and my friend Mary out of this place instantly, for tonight "they" are taking us both to a brothel to make a sight out of us for the men. I don't know what they've done with my cheque book but they are charging me up with all this whisky at the bedside, bottles and bottles, and this bottle [indicating a water bottle by her bed] is full of it. They knock off the heads to get at it quickly. They drink like fishes, so help me I've not had a drop of it, but I'm expected to pay. They put a twenty-one-day-old baby, a foot long, in a box into the bed of one poor woman who is too old to have a baby anyway, just to foist it on to someone else. They come in and drink every night from the little general shop just over the way – is it any wonder that one poor bitch jumped from the roof and crashed through my window trying to get away? All these dogs about the place – turn 'em out. The fire looks bright and cheerful but don't let 'em see you go for the cab . . .' And much much more in this strain, including 'doped food'. It was all very distressing.

I held her hand and stroked her hair and did all I could to comfort and pacify her, but I felt all the time that I wanted to take this pathetic, frail woman bodily in my arms and bring her home to die in peace of mind. At the moment I feel the recollection of this visit will haunt me for the rest of my days.

April 4th

THE THRUSH SOLOISTS AT DAWN AROUSED ME FROM SLEEP. OUT of bed at 6 a.m., a lovely sunny spring morning. My garden the chancel and choir stalls the trees, and what a chorus in that finest cool vibrant air. Bustling too, I was surprised to find at that early hour so many short-wave stations jiving musical numbers – about 7 a.m. A quick look round the greenhouse told me that I must pot up the schizanthus seedlings and prick out the ursinias. Then out with the dog to the old lodge by the willows. A hen mallard by the water's edge momentarily looked up then went to sleep again in her sunny corner. And out of the sweet joy that was mine this morning came the thought of many others who might share this emotion with me, and almost in reality there followed, as once the Pied Piper was followed, a procession of happy folk dancing in abandon the carnival of spring, which almost as quickly dissolved in other thoughts evoked by the appetizing smell of frying bacon as I entered the gate for breakfast. And so happily to work with Pont waving me a cheerful farewell from the lattice.

April 6th

THURSDAY NIGHT, WORK OVER AND FOUR CLEAR DAYS' RELEASE from official duties. The going has been strenuous and exacting these past few weeks. Problems and complaints. Problems are welcome, given a sporting time for their solution, but overseas complaints, often without warrant and not infrequently frivolous, are merely irritating and time-wasting devices born of ignorance or perverse officialdom, which, it seems to me, should be handled with less regard to official susceptibilities and squeamish nicety when something like aggressive firmness is called for. As a department I feel the respect is due that is properly the reward for efficient service. It is not all a matter of balance sheets.

April 7th, Good Friday

A GLORIOUS MORNING, BUT THE HOT CROSS BUNS LEFT EARLY ON the doorstep by the baker were stolen. Still, better that than indigestion.

I must arrange for the cushions to be re-covered. My father and his wife with us for tea and supper. The old boy looked extremely well for his eighty-two years and his new wife Agnes – my first sight of her – struck me as a bright, efficient, understanding little woman whom he was lucky in having to look after him. It was a pleasant evening we all spent together.

April 9th, Easter Sunday

A BRILLIANT GOD-GIVEN MORNING, FILLING ME, AS I STOOD IN the garden bathing my body and soul in the sun, with a mute joy expressed for me by the brilliant singing notes of the chaffinch's rippling song. Not yet seven o'clock and the long lonely morning before me.

Jauntily the starlings explored the sparkling lawn, leaving green brushing trails of their quick steps in the silver dew. The thrush and blackbird singing from their respective spray, quite undisturbed by my intrusion, swelled the chorus, while the old dog, in an abandon of comfort, blinked approval from the veranda mat. Reluctantly returning to clothe myself, Old Nell accompanied me to Willow Bridge as the bells of St Mary's invested the water meadows with a liturgical serenity. Like glad prayers intoned, the Mole softly sang its way over the shapely shallows. Later, with Pont, I motored over to Ethel, who happily is greatly improved mentally and, in fact, appeared quite normal. And so back to Shieling, where Pauline and Sid were waiting in the garden to take tea with us. Departing about 7 p.m., they left us with the rest of the evening, which we greatly enjoyed alone together.

April 10th, Easter Monday

ANOTHER WONDERFUL MORNING, DISTURBED ONLY BY VAGUE political dissensions, but the sun shines on – 'Only man is vile.'

April 18th

TONIGHT I WROTE TO FRANK TAYLOR AS FOLLOWS:

The reference in your most welcome letter of Monday to the state of trade on Tooley Street is an index of the universal moon ascending to heaven from industry generally in all parts of the country and confirmation enough of the lack of confidence which has arisen as a result of the world's political differences. I remember, in a previous letter to you, saying that goodwill is the strongest and most permanent force in the world and, in spite of all the present evidence to the contrary, I still believe that to be a great truth. But it seems to me that the world has periodically suffered the growing pains of international evolution. The few whose greed does not swamp their better natures are not enough to ward off these political upheavals, but yet are powerful enough to save the civilized world from going entirely and irrevocably to pieces. A sort of slow relay race between sanity and unreason where some measure of success for sanity is maintained even though many are bluish in the face. Thus humanity progresses over the ages a little and slowly. There is no more reason today to scoff at the ideal of the Brotherhood of Man than when the various great leaders of religion preached that gospel two thousand years ago. Wars don't endure, nor even their effects, immediate or remote. The tidal waves of mad passion eventually curl over on themselves and proceed to the more permanent and abiding levels of reason and good faith – even among savages. So far, old man, I have only touched the fringe of your letter, but a talk over a glass of sherry and a sandwich, if we can find time in the process of events, will rope in the rest. Keep a stout heart always.

April 24th

THE LUNCHEON APPOINTMENT WITH BERT TODAY I HAD TO PUT off to accommodate Frank, whose sister Grace and her husband from York had come to town. So to lunch the four of us. Grace: a woman growing old gracefully, well-informed, humorous and a good conversationalist. I can understand Frank's fondness for her. Her husband, who reminded me somewhat of Lord Snowdon, was more difficult to contact and not until we were well through lunch and after he had generally taken stock of me from beneath his sandy eyebrows did he begin to open out. I think Frank's reference to Santayana and the general discussion it provoked, and the mention of Gilbert Munsay's *Five Stages of Freak Religion* and Walter Pater's work and style,* which reflected the conversation into educational

* George Santayana was a poet and philosopher whose naturalist thinking, together with the writings of Walter Pater, the Victorian essayist, was important to Walter.

channels, drew him enthusiastically into the table talk. Afterwards, on our walk together to Charing X, where we eventually parted, his animated talk was very interesting. I was content to listen. As a professional educationalist he strongly condemned the pastime of cramming, adding that the examination system was a poor bet, that for education to be of any permanent value it must have its proper historical background, and that much of modern logic, especially of the Nazi kind, is a travesty of the real thing – and much more. A very cordial invitation to visit them at their York home accompanied our parting handshake, and so ended a very pleasant luncheon interval.

April 26th

HEARD THE CUCKOO THIS MORNING WHILE OUT WITH NELL FOR a pre-breakfast sojourn. I heard it first this year in mid-Surrey on Saturday. And with the visiting cuckoo comes, in this morning's paper, the Simon Cuckoo* to lay an enormous egg in the taxpayers' nest. Heigh-ho, what times we live in.

April 28th

VERY BUSY DAY AT OFFICE, HOME LATE, BUT IN TIME TO HAVE half an hour with Doris** who had been spending the afternoon at Shieling. She seemed thinner and looked better than when I saw her some months ago. I thanked her for her birthday gift of books, especially Richard Church's *The Porch*, which I had enjoyed so much. Later I saw her off at Hampton Court station.

* Sir John Simon, the Lord Chancellor, had introduced a new Purchase Tax. ** Clifford's fiancée.

April 30th

A QUIETLY HAPPY DAY AT HOME WITH PONT. OUR GOOD FRIENDS Bob and Betty called in the morning. Bob's salary maximum has been raised to £900 p.a., with annual increments of £50. From £300 at the CAS to £900 under the SCC in half a dozen years is good going. But the job's worth it and he's holding it down. I think a good career is assured him. He'll need it! Arranged for my print cushions to be sent to Dave Fender's for remaking.

May 3rd

WROTE FRANK TONIGHT AS FOLLOWS:

I've given some thought to the proposal you made to me over the phone yesterday in connection with your speeches at the forthcoming Dresden Conference, and while with you, I feel that we should do something more than merely discuss and write among ourselves about a matter of much vital importance as a return to international spiritual sanity, to adherence to a code commonly accepted by peoples with any pretence to ethical culture. Yet in a country where political and official integrity is a travesty of the real thing, the probability of even the most innocent of public utterances being wilfully distorted is full of potential danger, if not to the speaker, most certainly to his foreign friends and hosts.*

* This is probably the international conference mentioned earlier at which Frank had been asked to represent New Zealand. Frank appears to have been involved in representing the interests of the New Zealand farming industry, and to have suggested to his friend that he would use this as an opportunity to speak out against the Nazi regime while on German soil – and Walter's advice is appeasement!

No, old pal, I would counsel a policy of the 'greatest prudence'. There is so much that one would more effectively do here and with the million more acres to go into cultivation, quite possibly some opening with present stuff in which one sympathizes may find practical and effective expression. We are, both of us, quixotic, but I imagine that even the old Don himself, with all his romanticism, would hesitate at this juncture to tilt at the swastika windmill. If war doesn't come, and I don't think it will, the slow presence of business needs will eventually save the situation, and with it will come, I hope, some appreciation of spiritual values as ballast to human progress. But here, in our own country where some semblance of spiritual and ethical values still resides, is the culture from which the leaven can best work, and work it will in due course.

May 7th

ALREADY ONE WEEK OF THE MONTH GONE. FROM THE 1ST TO the end of the week in Yorkshire on official business and a record week of work done. Pressing invitations from my work associates Phil Gaunt, Charles Harmsworth – his mayoral year in Pudsey – and Steven Benedsall, for pleasant talk over lunch or dinner and for garden inspections, which for presence of work I had tactfully to decline under promise of acceptance at some more opportune date. But, 'the job's the job, still', and indeed I'm lucky not to be on the retired list. I was grateful for the weekend and, with it, rest in my own home and garden when, for relaxation, I can leisurely employ myself to the exclusion of all threatening official obsessions. To have Clifford to ourselves for a long weekend was, I think, as enjoyable to him as it was to us. Having planned to marry Doris next spring, the first refusal of a bungalow at Dartford, on which they seem to have set their hearts, makes its earliest purchase imperative.

From their account of it, it would appear to be an excellent bargain and suited to their modest needs. So why not an earlier wedding and live in it? But funds which would be available by spring for the great adventure have not yet accumulated sufficiently. After our pleasant Sunday evening visitors, the Hooks, had gone, Cliff and I talked frankly about ways and means. By assisting him with half of his 10 per cent first payment on the £600 purchase price as a wedding present in advance, I thought they could carry on without undue strain on their financial resources. With Pont's approval a cheque for £30 was handed over to him on Monday morning. I hope that sometime he too will be able truthfully and gratefully to say – with me,

My cottage with its garden trim
Abiding joy attends,
Where homely is the hearth that burns
And brooding care to laughter turns
To win the love of friends.

May 13th

SATURDAY AGAIN WITH US, AFTER A HECTIC WEEK OF OFFICIAL chores, but everything going well. A scratch lunch with Frank in the morning and Fred and Laura off to Eastbourne on Tuesday to recuperate till the end of the month. The garden, in back and front, is altogether delightful and much admired. The middle bed of crimson tulips and cloth-of-gold wallflowers is in Hampton Court's best tradition. A misty blue fringe of forget-me-nots makes a rare foil to the vivid green of the almost perfect lawn. The promise of the roses is a joy to anticipate. The rockery is just a wealth of colour, and above it the purple-red mary cascades and displays its bloom.

May 15th

MET THE CHIEF SCIENTIST OF THE *DISCOVERY* EXPEDITIONS, which, after two years' research on whaling and whales in the Antarctic, had just returned. It seems a pity such expeditions cannot go on indefinitely, or at least periodically, but apparently the industry which, with the help of the Falkland Islands, had financed the expeditions had come to the end of its resources. Surely matters such as this are the case of the whole world. Reflecting this during the conversation, my enthusiasm for the cause was in danger of outdoing my prudence when I answered a willingness to serve in any capacity in the event of another expedition of its kind being arranged!

May 17th

WROTE FRANK TODAY AS FOLLOWS:

This morning on my way to Kings X, looking at an Ovaltine poster in Leicester Square underground station, of a bonny lass, the picture of health, standing alone effortlessly, in the full vigour of youth through the countryside, I fell to thinking that her perceived delights had little to do with the beauty in or about her, but rather with that abundant vitality which found expression in her urgent need of learning to live physically. This I think must be the time of the many funny folk of both sexes to whom walking or hiking is the main, or perhaps only, objective. So often have I found their like to be inexcusably uninformed of the countryside – birds, trees, nature's signs and tokens. I feel that although I can no longer set out with their youthful abandonment to the sensual enjoyment of their physical powers, the delightful compensation for waning youth comes in increasing

Truly if you cannot make the world what you want it, You can think it so.

refinement of perception. I think I have said that the written word is our oldest and most enduring monument, but the spoken word has to come first and I am inclined to think that the development of organized language – speech – grew with and out of the need for better dissection in the first glimmerings of organized agriculture, the flocking of sheep, the herding of cattle, at the time perhaps when families were coalescing into the first social units and the more resourceful nomads developed into craftsmen of the field, the land, of tools and tribal management. Youth is seldom concerned with such reflections, but the simple beauty in the graceful vigour of the happy face of my station poster pulled the trigger for such of mine as I have set down for your entertainment and my own, arguably to occupy my time between London and Peterboro, en route for Leeds, my newspaper retaining still its virgin folds.

May 19th

WEDNESDAY, IN THE HEAVY WOOLLEN DISTRICT OF YORKSHIRE, was a day of bitter NE winds, the parching wind of Milton's 'Hyadus', and in my abbreviated summer underwear my legs were cold to the thighs. But a hot bath in the evening and long pants the next day remedied that. Today is the warmest of the week and promises continual and settled weather. At this distance from home it is especially pleasing to contemplate my weekend in the garden. Lunching with Chas. Harmsworth and his family in their fine old home in Pudsey – he is mayor this year – I was given a leisurely tour of their extensive garden. Lunch itself, apart from the delicious food, was a delightful event and quickly the four of us were in animated conversation that never fluffed until after coffee in the lounge when my host intimated his intention of conducting me around the garden in a tour of inspection while the ladies made ready to depart elsewhere. Mrs CH, matronly beautiful, is a woman of considerable charm and conversational ability and her daughter, too, of quick intelligence, with an engaging naturalness. We discussed at some length Phillis Bloome's work *The Mortal Storm*, which drew from me some reference to Louis Golding's *The Jew Problem*, to which the former is some sort of signal, all of which naturally led to the Hitler regime in Germany, and the larger and more fundamental issues involved, and finally to spiritual and ethical values.

And so we wandered in and out, up and down and round about, discussing this and that and generally comparing notes and finally I came away with a couple of pots of some seasonal and usable nasturtiums and cuttings of border carnations so that official Pudsey might be represented in my garden. A thoroughly pleasant break in the week's work. Very different is Charles Harmsworth, also a woollen and worsted manufacturer, from the fire-eating old Yorkshire baron Emmanuel Hoyle who passed away at Longwood a fortnight ago. He was reported in a South African newspaper as having said in a speech at some dinner that were it not for Prospect Mill half the British Navy would go naked.

I remember some years ago Sir Emmanuel threw out a challenge to me in respect of some serge I recycled, that it was not possible to dye it pure indigo. He even took the trouble to telephone to London to tell me so. I told him to send some pieces to a dyer, whom I would nominate, as a test, and that I would stand or fall by the result of his examination of the pieces on their return. I remained standing! In him Yorkshire has lost a son of force and character and, notwithstanding, personality.

May 21st

A HOMELY DAY, MOSTLY OCCUPIED IN RESTING IN MY GARDEN and quietly enjoying its beauty with Pont. Looking idly over the notes for the week, I am reminded of other Yorkshire friends. Recalling my early inspection days, I think of the Marsden brothers, five of whom worked together as a well-regulated team in the conduct of the cloth-dyeing and brushing industries of the Yorkshire Scarlet and Indigo Dyers, certainly the largest and best known and probably the oldest in Yorkshire which now, a quarter of a century later, is run by Eli's son, Willie Marsden. Such a combination in the direction and management of a highly technical business calling for perfection and craftsmanship must, I imagine, be almost unique in the annals of the textile industry. Philip: chairman, managing director, an artistic, fiery, hard-bitten Yorkshireman, a leader. Oliver: accounts and scientific direction: quietly efficient, wise, a soldier and nature's gentleman. Walter: mill manager and super-craftsman, a tower of quiet strength and white all through. William Henry: departmental manager, an amiable nonentity. Eli: supplies and transport, with whom 'orses is 'orses and a good story a good story. Utterly different types of men united by a supreme loyalty to the business and each other, which probably had its roots in their early beginnings at home where the Bible was the family book, obedience a creed, horsehair a sign of affluence, the aspidistra a symbol of severe respectability, and work a religion. To Walter I owe the technique of cloth-brushing and the tricks of the trade, and to Oliver the art of indigo-dyeing and dye analysis, which placed me officially in an unassailable position. Also to him, who until his death was sort of unofficial vice-chancellor of Leeds University, do I owe such cultural attainments as I possess. Unassuming almost to the point of effacement, he was naturally a cultured gentleman of the old school, yet not so divorced from the new that his sympathies were alienated.

From odd corners he would produce for my acceptance such books as Tennyson's *In Memoriam*, Milton's *Comus*, Plato's *Dialogues*, Lucrecia, one of Santayana's *Three Philosophical Poets,* and then came his gift of Walter Pater's *Marius the Epicurean*, which later gave direction to my cultural probings. Of all my friendly books *Marius the Epicurean*, the most thumbed, is perhaps the most treasured.

So from science to the classics, through history and philosophy to the poets, I come to the writing of poetry, essays, letters and, at long last, this intermittent diary. And later, after some talk on indigo-dyeing, the odd fermentation vat, the fierce days of the London indigo sales, when synthetic indigo, now in general use, was but a name, maybe some instruction in cochineal dyeing, or a discussion on dye analysis. Perhaps some little anecdote about the University of Leeds would emerge, or a reference to leaders of the old school, of cloth manufacturers now passed away – of Leonard Saint, a grand old Yorkshireman, of the fiery independence of John Halliday, the finest manufacturer of cloth of Crimean War days, who, having no use for receipts, disposed of them by a weekly burning, of old Fred Harper, bachelor and recluse, and the leonine Henry Booth, workers all. And now the back hole is full of dumbly articulate shadows, a whispering gallery of other days where I occasionally eat with the last surviving brother, Walter, than whom there is no more upright man in Yorkshire.

And as I write these notes Oliver Marsden emerges from the shadows, his old tweed cap 'resting' on his head, his pince nez half-way down his nose, his tie awry, to greet me with his slow smile and soft voice, as he strokes his small pointed beard, now white. 'Well, well, my friend. You will stay to lunch, won't you?' Others can have all the power and glory and wealth, but if amongst those I love, I can find him at the 'meeting place', I shall not be proud but just profoundly grateful. Thus in my

61st year the known prospects of the golden wealth in this beginning time of slow harvest, which, together with my health and home, itself the shrine of my domestic life, my garden, my heart's friends, my neighbours, my work and colleagues and business contacts, my pursuits and interests, are the expression of all that's best within me. Their continued cultivation must surely be a joy enduring to the end. So real to me is all this that those things I say now seem to have their roots so deep as never to have had a beginning, at least in me.

May 30th

WHITSUN OVER AND WORK BEGUN. A SUNNY HOLIDAY WITH A rather blistering wind. Instead of three days' slow boating I did the plenty there was to do in the garden. The iris, lupins and stocks are in full bloom, the roses coming on and the rockery, although past its best, is still a delight, with the double red mary as vivid as ever, the geraniums a knot of scarlet and bird-song around it, it was a quiet oasis in a neighbourhood of seething holiday folk who had come for the Hurst Park race meeting, the river, the fun-fair, cricket and Hampton Court. Clifford came to us on Sunday and later Bob and Betty called and announced the prospect of a glad event for Christmas.

On Whit Monday Clifford's friend Doris was, from noon to supper, on her hobby-horse of infant welfare and child psychology and nothing saw she that was not the outcome of careful thought. It smacked sometimes of the academies of welfare clinics, I thought; but that will help to correct the errors of too much maternal instinct when the time comes, so long as she surrenders that the babe must be fed according to its appetite timetable rather than Bradshaw's.

June 1st

PONT'S 67TH BIRTHDAY. AT 6.30 A.M. I PRESENTED HER MORNING tea in a dainty hyacinth blue Royal Doulton service. Her obvious delight in the acceptance of the surprise birthday gift was reward enough for me. And so off early to the west of England with official chores. A long, tiring day, which finished in the late evening at Dart Mill, Buckfastleigh, where now, for lack of rain, the weir is almost dry. Leaving the mill manager, Mr West, at 10.30 p.m. I stepped into the truly beautiful deep twilight of nearly midsummer with the after-sunset glow pale saffron behind the velvet black foothills of Dartmoor. I halted in silent wonder while time, for the moment, took possession and with me stood still. And by way of contrast, never, methinks, have I seen the pastures so palely luminous as when, this late afternoon travelling through Somerset, the glancing sun shone into the grass and made every blade glow like a green pellucid flame, suffusing the meadows with the cool, sweet light of hearty enchantment. Truly if you cannot make the world what you want it, you can think it so.

June 6th

A REALLY HOT SUMMER'S DAY. EN ROUTE TO LEEDS ONE COOLS down a little as the evening wears on but in the train I gently simmered for four hours. According to my weight I should require thirty hours to cook right through and be properly done. Nevertheless I was 'done' sufficiently for me in the shorter time, and if the meat doesn't come away from the bone, nobody noticed it for everyone was in the same plight, except that ladies of especially large proportion were rapidly approaching the melting and disrobing stage. I can't imagine

London being any hotter but it probably was. Anyway, for the first time in a long series of journeys I didn't write a single word; instead I gleaned idly through Hilaire Belloc's 'But soft, we are observed', light and humorous. My three travelling companions were as mute as I and probably for the same reasons. Stepping out of the train at Batley was briefly to change ovens, and to enter the finishing room of the mill was like standing in my own greenhouse in a heavy overcoat while the hot afternoon sun was doing its best to wreck the thermometer. How the many quite elderly women endure the slow, tedious task of mending faults in pieces of cloth, sitting in what appears to me to be their all-the-year-round clothes, under a fiercely burning glass roof with not a breath of air in the room without going to sleep just passes my comprehension. And in the store-hold almost naked men fantastic with slivers of shining sweat and corny white lines down their coal- blackened bodies, staring strangely at me from beneath dripping brows. Wow! It was Spurgeon who shocked his congregation one Sunday morning in the tabernacle by announcing as his text, 'Brethren, it is damned hot!' So it was. According to the *Yorkshire Evening Post* the shade temperature at noon today, recorded at Roundhay Park, was 90 degrees.

June 9th

TONIGHT FOR HOME, AFTER A DELIGHTFUL AND INTERESTING day in Keswick, which I reached last evening from Leeds via Newcastle and Carlisle. I was struck by the quiet beauty of the Tyne valley as I saw it from the train between Hexham and Carlisle but owing to the relatively long dry spell there was very little water in the river, which nevertheless reminded me very much of some reaches of the river Dart between Totnes and

Buckfastleigh. I felt that I would greatly like to explore it in some detail at leisure. But my early-morning pilgrimage to Derwentwater and Friar's Cray was the chief event of today's joys when in the sweet, cool air of the quiet sunny morning, the still water of the lake reflected the wooded mountain glory. Surely, I thought, all this is as much mine, at this moment, as anybody's.

June 10th

THE FIRST RAIN FOR ABOUT THREE WEEKS AND THE END OF A week's heatwave. The Hooks called this morning for a couple of hours. The big pot of *Lilium regale* with its wonderful blooms crowning the six-foot stems was greatly admired, as indeed was the whole garden, now a riot of colour with its Russell lupins, Oriental poppies, geraniums and a host of roses in full bloom set against the vivid green of an almost perfect lawn. Some useful work done, too, in bedding in lobelia, begonias, and dahlias. Schizanthus in the greenhouse are laden with painted butterflies. A walk to Hampton Court garden in the evening with Pont. Their flower-beds were very disappointing. Even allowing for the spell of hot, dry weather, there seems of late to be seasonal deterioration in the maintenance of its one-time excellent floral standard. Certainly the wallflower and tulip beds, now near to seed, should be brightened with new plantings; colour schemes are poor and lack boldness. The fact is that the master hand has departed.

June 12th

AFTER FIFTEEN WEEKS OF SICK LEAVE FRED RETURNED TO THE office today but he is far from strong. His abdominal sinus, a hole the size of a cherry, is not yet healed but his general health is good and he looks remarkably well after his convalescence in Eastbourne. Today is a decidedly cold day after last week's heatwave and I made a fire in the hearth this evening.

June 19th

SHEARING TIME. THE SHEEP IN THE GREAT PASTURES BY THE railway – as I travel to Leeds – gleam pure white in their nakedness against the rich green.

After reading the morning's news, with all its talk of trouble in the Far East, the Japanese blockade, of food supplies running short in the concessions, German troop movements towards the Slovak border, Arab and Jew at each other's throats in Palestine, riots in the British West Indies, Continental jockeying for alliances, armament-profit limitations and all that goes with the worldwide political dog-fight, the great countryside as I see it this morning helps me to regain poise. One is left wondering why mankind doesn't let well alone and pursue his peaceful vocations. But I fear that the conflict between nations is but a large-scale reflection of the conflict in man's dual nature that goes on within. Perhaps only when a more advanced stage of spiritual evolution is reached shall he achieve that poise which will enable him to develop those human attributes that alone make for real progress, i.e., the emancipation of self in service of his fellows.

But first the universal practice of a sound ethical code, rather than financial greed, must be the 'big business' of mankind. Perhaps his very remoteness from that is the measure of his martyrdom and his need. *Well.*

June 23rd

AT LAST A START FOR OUR SUMMER HOLIDAY. LEAVING WATERLOO at 11 a.m. we arrived at north Devon at 4 p.m. after a comfortable journey.

June 30th

A WEEK IDLING WITH COMFORTABLE QUALITIES AT MRS WILSON'S The Homestead, long, restful nights, excellent and abundant food, and easy rambling about the countryside overlooking the sea at Mortehoe. Pont's foot has improved every day and she can manage a five-mile walk without undue fatigue.

With the station three miles away and a wretchedly poor local train service we reached Barnstaple in time to attend the tail end of the local cattle market, but too late to find anything of special interest. But the rail journey was enjoyable because of the delightful sea and country views en route. It was sad to see the quantity of what appeared to be fertile land out of cultivation and running wild with weeds.

July 2nd

A DAY OF LITTLE SUN, CHILLY RAIN SQUALLS AND COLD, blistering wind. In the morning a walk to Morte Point; for the rest, reading, writing, and resting. A solitary yellowhammer sings his little song, 'a little bit of bread and no cheese', from a wayward spray of bramble, and in the quiet evening air the smell of new-mown hay recalls memories as fragrant as itself.

July 3rd

STROLLING ALONG THE CLIFF PATH TO BENNET'S MOUNT THIS sunny morning, a Mr Webb, a London man now resident here in retirement, whom I casually met, told me, apropos of the rabbit pest in the district, that during the winter some forty to fifty thousand are shot or trapped for the Birmingham and Portsmouth markets. One industrious local this winter accounted for 7000. This occupation is reckoned as the neighbourhood winter industry, and collection and transport are properly arranged to deal with such numbers. My informant occupies his leisure mainly with rough shooting – mostly rabbit and partridge and, when the frequent opportunity affords, snipe and woodcock. Of hares there are none; he regards raven and buzzards – of which he says there are not a few in the district – as enemies of the sportsman. A kestrel hovered above us as he spoke.

According to him, in the days of sail, as many as 130 small ships sheltered in Woolacombe Bay in gale weather. Then it was, so the story goes, that five shillings was the reward offered for the rescue of a live mariner and fifteen for a dead one. Be that as it may, he had no doubt that there was purposeful delay in notifying the authorities responsible for organizing rescue work for shipwrecked mariners by those who were interested in complete disaster: much of the flotsam and jetsam had disappeared by the time coastguards appeared upon the scene. Within fairly recent times he remembered that a copper-bottomed Spanish clipper, wrecked off Morte Point, spilled its cargo of oranges all along the beach, much to the joy of one old dame who stuffed a sack with the juicy spoil – to have it ripped open by a coastguard whom she could not evade when all the oranges spilled back again on the beach. The sort of rough penalty the law might have withheld, I thought. Many more yellowhammers here today, newly arrived immigrants. Letters from FHT and Doris, both very welcome.

July 4th

A LATE RAMBLE LAST NIGHT BROUGHT ME ITS REWARD. OVER THE cliffs by Bennet's Mount about 9.30 p.m. I saw a buzzard circling, majestically high, above the steep Kiniver Valley and, with my glasses, had a fine view of his graceful wing action. Shortly after, a flock of starlings, probably two hundred, suddenly appeared over the cliff face in my direction, flying so low as to almost skim the bracken. Standing stock still, I split their ranks. Noting the direction of their orbit I remained standing and, in a couple of minutes or so, they repeated the manoeuvre. And all this in the dusk of late evening when, to all intents and purposes, the entrance of moorland by the sea is a lifeless desolation.

July 6th

A DAY OF UNCEASING RAIN AND SQUALLY GALE-FORCE WINDS. From the window a grey desolation of sea and sky, which almost imperceptibly merge at the horizon. When I read 'fisherman: parties taken fishing, lobsters, crabs, prawns, etc.', I wondered not a little by what inducements other poor fish were encouraged to part with their 15*s*. per day with so little evidence of the means to successful enterprise. With a yard length of stout iron wire bent to a hook at one end and lashed at the other to an old broomstick one may go poking about likely pools among the rocks, combing a quite unspeakable length of foreshore in the process, and with luck land a 'lobster, crabs, prawns, etc.', by way of reward, which becomes the property of the finder. There are certain conventions to be observed before admission into the brotherhood. Apart from possession of the lethal weapon and a complete knowledge of crustacean folklore, there is the matter of the regulation attire without which no self-respecting prawn, lobster or crab would condescend to indicate, betray or declare his presence: a nautical peaked cap, disposed at the correct marine angle, a blue jersey with 'fisherman' embroidered in white worsted conspicuously across the chest; a very abbreviated pair of khaki shorts and white rubber shoes complete the ensemble. Nevertheless I'm not discouraged because of my lack of the orthodox equipment. Maybe a bathing suit and the crook of my old walking-stick will do equally well and I shall enjoy beginner's luck and the crab blowing bubbles.

July 10th

TODAY AFTER A PLEASANT JOURNEY WE ARRIVED AT SHIELING about 5 p.m., greatly cheered at the sight of our pleasant little homestead, shining with new paint, the garden in splendid order, thanks to the attentions of Benny, my henchman. The very trees around seem to have put on a green freshness of welcome. To fling open the familiar doors and windows was like shaking hands with an old friend. The joy of small jobs done to get us back on to the smooth rails of domestic fortune – resumption of newspaper and milk supplies, turning on the gas at the meter, clock-winding and dozens of other matters, like levers in the several parts of a machine that must be moved to start the whole in motion. And then, tomorrow, to collect the old dog from the boarding kennels. Slithering between my own good bed sheets, maybe Old Nell, you, my last thought before sleep.

July 11th

COLLECTING NELL THIS MORNING, I FELT THAT HER FRIENDLY greeting, after the interval, had little to do with cupboard love. All animals are pleased to eat and many give some sign of pleasant anticipation. But demonstration of personal affection by a dog for its master is of a different order and perhaps unique among animals, altho' in some cases the horse comes a fairly close second. Old Nell invariably inspects our visitors, but seldom remains in the room with them, not even in the winter when a quiet cosy fire is an especial attraction. Alone with me when the rest of the household has gone to bed, she is happily content to be at my feet before the fire, be I never so quiet, reading or writing. And much the same were the habits of our own dear old spaniel, Jim, who had the better intelligence.

A spaniel he
As brown could be
Whose gifts were love and loyalty.
May he see Rocco's grace and find
The paradise of a doggy kind.

By 10 a.m. I had started off to collect Ethel from Banstead hospital. The doctor, whom I interviewed, added but little to my knowledge of her case. Occupation, good food and cheerful amusement, he said, were essential to her continued progress. Enough of her liver was functioning to ensure reasonably good health and she is mentally sound, but alcohol in any form would now be quickly fatal in its effects. I promised that all reasonable precautions would be taken against her indulgence in it. She is to stay with us for six weeks then report to Banstead on 21st August at 10.30 a.m.

July 17th

RESUMED OFFICIAL DUTIES TODAY AFTER MY VACATION. FRED looked very well, I thought, if his physical strength returns but slowly. He was obviously pleased to have me back. As with home, so with work. One takes hold of the job as if holidays had never been. By the afternoon Mortehoe seemed so remote that there might have never been a break in the sequence of familiar duties, an effect induced perhaps by habit of mind, or by some measure of adaptability. But a greater zest for the job made the day happy.

July 24th

COME AND GONE THE WEEKEND AND ANOTHER MONDAY IN willingness surrounds my first port of call en route for Leeds. Lunched with Frank and Fred a week ago today. Never in the presence of a 'third party' do Frank and I get down to those intimate talks, those intimate silences, which are the gold of companionship. Never do we expand so naturally and spontaneously as when alone together. Then it is like being alone with oneself. Even after forty years of friendship I feel that I cannot say that of Fred.

Yet my regard for him is not less. Not in degree, but in kind does it seem greatly to differ. Looking back over the years to the Battersea Polytechnic days when I first met him – recently home from India – amiable with an indolent dependence, I find the Fred of today differs little except for the maturity that years bring, and perhaps because of this affection between us endures.

But the foggy night that brought Frank and I together on the Banstead to London train some seven years ago was the beginning of a friendship not less important to me in its consequences and much more intimate than my twenty-five years of friendship with Oliver Marsden. Oliver indicated the general direction of my cultural development, which, as the years passed, created its own nourishment and expanded eventually to discover its focus in my association with Taylor, who like some finely adjusted lens, enriched from its own glowing depths the clear, warm fires of reflection.

Affairs domestic have gone well with us all the week, Ethel seems cheerful and reasonably happy. Clifford came to us at the weekend and added a lively touch to events; his Doris came to lunch and for the rest of Sunday. Her *Oxford Book of Verse* accent, which outstanded itself on her first visit, disappeared on better acquaintance. She has a ready and ordered wit and her conversation is informed. She is level-headed, cool and deliberate in argument, possessed of a methodical mind and, I should say, has ability and brains. Be her other qualities what they may, Clifford won't lack for intellectual companionship in his domestic partner to satisfy one of his real needs.

July 30th

TODAY AND YESTERDAY IN THE GARDEN, WHICH IS IN GOOD form and much admired by a miscellany of visitors including Pauline and Sid who, with Bob Walker, took tea with us.

August 1st

SISTER FLORRIE'S BIRTHDAY. WROTE HER AT ZURICH WHERE, with her not unusual ill-luck, she is spending her holiday, sick. A neighbour to whom until today I had merely paid the usual courtesy, on the way to the station, said to me of another neighbour we had passed, 'He's a nasty piece of work.' Presuming he knew the man and asking his reasons for this gratuitous shaft it was disclosed that his prudence was born of impression without the authority of acquaintance. For no better reason than that the poor man was possessed of a small mouth, he must of necessity be nasty, as were declared to be all other possessors of small mouths. As a way of life I cannot imagine any attitude more cramping to human understanding. Aeschylus truly said, 'Learning is forever in the freshness of its youth, even for the old.' And so it is.

August 4th

MY INSPECTION OF PAPER FINISHED AT CROXLEY TODAY, I HAD A look around the mill and observed the many improvements made since my last visit in plant, layout and technique. Between them, their six machines now produce 600 to 650 tons of paper, each week refining for the process some 900 tons of raw material, 1100 tons of coal and 50,000 tons of water – and to reflect that we reach out for the scribbling block and tear off a sheet with the same unconcern that we turn on the bath-water. First made in China around the time of the Roman invasion of Britain – altho' centuries earlier the Chinese chewed rice straw and spat out the pulp to dry as crude sheets. Later, taking something like Marco Polo's route, paper next appeared in Samarkand. Slowly and laboriously trekking eastwards across Europe, it eventually appeared in England as the beginnings of a new industry early in the sixteenth century, every sheet made separately by hand. The first continuous web of machine-made paper appeared in this country around about 1775.

August 8th

BANK HOLIDAY OVER, AND NOTHING MORE EVENTFUL TO RECORD than two visits to Hampton Court and one to the cinema. To tea for the rest of the day came Father and his wife Agnes. The old man looked all of his 82 years and has shrunk visibly. I gathered that he had lost 28 lbs of weight in little over a year. On our visit to the cinema – myself, Pont and Ethel – I saw *The Wandering Jew* for the third time. That the subject should absorb my attention goes without saying; its mysticism appeals to that which is pagan within me.

August 9th

AN ACQUAINTANCE MADE THIRTY-FIVE YEARS AGO AND ONLY yesterday renewed is fast becoming a friend. George Ross during our river camping days together when I was about twenty-five years old introduced me, with much enthusiasm, to Hearn's *Stories of Old Japan*. Because of my respect for his more intense mind, his obvious good taste and perhaps, too, because of a consciousness of my own cultural inferiority, my interest was suspect rather than sincere. Only the author's name – possibly by reason of its halo of romance and the strange country of his adoption – remained as something dimly recollected. And now, on a chance walk from Red Lion Square through one of the narrow back courts to Holborn, in a shabby little bookshop I lighted upon Hearn's *Out of the East*. In this I thought I might now hope to achieve something of the delight in those bygone years that was Ross's; nor was I mistaken. Certain it is that Hearn now permanently resides with my other intimate friends, neatly to my service. He, too, must know of the 'meeting place'.*

Ethel wrote Tom today by register post, asking what steps he proposed to take to provide her with a home, what maintenance allowance he could afford and asking for some cash for immediate needs.

From the railway-carriage window, since my last journey to Yorkshire, the cereal crops have reached golden maturity and are ready for harvesting. Soft gold the corn against the vivid green of the all too prevalent meadows. Some day agriculture will come into its own.

August 15th

PUBLISHED IN TODAY'S *DAILY TELEGRAPH* IS THE WILL OF SIR Emmanuel Hoyle,** a comfortable fortune of something over £360,000 with bequests to many of his mill staff. Notification from Banstead this morning that I am 'requested to report with Ethel to the committee at 10 a.m. on the 21st August'. Spoke to her this morning before breakfast about her return recommending her to leave to the hospital authorities any action to be taken in respect of Tom, her husband. Clifford, who was with us on Sunday, spent a few hours on the river and announced the date of his wedding as 17th September.

* Walter often mentions the 'meeting place' as somewhere he will find all his heroes waiting to talk to him after his own death.

** The 'fire-eating old Yorkshire woollens baron' who had passed away earlier that year. Walter first mentions him in his entry of May 19th.

August 17th

IN A CROWDED TRAIN IN THE HEAT OF THE AFTERNOON TO Totnes. Perspiring humanity, for reasons of inclement weather and the anxious uncertainty of the international situation, appears to have telescoped its holiday travels into these few almost tropical days to sweat its several ways to the seaside in cheerful discomfort rather than postpone the annual pilgrimage any longer lest worse befall. But Devon in the sunshine after the long rains is a riot of luscious vegetation, and to wake up at Buckfastleigh at 5.30 a.m. on the 18th with the cool morning sunlight flooding my bed with amber and silver was a joy to be known only on such days of quiet beginning.

August 20th

TOM MCAWARD CALLED TODAY AND HAD A TALK IN THE GARDEN with Ethel, afterwards with me, about their affairs, the essential matter of which was his stated intention of making such provision for her as his means would permit. This, at my request, he reaffirmed. At 11 p.m. he phoned to say that on again turning the problem over in his mind he was prepared to set up a home with her on her discharge, but wanted my assurance that there were reasonable prospects of her abstention from alcohol. I gave him a qualified assurance – for nobody can be sure of anybody else – and he promised to call me at Shieling at 8.30 p.m. next Monday evening to discuss arrangements.

At 9.30 this morning I called on Florrie at Worcester Park and found her much better than expected and my niece Joy in quite good form. Apparently while in Zurich on holiday, my sister had been stung on the back of the throat by a mosquito and had suffered a bad time on account of her glandular infection.

August 21st

WITH ETHEL TO BANSTEAD THIS MORNING. A LONG TEDIOUS wait for the signal to appear before the committee, during which I write these and yesterday's notes. And now the interview over, in which I fear the committee got the wrong impression of me because of my refusal on Ethel's discharge to take her back with me to Shieling. She will now stay at an 'aftercare' establishment until Tom has got the home ready and sends for her. For obvious reasons I think it were better this: the onus is now on him to make ready as quickly as possible.

The spontaneous goodwill shown to Ethel on her return to the hospital by patients and staff alike left me in no doubt as to the friendliness of their relations. To whatever extent this happy state of affairs may be attributed to her own personality, it is greatly to the credit of an institutional policy that it fosters an atmosphere so sociable. Spoke to Phil this afternoon who promised to deliver up Ethel's papers and furniture agreement to me to pass to Tom when he needs them. To Tom I wrote as follows:

My dear Tom, I cannot tell you how glad I am for Ethel's sake, and our own too, that you have decided to start a home with her afresh. Having regard to the circumstances I feel that it is the only satisfactory course open to you. When I told her last night of your proposals to me on the phone, I felt sure her gratitude gave promise enough of happier times all round, especially for your two selves. I will acquaint the hospital authorities today of your intentions and report their arrangements to you when you come this evening to Shieling. As regards the future, I would like you to believe that you and Ethel can feel sure of a friendly welcome at Shieling at all times, and if good wishes count for anything at all, you are both assured of happier days. Yours very sincerely, Walter.

Tom McAward called this evening as promised. Clearly his intention is to push ahead with the house with as little delay as possible. Referring to his present mode of life, his bachelor existence: while it left him free to do what he liked with his leisure in the cultivation of his own little world, unburdened by domestic responsibilities and considerations, I thought it significant that he should remark that it never seemed very satisfying; though occupied, his evenings were often empty. On hearing these sentiments, I felt amply rewarded for the part I had taken in their affairs – knew my patience and caution to be justified. His fundamental needs are common to us all. I reported to him the arrangements made at Banstead for Ethel and insisted they both keep in touch with me as often as they wished. To Ethel at Banstead, I wrote telling her of Tom's visit and the gist of our conversation, urging her to wait patiently for Tom to fetch her home.

August 22nd

TODAY PHIL HANDED OVER ETHEL'S PAPERS AS PROMISED, WITH her furniture-storage dues paid up to the July demand.

August 31st

SINCE MY LAST ENTRY, DAYS OF GROWING SUSPENSE AND LIKE A rank weed, in the reeking atmosphere of conflicting passions, it flourishes vitally and we are on the brink of war with Germany. It would seem that very little now would start in the world a catastrophe too dreadful in its consequence for combatants and non-combatants alike even to imagine. One can only hope and pray for a return to sanity, that counsels of reason may prevail ere it is too late, that the principle of right over might will be acknowledged. In his letters to me, FHT supposed that I was recording in my diary the events leading up to this crisis.

I replied to him that the task of recording the mass of conflicting, partisan and exaggerated statements of the press, the mouthings of hearsay, the fantastic rumours and all the rest of it was quite beyond me. A gigantic tidal wave of political, financial and personal complexities surrounds almost to extinction the essential factors of dispute, which appear to me to be elementary and turn on the abandonment of a powerful few of those principles of sound ethics generally accepted, at least by the more entrusted races, the world over. But so it is and the 'man in the street' can do little to dissect the course of events except prepare for the worst while hoping for the best. With a philosophical acceptance of a situation in which he must trust his leaders, he works steadily at the task he is given, and as London evacuates its administrative centres and more vulnerable population, he plays his part in the various services organized to prepare the country for all eventualities.

September 1st

TENSION INCREASES. POLAND REPORTED INVADED, WARSAW AND other Polish towns bombed by the Germans, and Danzig under Nazi rule. A day of anxious suspense. England's participation seems now inevitable if we are to keep our hand with Poland. To know the worst would seem almost a relief. A wartime blackout in London tonight with continuance throughout the country until further notice. It seemed strange groping about one's own village in the unusual darkness, a darkness of the unlighted countryside at midnight, when only footsteps and voices can be heard coming out of the black void. All branches of the services have been called to their stations, vast numbers of schoolchildren evacuated to safe areas, the transport system put under government control, the press told by both sides of the House of Commons to exercise a decent restraint in the presentation of news – a tardy and very necessary rebuke – the public asked to put no unnecessary strain on the GPO, to exercise moderation in the purchase of foodstuffs. Warnings against food profiteering and other acts against the Body Politic. Hospitals are being cleared, safe accommodation being found for the blind; dug-outs and sandbagging and other precautionary measures are near completion. All ARP units are at their stations fully equipped in all branches ready for duty. And all going on with a quiet intensity which speaks well for confidence in the final issue.

September 2nd

ONLY FRED AND I IN ATTENDANCE AT THE OFFICE, THE REST ordered to remain at home 'on call'. And coming up on my usual train from Hampton Court I found London's sky scattered with silvery captive balloons, which form part of its air defence, each shining fully in the hesitant sunlight.

Saturday afternoon at Waterloo Station, the great booking hall full of perspiring humanity, the station with a miscellaneous crowd of people good-naturedly jostling each other in their eagerness to find departure platforms. A police sergeant leads across the station a posse of special constables conscious of their new duty, armlets over their civilian coat sleeves. A marching song grows louder and echoes under the glass vault of the station as a detachment of troops sings its way to the Aldershot departure platform. Everywhere piles of luggage and military kit, dogs, perambulators, loose clothing, bicycles – indiscriminately dumped and seemingly ownerless – litter the parade. The benches are crowded with waiting folk laden with luggage, most of them looking tired but cheerful and all patiently enduring. Tea trolleys and travelling milk bars do a roaring trade. A baby in a daintily upholstered box signals its arrival on the grubby platform floor while a small dog with expressive brown eyes stands guard. Presently a young couple disentangles itself from the crowd and each taking a rope handle on either side of the box with one accord lift and walk away with their precious burden, dog dutifully in the rear. I sit watching the eve-of-the-war crowd; the sounds become monotonous in their very variety. At the shrill bubbly note of a guard's whistle the Aldershot train, loaded to capacity with soldiers, slowly moves off and I make for my home train, thinking of the light-excluding blinds yet to be drawn at Shieling, the articles of extra clothing I shall require for the evacuation, and wonder vaguely what shall be my eventual destination.

And at home I was busy in the garden. I took a few cuttings, generally watered round and after a meal fixed most of the light-excluding blinds. The six o'clock news told of progressive invasion of Poland by Germany. I imagine the war is already on, at least, for them.

September 3rd

AT 11.15 A.M. TODAY THE PRIME MINISTER ANNOUNCED OVER the wireless that a state of war exists between England and Germany from this moment. Dreadfully disappointing for him. God grant that right shall prevail over might. At 11.31 the first real air-raid warning. At 5 p.m. a state of war came into

...full of perspiring humanity-

existence between France and Germany. At 6 p.m. the King made an affecting speech over the radio and gave this our crusade of right over might his blessing.

September 6th

THIS MORNING JUST BEFORE SUNRISE, LIKE SOME ROYAL ORDER in shining cloth-of-gold, the herald of day emblazoned low in the eastern sky. On a spray over the lawn, richly jewelled with pearly dew, my garden robin piped his cheerful melody. Almost immediately an air-raid warning shattered, as a thrown pebble might the still surface of some mirroring lake.

Exactly at 9 a.m. the all-clear sounded and the streets, which had been deserted, were instantly alive with people hurrying to work. A million of London's population, mainly children, have been evacuated to safer districts without a hitch, a marvellous achievement. A twentieth-century exodus.

Tom McAward called at Shieling immediately after the morning air raid – which was subsequently declared to be a false alarm – to inform us that Ethel had secured a flat for them both at Tulse Hill. I agreed that he should use my name as a reference. I then handed over to him the furniture storage agreement with Arding & Hobbs, storage-charge receipts and a letter of release together with an inventory of their furniture. On Monday night, too, Millie left for Worthing with the household animals, dropping Phil at Shieling on the way, and with us Phil will stay for an indefinite period.

September 10th

HAD SATURDAY MORNING OFF, WHICH GAVE ME THE WHOLE weekend. I spent most of it on garden chores. Took Pont to lunch at Kingston yesterday. This morning Tom McAward called and told me that he and Ethel enter into occupation of their flat at Tulse Hill on Friday next. I gave him a cheque for three guineas, which amount Arding & Hobbs said was owing, to clear the furniture charges, any excess to be refunded to me when the account was adjusted. In the evening, spent a pleasant couple of hours with the Hooks.

September 11th

A VERY CHEERY NOTE FROM FHT THIS MORNING, ENCLOSING A letter from an NZ friend and some verse which I much liked. With Clifford tonight, asking for news of his affairs since his weekly brief note to Pont did not come to hand as usual. A strange antipathy most people, especially young people, have to letter-writing of any sort. Business has slackened off greatly since war broke out, so the staff has busied itself with an intense 'spring' cleaning and the ruthless destruction of junk which has been accumulating this twenty years past.

Poland, according to radio and other news, is putting up heroic resistance to an invading horde of seventy divisions of German troops, some one and a half million men – poor Poland – but the Allied offensive on the Western Front between the Rhine and Moselle rivers is rapidly developing. Its progress on German territory should quickly relieve the pressure on the stout Polish army. For ourselves in England there is nothing more alarming to report than a general falling-off in business from the normal, the daily blackout, restricted transport and the sight of soldiers in unaccustomed places. The operation of the nightly blackout, in the opinion of many, is an unnecessary inconvenience and because of the sharp increase in road accidents, due to the nightly inky darkness, is likely to defeat its purpose. Since air-raid warnings should give timely notice of the approach of enemy raiders, it would seem that some sort of restricted street and other lighting might, with advantage, be permitted between raids, which could automatically be extinguished at the first note of warning. For households, etc., in occupation the continuance of the nightly blackout I think is necessary if only to inculcate a regular habit of protection in domestic routine.

September 15th

FOR A HALF-HOUR THIS MORNING I RENEWED MY ACQUAINTANCE with an unfamiliar corner of London, its walks, its miscellany of works and factories, dark old shops and street markets, its squalid old houses, its new blocks of flats and dwellings, posted alleys and the grim gloomy rampart of railway arches used as stores, warehouses, garages and sometimes factories. Running off Vauxhall Walk are to be found Gye Street, Laud, Tinworth, Jonathan and Salamanca Streets, and Randall Row, and across the far end from Vauxhall, Black Prince Road – a more modern but somewhat dingy thoroughfare. Opposite the Jolly Gardener, which, in spite of its dedication to Bacchus, looks anything but jolly, commences Lambeth Walk, a long thoroughfare of mediocre shops and costers' stalls. Turning off aimlessly from there towards the arches are Home Parade and Sellon Mews, degenerate sort of poor residential cum industrial locations, more curious than interesting. And towards the end, approaching China Walk, is Old Paradise Street, leading to Sail Street, continuous with the line of arches, and so through them to Pratt Walk, with its tortuous windings, past Norfolk Row and the far end of Old Paradise Street, against which the dark red-brick towers of Lambeth Palace come into view on the confines of this queer bit of London.

And I think of the sweet, clean ocean breezes of Mortehoe, but the war is with us. A poster outside a little general store announces the bombing of Polish towns by German warplanes and their slaughter of a hospital full of children. Never have Wordsworth's words had a grimmer significance than when he said, 'The world is too much with us.'

September 17th

AFTER RISKING LATE ARRIVAL FOR HIS WEDDING, THROUGH THE members of our own little party losing each other at Waterloo, today at noon Clifford was married to Doris at the New Gravel Pits Unitarian Church of Hackney. A quiet, cheery wedding, the ceremony was simple, touching and homely. A modest reception in honour of the bride and groom brought both families and friends together for a happy hour in the church room. Then making our way to Piccadilly, Clifford and Doris, her mother, Eve and Mary joined Pont and I at lunch to make the most of an hilarious last hour before departing our several ways. Clifford wryly commented on the necessity of carrying a gas mask to his wedding!

Today Russia invaded Poland – a further complication – and in the evening our neighbours the Hiscock girls and ourselves discussed the possible effects and developments of this new event in the war.

September 18th

HMS *COURAGEOUS*, AIRCRAFT CARRIER, SUNK TODAY BY GERMAN submarine, which was itself sunk by an RAF warplane piloted by a plucky South African. Half the personnel, some 680 men, were saved. The captain went down with his ship, standing at the salute. The Germans' first big 'bag'.

September 20th

TODAY I LEFT BY THE 10.30 A.M. WARTIME TRAIN FOR LEEDS, NO dining or buffet car, an interminably long journey, arriving at Peterboro' first stop at 12.30 p.m. For some of the crowd of passengers, a scramble for tea at the refreshment room; others besieged the tea trolley – no coffee available. Except that tea – and very poor tea – in bulk was ready, there was no organization for dealing with the rush, which should have been anticipated. Not until it was over did someone think to make ready several dozen cups at once for quick distribution, almost every one of which, because too late and unwanted, I saw poured back into large enamelled tin jugs – presumably for future use. At 3*d.* per cup it was ghastly stuff to have to scramble for. Eventually my train drew into Leeds at 4 p.m. I thought to listen to the radio commentary, repeated by the press this morning, on Hitler's Danzig speech made earlier in the day. I felt that in whatever contempt his utterances may be held in this country, we at least should not descend to the indignity of wrangling and recrimination like some ignorant slut of a fishwife, propaganda or no propaganda. If, as I believe, we are conducting this crusade for a principle, let us do so without stooping, be war never so terrible, lest in the wrangling we forget what we are fighting for.

During this long trip to Leeds, I seized the opportunity to delve for a while further into Dreiser's *Thoreau*, strong meat but wholesome. And so, by a lucky chance, one drifts away from the world that is too much with us, a world leprous with malevolent lust of power and spite, mendacious and beastly, to make it the larger and more beautiful world, a retreat, private and boundless. And so, lest suppression of spiritual emotion atrophies the soul, one must retreat to the cloistered seclusion of one's own making. One's inner self is one's special preserve.

September 21st

NO MORE THRILLING PIECE OF WAR NEWS HAVE I HEARD THAN today's announcement of the revolt of the Czechs, which took its spark from a series of labour demonstrations in Prague last week. Throughout Czechoslovakia armed revolt is sweeping the women no less than the men fighting for release from the Nazi regime. Bravo, Czechs!

September 28th

POLAND, NOW OCCUPIED BY GERMANY AND RUSSIA, WHO AT the moment are dividing the spoils, no longer exists as a nation. Here, income tax now starts at 7/6*d*.; increased taxation on tobacco, beer, cigars and other commodities; food, light and fuel to be controlled together with many raw materials, e.g., wool, and prices rising generally. Ordinary business shrinking daily, work falling off and employment for many in jeopardy or at a standstill. I can well imagine that almost any moment might put a period to my service at the office. A general blackout in real earnest, but one must face the conditions with a philosophical acceptance of their implications and adjust one's life accordingly. It is surprising how quickly, from our gimcrack complexities, at the first hot blast of war, like hops in a kiln, we return to the more simple existence imposed upon us by necessity. Invention is not her only child. Maybe events will stimulate a more lively exploration of ourselves to the discovery of the thread of gold within.

A letter from Ethel on Sunday, which seems to dispose of any doubt as to the prospect of her and Tom's domestic happiness. Some portion of the garden where they now live is her special charge. I have promised to help her stock it out of my supplies, this autumn.

September 29th

HAD A WORD WITH MY CHIEF TODAY, WHO INTIMATED THAT due to the falling off of official business, the question of my retention by the office may come up for review. It was not unexpected: I had already seen dimly the writing on the wall. But I'm not unduly concerned about the employment of my impending leisure. It doesn't frighten me. The most serious effect it can have will be upon my income, which will at once be reduced to one third of my current salary. By the exercise of a not too severe economy we still can live at Shieling in a style not far removed from our ordinary standard, which itself is modest. We have enough to keep the bed linen white, the carpet hoovered, the lavatory decent, the larder reasonably full, tidy and sweet-smelling, the bathroom inviting and doorsteps and windows clear. The domestic hearth is not an obscenity after the night before and generally the rooms are bright with flowers. A coat of paint finds application in good times. We prefer a home to a museum and place no finicky restrictions on the use of our best chairs. The kitchen being the warmest place in the winter, we breakfast there in comfort.

Pont reads to me the leading article in the *Daily Telegraph* to the soft music of the wind through the bare branches of the sycamores; moans the wind never so bleakly there is no more cheery homely place to sit and read or write than the log room. Yes, I think we can keep all that going and still have reserves for a rainy day. My wife will share my retirement so far as I may share her domestic duties. For the rest of my leisure, there will be the garden and the greenhouse and jobs about the house: always there will be some reading and writing and perhaps poetry too. But most attractive of all to the spirit of romance still lurking within me is the prospect of much country walking and exploration, perhaps for days on end, and the chance maybe of some overseas voyage when a quixotic imagination might clothe me with the travel-stained garments of a Marco Polo, or might I roam abroad, like David Grayson* as the caliph of Baghdad incognito, to find those adventures in friendship and understanding which he writes so seductively about. Yet must the homeliness of home be the permanent background to which all things shall be related. A splendid dream is that Shieling shall be the resting place of congenial souls, of whatever creed, age, sex, station or circumstances, who by their humanity and understanding shall discover in my home the touchstone for the gold within them. As Thoreau says, 'The richest gifts we can bestow are the least marketable.'

Probably the only 'Meeting Place' I shall ever know is the cloistered seclusion of my own inmost thoughts and emotions,

* David Grayson's *Great Possessions* is one of nine volumes of fiction entitled *Adventures in Contentment*, the first of which was published in 1908, in which a farmer writes about his walk across rural America. Walter would have responded to the traditional values of simplicity and appreciation of nature expressed in them.

that inner sanctuary full of the warm amber light of a sun that never sets.

October 2nd

ARRIVING IN LEEDS THIS EVENING AFTER A SOMEWHAT PROtracted journey, I just thought that I would spend a couple of hours at the cinema. *The Four Feathers* seemed an attractive title, but afterwards I decided that my own thoughts were better company and in the GPO telephone room revised my notes for 29th September and in the shadow cast by my own hand – for there was only one light in the room – wrote up my diary. Groping my way up the steps to the street I found myself in the Stygian darkness of City Square and felt my way to the Griffin for a meal. The ordering of a tankard of bitter beer to my supper reminded me of Pauline and Sid's call on Sunday at Shieling and Sid's tale of trouble in obtaining supplies of beer and spirits for his pub in Isleworth during the transition from peace to war, of the stealing of glasses by his customers – not less than twelve shillings' worth on Saturday night – who by all accounts are tough and sordid and mendacious; of his head barman, now dismissed, who robbed him, of the attempt by a customer during the blackout evening to steal his car, and the difficulties they have with two vigilant policemen and the nice tact that must be exercised when tempers are frayed and edgy over beams of light emitted from intermittently opening doors, and not least the dreadful atmosphere of the public bars as a result of lack of ventilation due to light-screening arrangements. A miserable business running a pub at such times in such a neighbourhood. It's a wretched affair making money on such terms, but needs must when the devil drives and one can only hope they'll be able to find more agreeable occupations soon. Fred seemed inclined to the view that the office authorities were not over-gracious in their consent to my Yorkshire journey this week. While I would not have him unhappy about their attitude, I remarked that the job had to be done as we had already inspected far too large a quantity of materials on samples submitted by the contractors themselves, which may or may not fairly represent bulk supplies. The war won't last for ever. He agreed, but not without some concern at my resistance to a policy with which, in principle, I disapproved. I felt that he was nervously diffident about hitching his wagon to a star – if only a tethered one.

The oleaginous and faintly acrid smell of frying fish as I walk along the Dewsbury Road is an offence to the darkness and me. More dark and silent still my lodgings when I shut the front doors on the vague and shadowy life in the street and grope for the switch. Eerie, too, the empty house, and strangely impersonal since Mrs Sheard* departed to Scotland a month ago to nurse a sick sister. The association of friendliness with household effects ceases in the absence of the owner, especially when there is no cheery face to watch the movement of my pen across these pages.

October 5th

DURING MY TRAVELS THIS WEEK I FIND THE REACTION TO MR Churchill's speech over the radio on Sunday night is everywhere satisfactory and, in fact, enthusiastic. It was in the spirit and temper that the man in the street could understand and

* Mrs Sheard was a northern friend with whom Walter stayed while on working trips to Yorkshire. She later became his housekeeper and companion.

appreciate. It helped him to feel that the country was doing something really definite about the war and that he himself was taking a not unimportant part on the Home Front in the crusade. That Poland should be submerged as a rock by a tidal wave was in the circumstances inevitable, tidal waves eventually recede – an excellent analogy and picturesque. A possible key to the Russian pact with Germany is to be found in Russia's anxiety to safeguard her boundaries against Nazi double-crossing, with Latvia, Estonia and Lithuania as pawns in the game. Our air force and naval successes had accounted for 10 per cent of German U-boat strength and had provided us with 150,000 tons of enemy cargo in excess of our normal stock, with a loss on our own part of less than half that quantity. Mr Churchill gave a touch of humour to his talk when he said that our navy was conducting the enemy submarine hunt with mercy but not without relish. He referred to the corruption among Nazi high chiefs. He rightly warned us that we were in for a tough time, that the ordeal would be severe but the price would be worth while. Above all, we weren't to get bored because for the moment there were no spectacular encounters. He declared that we should all find our right jobs in the scheme of the affair in due course. Spent a couple of hours over late tea with my friends Edmund and Maud Hoyle at The Hilliers. Wendy Hoyle, who has now left school and joined the VAD, is developing into a fine young woman, not without spirit of her own. I was greatly amused by her pert indignation when, her father somewhat caustically reproaching her for the slab of bread with margarine instead of butter which she brought into the dining room on a soiled plate to refresh supplies, she flounced out in a huff banging the door. I felt that the manner of his reproach, even before me, wasn't in quite good taste, but I was glad very soon to see Wendy, all shy smiles, demurely returning with her more successful effort.

October 6th

THIS EVENING I READ HITLER'S SPEECH TO THE REICHSTAG. THAT we are all now entering upon the final stage of the European drama, possibly the most terrible, appears certain. Having declared that we will have no truck with him or his kind, any reply seems unnecessary, yet as a matter of diplomatic courtesy and in order to avoid any misunderstanding by the world of our aims we must declare ourselves. In fact, we have already cut the banter. The direction in which the current of events will carry our fate is in the hands of Providence but of the worthiness of our cause we need have no misgivings. May our crusade go forward that the world may enjoy that lawful freedom which is every man's heritage.

October 8th

WITH A HEAVY COLD THAT HAS SUDDENLY DESCENDED UPON me, I am enjoying an extra hour or two in bed where, for the first time in several years, I have eaten my breakfast. I would never reconcile food and bed. Altho' this bedroom is my place of rest for at least half the year, not until this morning have I so fully appreciated its picturesque old-world charm. Through the open casement of the oriel window came the call to service from St Mary's, the sound of passing footsteps, the chatter of starlings and chirping of sparrows.

To me here as I write propped up in bed, sounds of lunch in preparation come up from the kitchen, so finishing my cigarette I rise and dress, hopeful that this pleasant idling will put me in good fettle for tomorrow.

October 16th

THIRTY-SIX HOURS OF CONTINUOUS AND SOMETIMES HEAVY RAIN during the weekend filled two of our rivers, the Mole and Ember, to their brims and made work in the garden impossible. Everywhere the yellow-brown of sycamore leaves against the brilliant green of the surviving grass imparted a sad beauty to the lawn as I saw it from the bedroom window on Sunday morning. Michaelmas daisies looked helpless and pathetic under the stinging lash of cold rain and queued in company with chrysanthemums, which bowed their heads in mute resignation and sympathy. Except for an occasional bedraggled tit, never a sight or sound of a bird to hearten our drowned world.

October 23rd

A LONG AND INTERESTING LETTER FROM FRANK THIS MORNING, full of reflections, comments and quotations. He refers to a book he recently picked up on *Friendship* by Hugh Black, commenting, 'It is because I like to think that someone thinks as I do on this subject that I express approval of this book.' Frank writes, too, of a book entitled *Winged Pharaoh* concerning the life of an Egyptian priestess who was joint pharaoh with her brother; of her parable of the wall, which she related to the farmer's wife estranged from her husband. 'I said to her, "Sebek, do you see that wall which has grown up between you and your husband until you can no longer reach him and how he is even hidden from your sight? Each brick is but a foolish word of yours, and even as you can no longer see him because of it, so can he no longer see you and of his loneliness he has taken unto himself the girl who tends the cows. Henceforward think well before you speak, and say only those things that you would like to hear said to you by one you love. Build no more upon this barrier and you shall find it crumbling before the love in your heart as a wall of unbaked mud crumbles before the inundation." ' A parable we can all take to heart.

October 26th

THE OTHER EVENING, CROSSING WESTMINSTER BRIDGE ON MY way home, I was struck by the curious almost unearthly storm light in the sky and the angry agitation of the clouds, which moved pendantly, grey-green and dull yellow, in rugged procession, trailing slaty blue wispy veils of wild rain, which here and there descended to the bleak windswept turgid waters of the Thames below.

October 27th

THIS MORNING, QUIETLY ENJOYING MY EARLY CUP OF TEA AND cigarette, my eye lighted upon this thought for the day in the *Sunday Express*, 'Lord, ere I start upon another day, I kneel to thee and in these words I pray, If I should fail in that for which I strive, grant from that failure good may I derive. And if I should succeed, then grant to me in that success thy guiding hand to see. But whether my affairs go right or wrong, grant me, O Lord, the grit to carry on.' Well, that is prayer enough for me.

During a pleasant couple of hours in the evening with neighbour Hook, apropos of seagulls, he told me that they sleep perched on the walls of our local reservoirs, secured from disturbance by gull sentinels, doing duty at each end, who raise the alarm at the approach of intruders.

October 31st

SOME THOUGHTS EN ROUTE FOR MANCHESTER. AS QUOTED BY Deacon Frye in an article of his I read in the *Evening Standard* recently, Goethe said, 'National hatred is always strongest in peoples of the lowest level of civilization.' The only good example which comes to my mind of 'national hatred' is that of the old Boers, which seemed to smoulder uniformly throughout their Africa, a deep sullen hatred of the mid-Victorian British, which had its roots as deep in their own stern Calvinism as ever it had in their resentment of our early colonial policy. The big, powerful, conquering nations of the past, often with less culture than the conquered, were fighters rather than haters and often victors and vanquished together enjoyed advantages and benefits ultimately resulting from the contest. Primitive peoples are not united enough and too simple for national hatred; generally they are laughter-loving folk, too close to the earth and inconsequential, I imagine, to be anything but merely wilful. For reasons of physical and mental inaccessibility, simple people don't lend themselves to effective hate propaganda, and the cultured can and do judge for themselves. Real hatred, like a poisonous weed, is an evil thing and wholly belongs to evil and, like the poisonous weed, should be exterminated for the common good, but I think there is relatively little of it of such detestable quality in the world.

In M'chester. Drawing my attentions to a small black dog, something of a cross between a smooth-haired terrier and a Labrador, the manager of E. J. Cook's leatherworks in the Blackfriars district of Salford told me that since its owner, an old woman occupying a poor cottage in a nearby street, died some three years ago the dog had patiently awaited her return. A home had been found for it, which it used merely as a dormitory; the leatherworks people provided the animal with food, and every day and all day between meals the dog remained in attendance on the old lady's cottage, a pathetic symbol of enduring loyalty, affection and patient hopefulness. I stood and watched for perhaps twenty minutes while the dog, after a short interval of sitting by the threshold, ran to the street corner and stood in an attitude of patient expectation, one paw raised, while it looked up and down the busy Salford Road. Then it crossed, for a short while repeated its anxious scrutiny from the works gate, soon to trot thoughtfully back to the cottage. Repeated several times as I stood watching, this, so far as I could see, was its whole waking existence.

The leatherworks, which I visited, I should think is almost unique in the kind of business it transacts. Here are received the pelts of walrus, seal, whale, shark, porpoise, crocodile, alligator, elk, moose, buffalo, bison, elephant, rhinoceros, hippopotamus and others I have forgotten. One year is the tanning time for the average pelt. Because of the war, walrus hunting as a commercial enterprise has practically ceased. Only the few hunted by the Eskimo are available, but to him the flesh and blubber are of chief interest as food; the pelt is therefore flayed with little care, in the crudest possible manner, is so damaged in the process as to have little value as a hide and is scarcely worth the cost of tanning. The commercially hunted walrus is flayed with proper regard to its pelt value as leather. Maybe the temporary cessation of whaling and sealing will afford these marine creatures a chance to restore their numbers through uninterrupted breeding. Some wonderfully soft elk hides from German pelts, resembling giant chamois leathers of the best sort and similarly tanned by an oil and fermentation process, were valued at 12*s*. per pound weight and cut into discs, rather like the cross-section of a pineapple. When threaded into a mandrel and revolved at high speed they are used to sharpen razor blades in bulk! Other of these curious hides are used for buffing and polishing in the cutlery, silver and other metal-fashioning trades. The manager said he couldn't buy walrus hides if he offered 20*s*. an ounce for them.

November 5th

WHETHER MY RECOLLECTION OF PAST AUTUMN GLORIES IS softened by the years or that my application is now in sharper focus is a matter for speculation. Maybe the years have brought some increasing refinement of perception, for I do not remember a Sunday so vividly colourful, so prodigal in variety of tints, so magical in effects of light and shade as this. And overhead the soft cumulus clouds sailing luminously across the blue made perfect the amplitude of fulfilment and quiet content. Such were my impressions in the Little Croft car through sunny Sussex to Fittleworth, there to lunch at the Old Swan with its gables and galleries, crooked stairways and odd mysterious corners all mellow with age and lore of generations long forgotten. There, too, is a copy of the group portraits by Herkomer of the selection committee of the Royal Academy of Victorian days, giving some clue perhaps to the identity of the distinguished revellers. On the staircase walls, a collection of police truncheons, batons, staves, rattles and handcuffs and an old pistol or two carries the mind back to the days of London's watchmen and Bow Street runners before Sir Robert Peel created the police force as we know it today and made of the 'bobby' or 'peeler', as he was then called, a public institution. Then lunch, the food good and generous to repletion, with cheerfulness abounding, and afterwards a stroll through the ivied archway, down to the Arun with its two old hump bridges, the picturesque old mill and lively churning waterwheel. Then leisurely on to explore Fittleworth church standing in its triangular acre of sunlit repose at the junction of the Pulborough and Petworth roads.

Finally a great half-hour alone with the old dog and Santayana's *Soliloquies on England*, before going to bed. Truly a day well spent.

November 11th

THE TWENTY-FIRST ANNIVERSARY OF ARMISTICE DAY – AND FOR ten truanted minutes I absented myself from the office, in Parliament Square, my tribute to the consecrated silence. Perhaps because of the absence of any organized ceremony, the absence of massed people, of directing police and traffic diversion, perhaps because of the restricted life of London, its wartime life, until 11 a.m. was taking its normal course, and it seemed that the observance of the silence was all the more serene and spontaneously represented. There was no maroon signal to declare the moment of observance and startle the pigeons into alarmed flighting circles over Parliament Square, no bowing of a thousand heads, nor at the end did the thin sound of the Last Post or the clarion call of Reveille cleave the silence, nor the roll of drums call the multitude to prayerful song to announce its close. But as Big Ben stated the hour of eleven, as with one accord every scattered vehicle stopped dead, every pedestrian halted in his stride and stood still, every soldier, sailor and airman remained quietly at the salute and the silence was of the stars on a still night. Yet some silly woman, so I read later, at the Cenotaph itself, most hysterically demonstrated her objections to the quiet proceedings and for her pains was promptly removed by the police. At two minutes past the hour, as if set in motion by some magic – as indeed it was – London resumed its life and movement.

November 13th

RECENTLY I LOOKED THROUGH THE STORY OF VAN GOGH, A book entitled *Lust for Life* by Stone. As with most frank stories of human life, much of it is sordid. His story differs in essentials from Victor Hugo's only in the matter of bank balance. Although his paintings have no appeal for me, I am content to accept his genius on the authority of others; Victor Hugo's remains unchallenged. Sex or alcohol or both seem often to bulk lazily in the slum life of the soul of men who achieve eminence in the artistic world. Their private affairs are caviar to the many who gloat with drooling jowls over the salacious titbits, mentally substituting themselves for the exalted one in the enjoyment of the pretty housemaid's favours. Yet fearful lest any should attribute to prurient motives their interest in the story.

The brandy bottle excites no such feelings. It is a curious fact that in certain sections of art, painting and poetry in particular, the animal in the artist is so over-emphasized as to distort the picture, often grossly. On the other hand in many cases great composers of music are so loaded with haloes that their lives are made to appear too perfect to be really human. Yet their art cannot be expressed except through emotions which, springing from the inner being and seasoned by experience, are too complex for simple statement. I doubt if any should escape some measure of slum life in its private world.

November 19th

MY FATHER'S EIGHTY-THIRD BIRTHDAY TODAY, SO WE INVITED him and his wife to lunch at Shieling. He looked remarkably well and moreover talked well. He carries his years lightly and looks forward to passing the 90 mark without misgivings.

On Saturday afternoon, after lunching with Pont at Kingston I took her to see the film *Goodbye Mr Chips*. We both thoroughly enjoyed this beautiful picture, which touches the high watermark of all-round good taste in conception and execution.

November 21st

TODAY MY PENULTIMATE TRIP OF THE WEEK TO NEWCASTLE. THE wagon covers of the goods train, which seems to step back as we overtake it, are so thick with hoar frost as to appear like spread bedsheets of the finest lawn. The smooth coats of the plough-horses gleam in the cold, hard light but it's good to see the sun after so many days of gloom and rain, days now all too short with the blackout commencing at 4.30 p.m. and no relief until 7.20 a.m. – nearly fifteen hours. A flock of still plovers, all facing the NW wind, flash their white breasts and wing parts as the passing train startles them into alarmed flight, but because of the rumble of wheels, I cannot hear their mournful cry. The sight of plovers recalls the engaging shy friendliness of a pair of dippers on Tuesday, which quietly flitted from beneath the old bridge at Hinchcliffe Mill. In short swift flightings low over the water they preceded me by some twenty yards from boulder to boulder down the moorland stream as I followed the companion footpath through the lovely little valley of the Holme to Holmforth. For nearly a mile we carried on this delightful flirting acquaintance as I walked quickly on making the most of the opportunity for sustained observation of these very proper and tailor-made birds. Tailor-made because they are so correct and immaculate in their brown-grey livery and wide expanse of boiled shirtfront with never a crease or stain. Rather smaller than the thrush, the dipper is similar in form. When poised on a rock in midstream it stoops and flicks its tail with the grace of a blackbird. It dives fearlessly. Because of its protective colouring it is elusive and, except for a shrill note, silent. It lives where it loves in the seclusion of lonely moorland water courses and, like moorland people, is shy of noisy strangers. On Thursday in the pouring rain, after a stiff climb up Duel Lane from Sowerby Bridge station, I found myself stranded for lack of transport to my first place of call at Mythomroyd some six or seven miles distant. On enquiring at a small general shop nearby, with gloomy relish I was informed that 'Some folk yesterday waited two hours and ten minutes for a bus.' But the driver of a passing lorry, responding to my hail of distress, drew up and with great good humour took me aboard. Off we humped and rattled down the long hill to Hebden Bridge while the rain beat through the cracks of his swaying cabin as I poised on each separate spring of his upholstered seat trying in vain to find a comfortable spot. In business for himself, the elderly driver had thought of getting a new lorry, but times were 'not as good' and anyway 't'owd lass could still show a good enough leg'. And so without undue delay I arrived at Rotcliffe's Mill and commenced what, after all, was a very satisfactory day's work.

November 26th

A WILD, STIRRING MORNING AND AT WILLOW BRIDGE THE MOLE, turgid and brown, rushes headlong down its briny channel, swirling and eddying beneath the old bridge flecking with white spume its broad, smooth expanse at the bend. The old dog sniffs the air in complete enjoyment and I feel tremendously alive. For lunch came Ethel and Tom to Shieling and remained until the blackout announced the time for their departure. A very pleasant and quietly happy afternoon we all spent together round the fire after Pont's excellently prepared meal, which for a short while inclined us to somnolence. Pleasant conversation and a hand at whist rounded off the visit. A very promising cyclamen, which should be in full bloom by Xmas, and a tin of sweetmeats remain with us as mementoes of their visit.

November 27th

I RECEIVED TODAY THE FIRST OF FRANK TAYLOR'S NEW SERIES OF personal letters – a generous effort of something over 3000 words and every line of interest – of which series he is now preserving carbon copies for future reference. In it he refers to his first dip into Robert Burton's *Anatomy of Melancholy* from which he quotes – 'Here now, then there, the world is mine, Rare beauties, gallant ladies shine, Whate'er is lovely or divine, All other joys to this are folly, None so sweet as melancholy' – and promises more.

December 2nd

'PEACE ON THY HOUSE, O PASSER-BY.' THIS IS THE GENTLE inscription, carved in stone, over the portal of No. 2 Barton Street, SW1, a retreat of quiet refinement in the heart of Westminster, where the plane tree boles gleam with the dappled glory of buff and olive, and fat, leisurely pigeons find sanctuary in the secluded precincts of Westminster School, above which the venerable twin towers of the Abbey shine greyly in the autumn sunlight – a symbol of peace and culture so real, so established and abiding, that the news of Russia's invasion of Finland seems fantastically and cruelly absurd. It is more than an inscription, it is a Presence. And a curious train of thought drifted me on to Professor James's book *The Stars and Their Courses*. In it James quite properly reminds us of our relative unimportance in the great scheme of creation. But as Thos. Hardy, speaking of the stars, says of man, 'He is one with us, beginning and end.' And I for one find it difficult, if not impossible, to divorce emotion from science. If we are to believe the evidence of astronomers and biologists, geologists and historians, and the rest, there seems to be nothing inconsistent in the conclusion that all creation is ever a-waxing and waning. That is the stuff to which our senses and perceptions ultimately respond. It has the sanction of reason and intuition alike, and authority, too, in the finality of conviction, expressed by the old psalmist with such simple grandeur: 'As it was in the beginning, so now and ever shall be, world without end. Amen.'

December 4th

THAT THERE IS NO REAL HATRED CONTAINED IN US FOR THE Germans is evidenced by the opinion finely expressed by many that we may find ourselves and the French fighting in company with Germany to overcome the menace of Soviet Russia. A menace openly revealed in her efforts to secure by an attack on Finland the desired strategic, military, naval and air bases in the Gulf of Finland, which geographically is but an extension of the Izvestia Baltic. This is all of a piece with the plundering of Poland, of Russia's domination of the eastern Balkan states and the victimization of Germany itself. And all with a basely cynical disregard of the decencies, which leaves us with little doubt of her ultimate intentions eventually to achieve

European domination, a worse evil ever than domination by Nazi Germany. The growth of Nazism has been so fierce, so over-stimulated as to exhaust the fertile soil of enthusiasm and must needs live upon its own declining tissues. Maybe a chastened Germany will rise from the remains with its roots in the best German tradition. This is the Germany we can and will live with. But with Russia the problem is different, the country so vast, its people more primitive and, with their Mongolian mentality, their reactions even less predictable than those of the Germans. Its leaders are more astute, more wary, more subtle and callous and, in their control of their peoples, more absolute. Out of the welter of conflicting political creeds will emerge, we hope, a chastened and homely Europe to endure in friendliness and prosperous peace. But it's a long, long way to Tipperary.

December 5th

WITH OUR FEET FIRMLY PLANTED ON MOTHER EARTH – FOR THERE is no tradition without the soil – with hands and hearts actively employed about our daily affairs, with our imagination reaching out to the stars, we are in possession of a happy credo. This is my enchanted garden, full of all that is most worthwhile. Such was the introductory note of my letter to Mr Barr, whom I met this morning quite by chance while drinking a hasty coffee in a Praed Street Lyons before boarding my train at Paddington for the West Country.

A bright-eyed, cheerful, active little man of 73 years of age, he sat at the next table philosophizing that we should live less in the past and make more of the present and future. I told him that I subscribed to his sentiments, that I myself talked this stuff to all who would listen but found, generally, that men were more responsive than women to my overtures. 'But why,' he asked, 'do you say that?' I replied that I believed the aversion of the generality of women to such a creed was an attribute of sex that expressed itself in a material conservatism too deeply instinctive to admit of appreciable modification – and because of this they tended to live much in the past. But my train wouldn't wait for me, so we exchanged cards and with them a promise to continue a talk so mutually agreeable. On his I read, 'J.W. Barr FRHS, land, estate and horticultural technical adviser, 20 London Street, London W2.' On enquiring, he told me he was of the well-known firm of seed and bulb growers of King Street, Covent Garden.

And now my train is just drawing out of Bath station on its way to Bristol, my first port of call. The day is cold. A thin sprinkling of snow lightly veils the Wiltshire countryside, the high downs gleam whitely under the uniformly grey sky. Inside the bus to Buckfastleigh it is comfortable and warm enough, with ample light for reading, but I don't envy the driver his ten-mile drive in the utter darkness. With a gadget resembling a miniature piano strapped to his chest the conductor approaches, turns a handle and grinds out my shilling ticket.

December 10th

YESTERDAY WE SPENT A PLEASANT AFTERNOON AT NEIGHBOUR Hook's, during which he commented on my diary entry of 31st October on the subject of hatred, which he had read earlier in the week. He told me that he had found confirmation of my views in his concordance.

December 16th

EN ROUTE FROM LEEDS I TAKE MY THIRD LOOK THROUGH Frank's last letter, four greasy mechanics play solo whist, and except for the chink of small change the carriage is quiet. They smell a little of stale motor oil but a stroll through the fish truck behind tells of worse, so I sit comfortably in my corner and make a note or two.

December 19th

TO TOWN FOR LUNCH WITH PONT. FRED JOINED US FOR A HAPPY few minutes of reunion over a glass of wine – Pont and Fred hadn't met for over eighteen months – and then to the Army and Navy Stores for some Xmas shopping. A very comfortable place for leisurely marketing. Their wares are of the better sort, as in the main are their customers. But much of the Xmas stuff displayed can only be described as useless, and expensive at that, articles that can only serve the most transitory purposes, weeds of the industrial world, scarcely ornamental and never useful. Collectors of dust and dirt in the home which, on first presentation, bring to the lips of the recipients a spate of ecstatic superlatives – 'How cute', 'So quaint', 'What a dinky thing' – then later, the lumber loft or the dustbin, or maybe inflicted upon the charlady for decent burial. Labour and material just wasted.

December 24th

LISTENING TO THE MORNING RADIO SERVICE I HEARD, 'THE spirit of Christ can only remain in the affairs of men so long as it takes command of their hearts.' That statement is essentially true. I hoped that it was more than the utterance of a wishful thought when the speaker declared that in this country the war was bringing us to a more lively appreciation of spiritual values. With my niece Joy I visited Florrie at the homeopathic hospital this afternoon where she is under observation pending a possible operation. She seemed pretty cheerful and confident. The enforced rest will do her much good. Decorated for Xmas festivities, the wards looked gay and even sparkling.

And so out into the finger cold gloom of foggy twilight for home calling en route on neighbour Hook to wish his house a merry Xmas. Over a glass of sherry, enjoyed some talk about Thoreau, whom he thought resembled Emerson in his writings. Ethel and Tom had arrived by the time I reached home and we all spent a happy evening at solo whist. Taking the dog out at 11.35 p.m., I found the fog much cleared and the moon shining brightly over a freezing world. We enjoyed together a stroll to Willow Bridge where we remained looking at the quiet, still scene until the Hampton Court clock tolled the midnight hour.

December 25th

A SLOW, RELUCTANT DAWNING AND, EXCEPT FOR THE PATTER outside of drops from the mist-shrouded trees, very still. The household sleeps on as I quietly prepare the early-morning tea. After breakfast wishing Little Croft, Heathfield and Lyndhurst a merry Xmas I returned to Shieling, set the wine before the fire, put on the yule logs, which I had reserved for the occasion, and made preparations for carving the immortal bird. Putting calls through during the interval to Fred and Frank, I found them engulfed in the same pleasant duties. Pont, Ethel and Tom are in good form and so to the feast of the year, and with the time-honoured toast my thoughts reach out to the many about this island of ours whose goodwill and friendship it has been my privilege to enjoy over the years. To them and to all I wish a merry Xmas. I could wish that none were less blessed than we ourselves are at Shieling this day. Our dinner was a truly merry event, a feast for the Gods which made all the more agreeable the restful afternoon by firelight. A walk along the riverbank with the old dog in the early evening under a hazy moon afforded pleasant exercise and I discovered a heron quietly fishing.

And so back to the brightness, warmth and good cheer of Shieling and an evening of cards, to be rounded off by Gracie Fields on the radio, that wonderful songster somewhere in France who, with characteristic enthusiasm, is entertaining the troops and us. Thus passed Xmas Day most happily for us all.

December 26th

CLIFFORD AND DORIS FOR LUNCH AND THE REST OF THE DAY. IT was good to see him, his first visit to Shieling since his wedding day. A merry meal and reposeful afternoon. Some talk about words in the evening and some agreement about the flexibility of the word 'unique', Doris contending that any qualification, such as quite, as in 'quite unique', was redundant, myself holding that in certain applications the adverb is permissible in emphasizing the quality and extremity of uniqueness in the relation of rare object to a like neighbour. We agreed to differ on the grounds that for the purist she was right, yet for the purpose of verbal currency there was nothing inconsistent with good taste in the use of the adverb. Not only is the slovenly use of words in conversation, as in writing, an offence to the mother tongue, but it brands the user with the measure of his defects. Yet outside the lecture room, a too precise regard for exactitude makes of the purist a pedant and exposes him to the charge of verbal snobbery. The woman is dubbed a schoolmarm, the man a prig. We've got to live together so we may as well be comfortable with each other.

1940

January [illegible]

[illegible] New Year's [illegible] fully [illegible] occasion [illegible] years that the crisis [illegible] without having [illegible] cannibal[illegible], imprisoned [illegible] wanting their [illegible]

A very different story [illegible] when this [illegible] calamities [illegible] now, from this night it is not easy [illegible] present-day political and military [illegible] of the fantastic stories of the planned [illegible] Jews by sterilization, of the [illegible] into the mouths of prisoners in concentration camps [illegible] gaps and suicides by concentration [illegible] still going on behind the scenes [illegible] cal domination. In the [illegible] of the [illegible] distribution of wealth, spreading [illegible] social

January 1st

I LOOK OUT OF THE WINDOW INTO THE FOG AND GLOOM OF A New Year's morning. So much as I can see of the garden gleams fully of congealed snow. No sound of bird nor any sign save a confusion of claw prints about the terraces of the rockery where yesterday the birds were fed. A bitter cold and still silence prevails without having the rumourless indifference to life of a maiming cartwheel, unpersonal as the earthquake in Turkey, as relentless as warring man's inhumanity to man these troubled days.

A very different story is this from my entry of a year ago when first I started this diary; nor could one then see the calamities upon us. Sitting by the comfortable fireside of my cosy room this night it is not easy to realize the horrors of present-day political and military events, or the truth of the fantastic stories of the organized mutilation of thousands of Jews by sterilization, of the urination by their guards into the mouths of prisoners in concentration camps, of awful floggings and suicides by compulsion and all the rest of the sadistic stuff going on behind the scenes in the name of war for political domination. In the twentieth century, in spite of the better distribution of wealth, spreading education, improved social amenities, general material advancement and wider culture, we are back to the bestially crude indignities and violences of the Dark Ages. Faith in the ultimate goodness of mankind needs to be deeply rooted to withstand 'the thousand natural shocks that flesh is heir to'. We can only hope that faith dwells with the majority, lest life for the next few generations be utterly without saviour, barren and bleak. I could have wished that this New Year's Day had heralded the beginning of better things, that mankind had begun this climb out of the valley of shadows into which he had been so wilfully driven, but the journey is before us and the way long, difficult and dangerous. So I look through the year's events and communiqués as recorded in this diary for 1939, a sort of personal log book registering my approximate course, and realize how full of interest the journey has been. Yet, in the light of experience, I am conscious that the sails of my barque will forever need trimming if the desired course is to be maintained.

January 4th

PROTESTS INCREASE DAILY AND BECOME MORE VOCIFEROUS amongst civil servants as the scheme for the evacuation of their offices from London is more widely applied. The recent removal of the personnel from the Ministry of Health has brought a spate of objections from individuals, mostly female staff, on the grounds of the economic and domestic hardships it imposes. The popular press has not been slow to take advantage of the event by the publication verbatim of individual protests, more colourful than discreet, and certain pretty girls have achieved, in the publication of their photographs, a fleeting notoriety. It imposes real hardships on some of the junior married men who now have to keep two homes going, an avoidable expense to them and the nation.

January 6th

I RETURNED TODAY AFTER AN ICY BUT OTHERWISE SINGULARLY uneventful week in Yorkshire. With the temperature somewhere in the twenties getting about was difficult and in the blackout even dangerous. During my journeyings, despite the county's basic need, I saw little being done to give effect to the Minister of Agriculture's appeal to farmers to put more land under cultivation, and there was little or no evidence of any extension of allotments. To expect private householders to tear up their lawns for potatoes, to root up their herbaceous borders and flower-beds for cabbages by way of setting an example of home food production, is to begin at the wrong end. As if war stuff is not ugly enough we have to make unsightly our little oases of quiet delight in this desert of strife by amateurish attempts to convert them into potato patches. Surely a well-cultivated ornamental garden has some aesthetic value – some beauty is required to offset the ugliness of war. Man does not live by bread alone. No. Let the farmer set a good example with his land, it is his job, his responsibility; let all idle plots be converted into allotments – even without rent – and then as a last resort, if supplementary efforts are required, the home flower gardens and lawns might be savaged in the name of patriotism. Farmers grumble and declare that farming doesn't pay but the fact of the matter seems to be that many of them are lazy, unimaginative and unprogressive. Moreover, many have become urbanized and have lost the land tradition. They might well take a lesson from the examples set by the small farmers of Holland, France and Belgium who work wonders with the land which, because of their industry, supports a large and contented peasant population.

January 12th

A RISE OF OVER TWENTY DEGREES ON THE TEMPERATURE OVER last weekend made Sunday comfortably warm but since then the thermometer has never been above freezing point and often ten below.

The barrage balloons, which are much in evidence again, gleam frostily in the upper air. But it is comfortable this night sitting by the glowing fire as I conceive plans for my small hand loom, the construction of which I want to begin as soon as possible. It's good to occupy myself during these weeks of war and political dissension with interests so remote from events. The knitting I had undertaken is too monotonous for my taste, but I wouldn't myself refuse a task that others had so willingly agreed to share for the common cause, yet 70 stitches per row for the khaki woollen scarf I am making seems interminable. It is devastating to reflect that some 14,000 stitches are required for the whole job, representing – at my rate of progress – about 34 hours of continuous work. However, I must persevere.

January 18th

PAULINE TO LUNCH WITH PONT AT SHIELING TODAY. ON MY return from the office I found them both comfortably knitting by a bright fire. She is greatly improved in health, and although the war and blackout has brought serious reverses to her business of the pub, she is cheerful enough.

January 20th

A ROSY FLUSH SUFFUSING THE EASTERN SKY PORTENDS A CLEAR, cold day. The high arch of morning is cloudlessly azure. My thermometer registers 16 degrees frost.

During my walk along the Albert Embankment, Lambeth Bridge greyly develops through the foggy veil shadowing the river as might some slowly intensified image on a photographic plate. Over the train of lumbering barges mooring downstream a flight of some forty mallards in formation comes swiftly into view and as swiftly passes. With crowds of shuffling mortals I hurry along Millbank to the more genial warmth of the office. Food and warmth seem to be the only essentials this cold January when, as the *Daily Telegraph* reports, Finland records 100 degrees of frost and all Europe to the Mediterranean is in the grip of an implacable cold. Our friendly Gulf Stream spares us the rigours of such polar conditions.

January 26th

MY BROTHER'S BIRTHDAY. I DULY WRITE HIM. AFTER A WEEK OF frozen travel in Yorkshire where, near Leeds, 28 degrees of frost was recorded last weekend, I am today on the homeward journey.

News from Alice Mary during the week comforted me with the thought that all is well at Shieling and that my greenhouse children, which, when I left on Monday morning, in spite of a fortnight's bitter frost, were still doing well.

Taking a leisurely look over Frank's letter as I journey home, I am amused by his gentle banter concerning my knitting. With my knitting needles and spectacles, all that I need, says he, to complete the picture of domesticity is a skirt and over

...some beauty is required to offset the ugliness of war—

my shoulder a shawl. Be that as it may, this have I discovered: an hour or so of knitting has a soothing effect, which comes from a gentle absorption in the task which promotes tranquillity. Anyway, it's gratifying to record that the quality of the work of my knitting circle has been praised by my Halifax friends to whom the various articles – mittens, scarves, helmets and pullovers – have been sent for distribution through Sam Hoyle, now expecting his captaincy, to his company of the 7th Duke of Wellington's Regiment. The compliment has been duly passed on to all concerned.

And still browsing through Frank's letter; in a kindly reference to my own verse story of Cupid and Psyche,* he introduces, relative to the poet's attitude to his readers, some extracts from the Russian poet Pushkin which not a little remind me of Alexander Pope's essay on 'Criticism: The Critic's Task'.

A little learning is a dang'rous thing;
Drink deep, or taste not the Pierian spring:
There shallow draughts intoxicate the brain,
And drinking largely sobers us again.

As I approach the end of my journey so I reach the conclusion of his letter in which he tells me, 'Midnight has chimed on the grandfather clock and the fire is now getting low. Possibly Tom and Alice Mary have retired ere this and are sound asleep. May your sleep be refreshing to your dear old bodies and the wintry sun rise and shine upon a little home full of love and happiness. Cheerful thoughts and happy working hours be thine.' Good will in abundance, what more does a man want from his friend?

* Walter was composing a long poem on the story of Cupid and Psyche.

January 28th

THREE INCHES OF SNOW GREETED MY FIRST GLANCE OUT OF THE window this morning. For the first time since the war, weather today is front-page news, much prominence is given to the freeze-up, somewhat belatedly, I thought, after three weeks of the severe weather, but it's a change from the war news.

January 29th

MORE SNOW FELL IN THE NIGHT; THE SERVICE OF TRAINS FROM Hampton Court was practically suspended. By bus via Kingston to Surbiton where luckily I picked up a main-line train which by chance stopped at Vauxhall, my journey to the office occupied 2½ hours. The electric trains were attached to steam locomotives to ensure progress. The snow has brought about a state of chaos in the railways. Incessant flashes of blue light from the electric conductors fill the night sky with a spectral radiance and light up the snow-covered landscape with a ghostly glow. The *Daily Telegraph* reports the Thames frozen over for eight miles between Teddington and Sunbury, and at Edgbaston a minimum temperature of three degrees below Fahrenheit, and amongst its items of special news, 'The sea froze as it lapped the shore at Felpham, near Bognor Regis, a line of ice stretching along the coast for 300 yards.' A woman found dead in her bath in Islington was sitting in a block of ice. In the Capil district snow reached the rooftops of some homes – families found themselves trapped until they could cut a way out through their doors. Many sheep were frozen to death on Romney Marshes. It is reported that the death toll through cold is considerable; frozen waterpipes and boiler explosions announce many casualties. My evacuated next-door neighbour arrived home this weekend with his family from Whitchurch, Hants, and found all his radiators cracked, his kitchen boiler burst and lavatory pan with the bottom out. A sorry state of affairs. A hot-water bottle left in his children's bed, although covered with four blankets, was frozen solid. We did our best to help them over their troubles. By way of consolation the *DT* concludes its weather news by reference to the fact that 'Dec 4th 1879 holds the record for the coldest visitation in this country. On that date 55 degrees of frost was registered in Berwickshire.'

February 1st

YESTERDAY A THAW SET IN AND CONTINUED THROUGH THE night, and today it still holds. During the night, avalanches of snow from the roof at Shieling seemed to be dragging the tiles with them as they crashed to the ground. But a hurried inspection this morning discovered no damage. Everywhere in town the streets are wet and slippery while at home half-melted snow makes the going treacherous. Snow piled in heaps along the roadsides awaits a final turn in the weather. Looking through the January edition of *State Service* this evening, I read that the first civil servant of whom English history has preserved clear record, the respected founder of the Exchequer and creator of the service, was Father Roger, a humble parish priest of Caen, Normandy, in whose little chapel during a declaration of mass, Henry I took shelter during a storm while hunting. The speed with which the priest concluded his service commended itself to the irreverent but industrious king, who appointed him to his service as chaplain of the Royal Household. Because of his literacy, zeal and ability the new chaplain rapidly achieved promotion, and in 1101 Henry made him Chancellor, i.e., head of the clerks who drew up the King's

Writs. In 1102 he was appointed Bishop of Salisbury and later the king conferred upon him the Justiceship, the highest office under the crown. His reforms quickly reduced the kingdom to order and its barons to obedience, which achieved for the Crown 'both the law and the profits'. From now on all the financial business of the Crown passed through the hands of a trained permanent staff and there began the work of the first organized civil service since classical times when, such was the good order of the state, 'a single man might carry gold from one end of the country to the other, in peace'. Roger, Bishop of Salisbury, left a memorial more lasting and permanent than the tomb, suspected to be his, which is shown to this day in Salisbury Cathedral.

February 4th

THE GREAT FROST IS OVER. THE THAW BEGAN OVERNIGHT. THIS morning everywhere drips water, a slight rain falls, the snow lies as sloppy obscene mush, almost pathological. The fine pebbly ballast strewn a fortnight ago to afford foothold on the icy paths no longer serves its friendly purpose but, lying menacingly on the wet pavements, threatens to penetrate the strongest boot soles to torment the feet. For all that, the change from Arctic conditions is very agreeable. The sun shines weakly and the bland wet air gives a far-off hint of spring. From beneath vestiges of snow in the garden the delicate new green of bulbs emerges bravely, even the birds are singing. The thermometer in the greenhouse stands at 50° without any assistance. It's nice to sit with a book this afternoon and feel comfortably warm all over.

February 10th

ON 4TH FEBRUARY I WROTE THAT THE GREAT FROST IS OVER, BUT I was not so sanguine as to suppose that we had suffered the last of the cold weather. After all February is our most wintry month and so early in the month one couldn't expect spring to make a real beginning. Yesterday a chill nor'-easterly brought the temperature down to freezing; the ground is again as hard as iron and seems likely to remain so for a few days. But the sun shines promisingly.

Following President Roosevelt's broadcast call for peace among the warring nations, and the much talked-of sympathy of the United States for Finland's heroic resistance to Soviet aggression, and the declaration of principles that should govern the relationships of governments the world over, there was something cynically ironical in the *DT* this morning of the shipment by America on Norwegian steamers of such war essentials as copper to Russia. Nonetheless, better the irony that Norway's ships should carry to a potential enemy material that might well be employed to effect her own destruction – and all in the sacred name of big business, which debases man's every precious possession in order to achieve gilt-edged solvency, power and fat dividends.

February 12th

IN A FLURRY OF SNOW TODAY I LEAVE PADDINGTON FOR THE West Country. With me I take Frank's last letter, which is concerned mainly with the celebration of New Zealand's centenary at the Mansion House on 6th February, presided over by the Lord Mayor of London, at which prominent members of the dominion, official and civilian, were welcomed by the King and Queen in introduction by Mr Jordan, NZ's high commissioner in London. Taylor writes enthusiastically about the simple and informal appearance among the crowd of guests of Their Majesties.

And so this afternoon more links had been forged that go to make that great chain which binds the Empire. Sitting in my fireside chair on the night following these centenary celebrations, I let my mind wander back to that faraway dominion of the southern seas where, as a lad of some fifteen summers, I had arrived without kith or kin as an English immigrant determined to carve a career for myself in that young country. How well I recall the sunny harvest day when, shortly after my arrival on the South Island, I strolled into a large paddock in which a crop of wheat was being harvested. I can almost hear the clatter of the reaper and binder as it cut into the standing corn and automatically delivered the neatly tied sheaves, tossing them to the ground where they lay in ordered rows like soldiers on a parade-ground. In the far corner of the paddock I noticed two farmhands busily engaged 'stooking' their sheaves and I thought, in my boyish innocence, what fun it must be. Nearer and nearer approached the binder until, with a lusty 'Whoa' from the driver, the team was brought to a standstill. Yes, I can recall the acrid perfume of those foam-flecked Clydesdales, dripping perspiration from the heat of their toil. I almost felt that I had done them a service by bringing their driver to a halt. Something in the cut of my English clothes must have roused the curiosity of the 'Cockie' for he asked what he could do for me and where I had come from. As I look back on it now I am not surprised that he burst out laughing when I informed him that I wished to learn farming and could he give me a job? In which he undertook to teach me something about farming and the very next day I was busy picking up those sheaves and raising blisters on my hands. To say the least of it, the going was hard. As cowboy, roustabout and general nuisance, one of my tasks, after having milked the cows, was to clean the children's boots prior to their going to school. I mention this because it has its sequel: Mary, a little toddler aged five, appeared to add to the enjoyment of her walk home from the village school by putting her boots in the creek and generally covering them with mud – how I blessed her. I can still see her mother looking at her unpolished boots with a scowl that clearly indicated my unpopularity and seeming uselessness. Yesterday I met Mary at the Mansion House. She is now a doctor of medicine in London and I – well, I'm also in London, engaged upon a task not so far removed from that which her father set out to teach me! Adventure enough for most, I imagine.

February 13th

THIS MORNING EARLY, IN THE GARDEN OF THE WHITE HART INN at Buckfastleigh, I saw my first crocus of the season in bloom, their orange-yellow petals warm above the still frosted grass. A few early lambs, sheltering with their ewes in the hedge corner of an upland meadow, tell of the season's beginning.

February 18th

A. P. HERBERT ON THE RADIO LAST NIGHT MADE TIMELY, IF somewhat scathing, reference to the growing tendency of Whitehall to what in glib official language might be described as verbal circumlocution, i.e., simple statements wrapt up in high-falutin language that not only confuses and irritates plain folk but often defeats its object, wastes paper as well as words, and stamps the author as a verbal snob. If Nelson's immortal signal had been written by one of our fat word-breeders in Whitehall, Herbert said, it would probably have read, 'England anticipates that with regard to the current emergency, personnel will duly implement their obligations in accordance with the functions allocated to their respective age groups.' Mr Churchill had shown, he added, that it was unnecessary to speak of big things in 'long woolly words'.

The rescue by HMS *Cossack* of English seamen on Saturday from the German naval auxiliary *Altmark*, one-time supply ship to the *Graf Spee* to which that ill-starred raider, now reclining on the floor of Montevideo harbour, transferred most of her captives, was a job well done in accordance with the best tradition of the British Navy. With a fine courage and a daring insolence worthy of Drake, the destroyer's company of merry men after cornering the *Altmark* in a Norwegian fjord boarded her and ran her stern just on to the rocks, and with great glee released from her stinking holds the three hundred or so prisoners who for weeks had suffered under its tyrant commander hardships and indignities reminiscent of the days of slave dhows. All the Empire and half the world chuckles over the swift success of our exploit, which so neatly at the eleventh hour turned the tables on the enemy, who had planned to stage the dramatic spectacle of a march of captive British PoWs thro' the streets of the German capital – who knows, perhaps in chains and barefoot.

February 20th

TO QUOTE FROM A LETTER JUST RECEIVED FROM DEAR OLD Brackenridge, whom I met when we were together in the metallurgical section of the Salvage Disposal Branch of the

War Office in 1918. A great old-timer from the Australian bush. A white medicine man, still remembered by the natives for a thousand miles of the Upper Amazon, prospector in the Bolivian Andes, mine surveyor in Zululand, who with a bunch of toughs joined the Canadian Army in Canada for service in France in the Great War and was discharged with the sight in one eye destroyed by shrapnel. Now a maker of optical telescopic sights for rifles. He is too honest ever to be rich, too independent ever to be poor, too kindly a philosopher ever to moan, a man of the primitive wild, white all through, but broken, a shadow of his former self. Writing about present events he says, 'There will no doubt be a new order of things to emerge from this terrible crisis, but what it will be, who can foresee?'

February 24th

TWO OR THREE DAYS OF SPRING-LIKE WEATHER HAS CHEERED everybody and done much to restore general confidence, which best expressed itself in the splendid welcome by the crowds to the crews of HMS *Ajax* and *Exeter*, heroes of the *Graf Spee* engagement, who yesterday marched thro' London to the Guildhall to be received by the Lord Mayor and receive the King's Honours. Mr Churchill said, 'Warriors of the past may look down on us now without any feeling that the island race has lost its daring.' Well said.

Taking a sunrise look around the garden this morning I spied a thousand green things breaking through the brown moist earth for a first greeting, and urgently within me grew the need to express my never absent wonder at the miracle of life, its tenacity and regeneration.

February 27th

ENTERING MY LOCAL NEWSAGENT SHOP LAST NIGHT, I RAN FULL tilt into an animated discussion between the proprietress and a customer on 'the difficulty in living up to the teachings of Christ' in this severely competitive world. A discussion which lost none of its friendly vigour because of my intrusion. Notwithstanding the lofty remoteness of the Divine Ideal they agreed that each should do his best, however humble the effort, towards its attainment. Here, I thought, is first-hand evidence in a place of public business of the beginnings, at least among the rank and file, of that spiritual awakening of which the Dean of Durham had written some four days ago in the *Daily Telegraph*. And to me came the thought of my lunchtime conversation with Frank, on Tuesday, concerning the probability of a post-war reaction of nations surfeited with political chicanery, waste of life and wealth and opportunity, which with proper leadership might be directed towards a more ready acceptance of Christian standards and ethical redemption. Few seem to recognize that all evolution is a painfully slow process, that every effort to speed it up brings disaster in its train, that the meagre net gains to mankind are seldom worth the price of his hurry. The things that matter in life are more permanent than the slow hills and as seldom we regard them. No great teacher better demonstrated these truths than the Nazarene, Himself a leader of men, whose supreme sacrifice, after two thousand years, seems to have counted for so little. And before Him, Plato. Science has afforded us many conveniences but few consolations – 'whither goest thou' is still on every tongue.

When, during the discussion, I was asked if I believed in a Hereafter, I enquired exactly what was meant by a Hereafter. I could elicit little but vague nothing. With the conventional heaven and hell I have scant patience, except as mythological conception.

March 6th

EN ROUTE TO HUDDERSFIELD AND HOLMFIRTH. WHETHER IT IS the end-of-winter feeling, the effect of the blackout, the news yesterday of Fred's sudden relapse or too much heavy reading – or maybe, when every man in my department except myself has been absent on sick leave this winter, I am a little tired with extra duties, I don't know, but certain it is this morning that I lack my customary buoyancy of spirits. Possibly it is the cumulative effect upon me of all these things that my outlook at the moment should carry a somewhat jaundiced tinge. But the very act of writing these notes, as I travelled, attested to the unreason of my gloom and slowly medicined me to a more cheerful frame of mind. From the bus I stepped into the gold of the sunshine to follow on foot the pleasant river path through the valley bottom to Hinchcliffe Mill and the banishment of melancholy.

March 8th

GRIMY AGAIN. HUNSLET PARISH CHURCH WAS CALLING THE FAITHful to prayer at 7.15 this morning as I passed in the tram on my way to the station. Public worship seemed unreasonable at that dark hour of cold dawn, and alien, like the pungent reek of coarse tobacco pervading the tram top from foul pipes stuck into tired faces of listless workmen. And inside the tram crowded somnolent women, and with them resides the smell of unwashed bodies, the stale oiliness of weaving sheds, the unmistakable damp, steamy heaviness of clothing-factory pressing rooms; faint whiffs of carbolic and eucalyptus followed bursts of smothered coughing and, as a background to this assortment of odours, the smell of a hot axle bearing, which, I noticed on alighting, sent a plume of faint blue smoke curling from under the chassis.

Queerly enough, through my head all the time runs insistently the lilting jingle of 'Tiptoe Through The Tulips With Me'. Still it lingered as I made these notes on the morning train to London.

A platform full of soldiers takes possession of my train at Doncaster. It is now too crowded for writing, so I read a little more of Plato, himself a would-be dictator and perhaps not so benevolent as such. I prefer Pericles: he was more human and less highbrow. Passing Peterboro', the strains of 'Pack Up Your Troubles In Your Old Kit Bag', sung with more gusto than harmony, came in chorus from the soldier boys in the coach behind mine.

March 12th

HOW VERY ELUSIVE IS THE SOUND OF THE WOODPECKER AT work. During my early walk with the dog this morning his rapid tapping at a hollow tree trunk sounded as might the quick action of a wooden machine-gun firing wooden bullets. In the treed space of a quarter of a square mile I diligently searched the bare upper branches; the wooden drumming sound seemed now here, now there, so local it appeared, so close, I felt he couldn't escape my search. Yet never a sight of him did I enjoy. Still, it was good to hear him, to know that he is still with us.

March 13th

NOSES ARE QUEER THINGS – AT LEAST, SO I FOUND MYSELF vaguely thinking when on Saturday our little party sat chatting pleasantly round the luncheon table. Not even the observant Frank could have guessed the object of my puckish thoughts.

Again this morning, in the train from Vauxhall, a whole row of noses obtruded themselves upon my attention. Anatomically the same, they offer the same infinite variety of form as do feet, ears, even potatoes. Without a good supply of noses, the handkerchief industry must perish – Manchester and Belfast would be on half-time. The beauty business would go into mourning, distillers would languish and barley-growing cease. Vineyards would no longer inspire the muse. Without a natural support for spectacles, the manufacturers would cease to exist. What should we do about sneezing? Every kind of nose must sneeze sometimes if only to dislodge that fly from a reposeful face. As a chemistry student my sense of smell was the final authority in the identification of the contents of bottles from which labels had disappeared. But an acute sense of smell is not an inured blessing as witness my unpopularity when, from the bedroom, I give warning of far-off scorching toast, of milk boiling over and other trifling domestic events. And what better than the intoxicating fragrance of some other body's good cigar on a frosty morning. Then is it 'follow your nose'.

March 16th

MY OWN NOSE HAS BEEN A BANE JUST NOW. FIGHTING A COLD for the better part of a week, I managed to hang on to the official chores till Friday was done and now here I am with a whole day in bed to my credit. And here I must remain for the most part, at least, of tomorrow. My creature comforts are the unremitting care and secret joy of my wife, and I am content to relax and abandon myself to her ministrations.

March 19th

SO OFTEN DO I READ OR HEAR ABOUT THE AVERAGE MAN THAT I am a little curious about a phrase that is so much taken for granted, since it neither describes nor defines him. Yet hypothetical as he is, in a loose way we all know when the stomach warms up that it is somewhere about lunchtime. He is the man for whom the state budgets and legislates. He is the man in the street of the press, neither brilliant nor dull, rich nor poor; neither saint nor rogue, tiger nor worm, merchant nor mendicant, whose heart and brain step in double harness along life's highway. On reflection, if left to himself, the Average Man might make a better job now of the governance of the world than the specialist. After all, with each intent on cultivating his garden co-operatively, there might come sustained peace and steady achievement towards an average world. To be average is not to be mediocre or static. It is to eschew extremes.

March 26th

ALICE MARY'S NIGHT-LONG FIT OF COUGHING HAS GREATLY disturbed and exhausts her. One can only hope that this bronchial attack will subside as suddenly as it happened. Her patient endurance of the ordeal and her concern for my rest fills me with a great tenderness and admiration for her selflessness during her affliction. Such events it seems provide occasion for the supreme expression of mutual affection.

March 27th

MY 61ST BIRTHDAY. I AM STILL NURSING MY COLD, WHICH stubbornly persists. Pont is much better after a relatively tranquil night. Frank's letter this week makes considerable reference to Havelock Ellis, who died a few years ago and whose autobiography has just been published. Ellis was ahead of his generation and ours too for that matter in his psychology of sex. Even now most people are nebulous about matters that belong to the deeper problems of life. 'Know Thyself' is still the problem. Women in the main instinctively dodge the issue in any discussion on the subject and cannot get rid of the taboo obsession or become belligerently irrational. Most men won't be bothered, the philosophy of it bores them. People generally prefer to discuss the other fellow's affairs rather than their own. They seem to be as much averse to the discussion of matters so fundamentally personal as they are to their own family skeletons. What decides for a young man his choice of a woman – when she doesn't choose him – is not companionship, not identity of intellectual instincts, although a few might so deceive themselves, not social status and not so very often worldly possessions. Least of all is it domestic efficiency. Where the choice is free and uninfluenced by these or other considerations, some esoteric attraction of the physical side of sex pulls the trigger for most of the events that follow. There is no real companionship without affection. With the affections centred on each other, the mutual satisfaction of sensual desire is an emotion of supreme delight that no reaction can sully. The companionship that grows out of it is one of the loveliest things in life. Enriched by the memories of other days, life for the fortunate grows sweeter and more tranquil as the years advance. There is tender tolerance and mutual understanding, which is less concerned with identity of interests than with the deep and abiding regard fertilized by other years.

April 1st

FRED'S BIRTHDAY (59) AND I RETURN TO DUTY AFTER A fortnight's sick leave feeling all the better for the enforced rest. Pont, too, this soft spring morning is greatly improved. Our general well-being is of a piece with that of the almond tree, radiantly in flower at the garden end. All life is stirring to the urge of spring. Everywhere the rich brown earth of the herbaceous borders is broken by the aggressive vigour of new generations of plant life exultant in their emergence from the conserving darkness. The small birds are ceaseless from dawn to dusk in their fetching and carrying for their nests. The larger birds and aquatics are all excitement in their courtships. Doris Walker at Shieling this afternoon for tea with Pont. Looking remarkably well, it was good to see her after so long an interval.

April 2nd

HERE I AM ON THE AFTERNOON TRAIN TO LEEDS, GLAD OF THE opportunity for rest and quiet that the journey affords. A crowded train with every compartment packed to the limit makes difficult the writing I had intended but with some reading the five-hour journey is soon over. During my sick leave, I read for the second time Armstrong's *Lord of Arabia*.* With patient wisdom and the help of his own strong right arm he welded together the scattered tribes of the vast desert lands,

* This is H. C. Armstrong's famous biography of Ibn Saud, King of Saudi Arabia (1880–1953), whose unification of proud and warring tribes laid the foundations for the modern state. His unique combination of faith and respect for tradition while keeping up with the progress of technology would have appealed to Walter.

raiders and fanatics, shepherds and bandits into some semblance of the homogeneity of the ancient Arabian empire. His was a personal government based on Islamic tradition and customs of the desert peoples, a kind of benevolent dictatorship with democratic tendencies, which because of his infinite patience, outstanding ability and innate sense of justice eventually achieved for him recognition of his sovereignty by the world powers. A mighty man of the calibre of Philip of Macedon. The man of whom the much-published Lawrence of Arabia, touching only the fringes of that implacable country, knowing nothing of its inner desert and deceived by the crafty, self-seeking Hussein, overlord of Mecca and the Hedjaz, who aspired to the caliphate, neglected to take account and so lost for England what might have been, during the Great War and after, the solid backing of a united Arabia. I confess to the little man's admiration for the big man. Maybe such admiration is tinctured by the schoolboy romanticism that lingers life-long with most of us. The big man of diminutive stature, like the captive elephant, is a pitiable object.

April 4th

THIS IS A SHORT WEEK OF JOURNEYING. OFTEN I HAVE NOTICED that with Monday and Tuesday out for the week's travel, the other days seem several hours short of the twenty-four. Even a whole day may miss its sequence in the earth's turning and be lost. At least, so it feels to me tonight as I write my weekly letter to Fred. Not until Saturday will it reach him, when the week is counted over, yet to me it is scarcely begun.

April 9th

'SIR,' SAID JOHNSON, 'ALL THE ARGUMENTS WHICH ARE BROUGHT to represent poverty as no evil show it to be evidently a great evil. You never find people labouring to convince you that you may live very happily upon a plentiful fortune.' This is Dr Johnson quoted in George Gissing's essay no. 5 from *The Private Papers of Henry Ryecraft*, which I have again been dipping into recently. But all things are relative. Johnson's strictures more properly apply to the poverty that is destitution. Conversely, riches do not invariably bring happiness. Perhaps Sappho of Lesbos in that lovely fragment of hers which has been preserved for us shows how comfortably balanced are needs with rewards where contentment resides. 'So Pelagon Meniseus gave,/This oar and basket for his grave,/That those who pass his tomb might see/How small a fisher's wealth can be.' Very largely the intellect feeds upon itself. Few of the world's great thinkers and fewer still of its philosophers were rich in worldly possessions. As things are in our world, the larger incomes after which the Ryecrafts hanker must be sought for in markets promising the easier rewards, but even here ability must step with ambition. If reasonably happily earned there can be no real poverty. All expectations are not needs. When people are asked what they want out of life, few seem to have any definite idea. Many who sigh for a good time cannot define it, and whatever form it takes, it is expected to fall, like manna, from heaven. To them Dr Johnson's standard of comparison conveys little or no meaning. The standards of the well-to-do are not valued for the poor. The quality of the vine isn't judged by comparison with a gooseberry bush. Those who want grapes must grow them, and those who want them badly enough will take the doctor's advice to avoid the poverty which, without grapes, might be theirs. Yet on grapes alone we cannot survive and live a full life. I have noticed that for many they are not infrequently sour.

April 16th

A WEEK OF CROWDED EVENTS SINCE MY LAST ENTRY, POLITICAL and naval events, but so diluted with rancour, conjecture and speculation that it has been impossible to disentangle fact from fiction. And now, with the sudden and complete invasion of Denmark by the Germans through a confidence trick made possible by traitors within, with Norway invaded at several points and Oslo occupied by the application of the Greek plan, when Ulysses made entry into Troy inside a wooden horse, the Germans had hoped to be within easier striking distance of our shores and to replenish their stock of raw materials and other supplies from the mines, factories and larders of Norway and Denmark. But this was not effected without the distribution by our navy – altho' a little late – of part of their fleet and several of their troop and munitions laden transport intended as reinforcements to consolidate their gains in Norway. The loss by drowning of many enemy troops and sailors inspired in Frank, according to his letter this week, the thought that the drowning of the whole German nation might not come amiss to the rest of the world. He suggests that the acceptance of government by criminal gangsters demonstrates that the German people themselves are gangster-minded. Disraeli said, 'A people gets the Government it deserves.' For a democratic people this is largely true, since the choice of a government as well as the power to change or dismiss it is theirs through the expression of public opinion. But Germans never have been free in a democratic sense. Under Prussian supremacy Bismarck made war for Germany a national industry, which made its first big bid for power in 1914. Dictatorship has gradually reduced whatever freedom was theirs until now it is at vanishing point. Political and military bondage is complete. As Anthony Eden said recently in a speech at Birmingham, 'Hitler is not something distinct from the German nation, he is the direct expression of a great part of it,' and Hitler must presume that his vast following is not unhappy under his leadership. Nevertheless his actions are contrary to generally accepted standards the world over, and thoughts of retaliation in like kind are our immediate reactions to his unscrupulous conduct of the war, which ignores all the acknowledged rules of the game. The moral and ethical precepts to which we declare our adherence we must practise as well as preach lest England, too, is counted lost to all sense of decency. Frank's subsequent thoughts must have taken something of this direction when, later in his letter, he referred to the common bond of grief that unites women the world over in the loss of their menfolk in war. For that and every other good reason, if we must kill let us kill cleanly: there will be less hatred in the grief and the peace to come will be all the sweeter. For ourselves, let us keep our minds on the permanent things, however remote they seem in the storm and heat and confusion of immediate events. The soul of a nation is its peasantry. Often the horse knows the road better than his driver.

April 21st

SUNDAY. A WONDERFUL SUMMERY WEEKEND. REAL OUT-OF-DOOR weather from sunrise till dusk. In response to the national slogan 'Dig for Victory' I took over a section of Ockwell's district garden to cultivate for the Home Front and grow more food. It was choked with weeds, littered with old iron, bottles, jars, broken glass, brickbats and rubbish generally, a disgusting cabbage patch that appears very fertile and in good condition. With help I am now getting it cleaned up, dug and ready before the season is too far advanced for planting as a vegetable garden. On the basis of Pont's greengrocery purchases at £1 per month, I think the enterprise will be profitable.

April 23rd

GENERALLY I AM BLESSED WITH THE ABILITY TO SLEEP WELL. After some seven or eight hours of tranquil slumber, which is my normal quota, my mornings are almost always a joy. Seldom am I troubled with dreams and still less often do I remember them, even vaguely. But my dream of the old dog last night was vivid enough to awaken me and trouble my morning. The recollection of it is still clear in my mind. Out for a walk in the country with Nell, Pont and I overtook another couple accompanied by a large grey dog resembling a Saluki whose presence seemed greatly to disturb her and which, as we approached slowly, assumed the form of a gigantic dog-faced baboon now covered with brown fur and erect upon its hind legs, beckoning to Nell to advance towards it. It was pitiful to see my old dog's agitation and acute distress. With a terrified resignation to the inevitable she hesitantly drew towards the creature, and went slowly and reluctantly out of our lives. Helpless in my dream to prevent it, my grief at her going was very real and obsessed me until on rising I found her as usual waiting for me at the foot of the stairs. I confess to the thrill of emotion that was mine when I felt her warm, soft, hairy body pressing against me and her muzzle buried in my arms in greeting. This same attitude of cowed resignation to the inevitable attracted the attention of Pont and me to her when, some five or six years ago, we discovered her during a winter walk to Kingston for lunch. A large brown Airedale bitch, long in the legs and with a gentle friendly face, lying deserted in the long grass. I ran my hand gently over her body and discovered her emaciated condition. Abandoning our projected lunch and, weak as she was, we managed to get her home to feed and nurse her. A better house dog, a more loyal and affectionate pal to my wife and I it would be hard to find. Yet even after five years of understanding companionship, the friendship of our neighbours at Little Croft and neighbourhood popularity – for all the village knows and has a kind word for 'Our Nell' – recollections of some early brutal testament still haunts her days. She hates small girl children to touch her and quickly snaps if any do. She is instantly cowed by a harsh word and is genuinely distressed. Often have I noticed that her approach to food is hesitant and apprehensive, as if during some early part of her life crusts and curses were served up together. So many things we have observed about her seem to point to the probability that her early life was tough and terrible, but she can't tell us. That for us is reason enough, if no better could be advanced, for making her declining years, now approaching blindness, comfortable and happy.

Thus I occupy the Peterboro' stage of my journey this day from London to Leeds. The picture in today's *DT* of a grey-whiskered old seal, sitting sunning himself on the muzzle of one of the *Graf Spee*'s eleven-inch guns, now covered with the gradual sinking of the scuttled battleship into the mud of Montevideo Harbour, is, I hope, a good omen of the impermanence of Nazidom. An excellent subject, I thought, for one of Low's cartoons, with just the outline addition, on the gun barrel, of Hitler's features, slowly but surely being submerged and obliterated. For all his power, this mighty gun, so recently belching forth death and destruction, is now but the perch of an inquisitive old seal, adding insult to injury – the injury to German prestige in the tragedy of its gallant commander, who shot himself because of the betrayal of his honour in the ordered scuttling of his scarred and battered ship, the pride of the German Navy.

April 24th

NOW IN YORKSHIRE AND THE NORTH GENERALLY THE WEATHER is cold, bleak, wet and thoroughly uncomfortable. At Dobcross today I visited an old stone cottage where I found the last of the neighbourhood hand-loom rug weavers at work. Most of the light of this gloomy day coming thro' the narrow stone mullioned windows was absorbed by the age-old grime on the rough walls of the low, beamed room, once a living room and now, perhaps for a century, a workshop. I fell to thinking that such were the conditions of grime and gloom and discomfort in the days of cottage industry. But most interesting of all was that my visit solved for me the problem of the balanced lifts for shedding the warps in my small loom, a simple device that I can construct myself. On the high moors across from Dobcross to Holmbridge the wet mist in no way softened the grim unfriendliness of the fells, brooding, wild in this desolation. Yet in the Holm valley I saw my first swallows of the season, twenty or more in swift erratic flight low over the millpond hawking for flies, and immediately beneath them small fish rising to the same bait. Evidently the birds and fish together were aware of the feast at hand although I hardly expected the flies to be abroad on such a cold day. Anyway, for a few minutes I stood and stared while the birds entertained me with their dextrous wing work and the flashing of their beautiful indigo and white forms, in speedy flight.

April 26th

ALREADY THE PORTER HERE AT YORK HAS ANNOUNCED THAT passengers must take their seats, that the train stops at Northallerton, Darlington, Durham, Newcastle en route for Edinburgh and now we are actually moving northward out of the soft gloom of the station into the sparkling sunshine of the best day of the week. As I glance from the window a Normandy poplar, graceful in its elegant nudity, stands boldly against the background of a slow-sailing cloud of fine fleece, set in azure, a lovely sight to behold, just the sort of composition of which Frank would make a picture for keeping. Strange, isn't it?, that man and woman seldom grow so ruggedly beautiful in old age as do trees. Glancing through the *Daily Express*, today's titbit is a reference to Captain Edwin Unwin, VC, RN, now 76 years. One of Gallipoli's heroes, 'a giant with rugged purple face, a hurricane laugh, and arm muscles like steel', just lately refused by the Admiralty for service in Norway, he is reported as saying at the Anzac Day lunch yesterday, 'As I told a boys' school the other day, when I was a young lad I begged a maiden ten years older than myself for a chaste embrace. She said to me, "Boys ask for kisses, men take 'em." I've never forgotten that lesson.' Well, it's the go-getters who do the rough-and-tumble jobs and often retrieve the scorching chestnuts – but mainly go-getters are born not made.

It requires a lot of moral courage to eat a scratch meal out of a brown-paper bag in the first-class carriage of a main-line train, especially when the dining car is only next door. With a very elegant and somewhat severe old lady in one corner of my compartment, a lordly fusilier major in another, in the third a forbidding, silent old man behind a barricade of official-looking satchels, shiny with locks and buckles, in the opposite seat a large German-looking cove stuffing himself into the armrests, and by my side, jiggling my elbow, an industrial nabob, oozing prosperity, each unwinkingly immersed in his own affairs, I felt that to produce my nosebag, I should draw upon myself the most devastating stares of disapproval and incur the corroding odium of the elect in their travelling sanctum. No, I just couldn't face them with it. Yet I must eat. I couldn't afford, on my 15*s.* per diem subsistence allowance – the same now as twenty-five years ago! – to indulge in a superior 6*s.* meal in the dining car and be one of them, even in theory. Neither did I need such a heavy meal, nor do I need to eat to while away my travelling hours. I have other interests. No, I had not the courage to produce before their gaze the food which I had bought in Newcastle to sustain me on my eight-hour journey; the bunch of watercress surreptitiously washed under the lavatory tap at the mill and wrapt up in a clean handkerchief, the fourpenny Melton Mowbray pork pie and the box of P&L dates – total cost 1/3*d.* – all bundled together in a fruiterer's bag.

I couldn't imagine myself screwing off the coarse stalks of the cress and strewing them over the carpeted floor, or flinging them under the seat, or dissecting my pork pie with a none-too-bright penknife, shedding crumbs about me, or noisily sucking my fingers after my dessert of sticky dates and drying them on my handkerchief. Outward dignity, at least, must be maintained. On the altar of respectability must be sacrificed my comfort, so to the corridor I accompanied my brown bag and there in the recess by the open window I stood and most solemnly devoured with deliberation, while watching the fleeting countryside, the watercress and pork pie in alternate mouthfuls and finally half of the box of dates, spitting the stones at telegraph poles as they flashed by. Unwanted cress followed the stones and then, lighting my after-dinner ciggie, I felt restored and reconciled to the company of first class. But the lordly major wasn't so lordly after all: having returned from the dining car, he settled down in his corner and, behind his book, commenced a considered finger attack on his nose, looking intently at his finds before chewing them off with relish! Well, well.

April 28th

THIS MORNING AT HOME I HEARD THE CUCKOO FOR THE FIRST time this season. The wandering voice with a welcome message.

May 4th

LAST NIGHT FOR THE FIRST TIME THIS SEASON I SAW ANOTHER OF our summer visitors wheeling high in the sky, the swifts on their scythe-like wings, and what a feast they must be having. Only the night before clouds of gnats hung like a moving veil above the Mole at Willow Bridge – indeed, it was unpleasant to pass through them on my way across. I remember saying to myself at the time, 'The swifts will soon be here to thin them out.' A wonderful dawn and brilliant sunshine, the best morning of the year. Looking over the paper while sunbathing at the greenhouse door, I found the journalist Godfrey Winn telling the following story: 'A Bradford man, as a speculation, acquired some property in the Lake District. One day he sent his bailiff a telegram: "Start shearing, wool rising." To which came the brief and terse reply: "Sorry, cannot, lambing." This stung him to the answer the bailiff received a few hours later: "Who's boss? Stop lambing and start shearing!" ' As Winn says, 'We may think that war is the most vital event of all in the world today. But is it? Today in many parts of the countryside, the really important thing is that the sheep are lambing. Our sheep population is thirty million!'

Saturday, and today is devoted to the garden and greenhouse. All the seasonal chores are now well in hand. The internal redecoration of the house is now finished so everything has come together most satisfactorily. Our little homestead, inside and out, pleases the eye and gladdens the heart. I almost believe our nearby neighbours enjoy it all as much as we ourselves do.

May 10th

AND TODAY WE AWAKEN TO THE NEWS OF GERMANY'S INVASION of Holland, Belgium and Luxembourg. Events move swiftly. I fancy we are on the threshold of nearer events, the beginning of the war for us.

I spent Wednesday evening with Phil Gaunt and his wife – the Lady Isobel – at their lovely home, Wood Hall. Built in the seventeenth century in a secluded bit of high country between Leeds and Bradford, surrounded by wooded parkland and intensive gardens, this stone-built many-gabled house, with its mullioned windows, richly panelled hall and staircase, the spacious dignity of its shining refectory, its stained glass and quietly tasteful appointments, is, for me, the ideal ancestral home, a place to be born in, to die for, fighting, in shining armour.

May 13th

IT WAS ANNOUNCED A FEW DAYS AGO THAT WHITSUN BANK Holiday was officially cancelled. So on the day which normally would have found all the world and his wife holiday-making, business as usual was the slogan. With the horror of events

...a place to be born in, to die for, fighting, in shining armour.

crowding in upon us, there could have been no really carefree holiday for anyone. Ethel and Tom were with us the other weekend, and with Tom's help I overtook all areas of garden and greenhouse where everything is beginning to look very summery.

May 14th

ANTHONY EDEN, MINISTER OF WAR, ANNOUNCED TONIGHT THE formation of Local Volunteer Forces throughout the country as a precautionary measure against possible evening parachute-troop operations.

May 15th

BY RADIO CAME THE NEWS AT 7 A.M. THAT THE DUTCH HAD LAID down their arms in the struggle against German invasion, which overwhelmed much of their country. The Hague is in the hands of the enemy. The Dutch Royal Family seek sanctuary in England. The war creeps nearer.

May 16th

THIS MORNING AT MOLESEY POLICE STATION I ENROLLED IN THE Local Volunteer Force.

May 20th

WHAT SHALL I SAY OF MYSELF, WHOSE DECLARED PHILOSOPHY creaks and groans under the strain of my reaction to events, of the black depression that descends upon me with every attack of nervous indigestion, of my revulsion even to the radio, of the morbid gloom that submerges me like some quick tide whatever my opposition to it? Where has gone my cheerfulness and confidence? My wife shames me with her splendid example of quiet assurance, courage and repose. These past days I have sustained myself through her when I should have been the fount of her strength. I despise myself for this weakness and literally this morning was sick with a stomach and soul that seemed at intervals to paralyse my volition. But I must go on fighting this pathology of spirit, fight myself into a healthy state of body and mind.

May 26th

I'VE TURNED THE CORNER. MY SPIRITS ARE IN THE ASCENDANT. I face the grim realities and possibilities, and rally my inner defences. Today, busied myself at Shieling with precautionary arrangements against air raids, contriving a greater security for Pont in case I have to go away from home. I bring all the cheerful comfort I can to her who is sticking it so bravely. We are engaged in a Titanic struggle. It cannot be that our cause is not just: right must prevail, whatever the nation suffers. Surely that is our strength and our ultimate salvation.

From Shieling's peaceful gardens the war is altogether remote. A calm sunlight sky smiles down upon bird and flower, tree and lawn. The bells of St Mary's seem to sanctify, this morning, all that it stands for in the quiet joys of our home life. If in the back of the mind there still lurks the thought that the peaceful security we believed was ours is a conditioned thing, we must make the best of the conditions of stewardship and be glad. At the first call of St Mary's this morning Pont and I attended divine service, there to add our prayers to the national cry to high heaven for strength and endurance and courage in this time of trial and testing, and to crave a word with God on our own account.

June 1st

ALICE MARY'S BIRTHDAY, AND HAPPILY THE DAY STARTED WITH greetings and good wishes. A week gone since my last entry, a week of horrific events and heroic endurance, commencing with the shameful surrender, without warning, of the King of the Belgians to the invading Germans, thus exposing the BEF to annihilation through complete encirclement by the enemy. Every hour of the day and night brought intense anxiety for the safety of our brave lads who it seemed might be lost. But the miracle happened. Screened by the RAF bombers the gallant French hewed a pathway through the encircling Germans along which our men, fighting all the time a fierce rearguard action, made their way to the sea and the ships of all kinds waiting to bring them home. We can never count what we owe to the conception and execution of such spur-of-the-moment plans, which made possible an evacuation so successful as to be described as a splendid deliverance. And today we are told that 80 per cent of the force of thirty divisions is already back in England to fight another day. This weekend we can at least breathe a little more freely and give our minds more fully to other things. For this and the miracle, we lift up our hearts in thanks to the Lord.

And so the weekend was occupied in the garden, kitchen plot and greenhouse. Ethel and Tom stayed with us over the weekend and made themselves very useful. Tom was particularly helpful in the garden – without him I could not get so much work done. I arranged on Saturday with Marney's, the tree-loppers, for the felling next week of the giant black poplar next door, which is diseased and overhanging Shieling and is a potential danger to my property. Some six months ago I informed in writing the agent for Ockwell's district garden of the condition of this forest tree and its threat of destruction to my house but received no reply. The owner does nothing for the preservation of his own property and as he is little likely to do anything for it that concerns mine, I must take the matter into my own hands. The charge of £5 for the felling and removal of the tree is a trifle compared to the damage it would cause in falling. A blast of high explosive in some air raid might easily cause it to topple and crush my home.

During their visit this weekend we discussed with Ethel and Tom the effect of my evacuation with the office staff from London and they agreed that in the event of my leaving Alice Mary at Shieling they would take up residence with her. For me, while away, the knowledge of all this would bring me a greater content and ease of mind. The question of their contribution to the household expenses is a matter for friendly adjustment if and when the need arises. To round off these weekend notes it is pleasant and fitting to record the birthday luncheon Pont and I enjoyed together in Kingston on the 1st, with a lashing of sparkling Moselle to mark the occasion. We felt that the event had passed not unworthily.

June 8th

OFTEN THE UNEXPECTED HAPPENS. WHY I SHOULD ANTICIPATE hostility from my neighbour over the removal of his tree I hardly know. I wrote him on Tuesday intimating my willingness to share with him the cost of its removal arranged for today. Thursday brought his reply – an acquiescence to my proposal. This morning the felling had commenced and when I returned from the office this giant black poplar lay pitifully across the ground. A nest of blue tits, still intact, was found in a hole in the trunk.

June 11th

I CAME IN FROM EARTHING UP THE POTATOES TO LISTEN TO THE nine o'clock news and heard that Italy had at long last declared war on England and France. Surely no nation in this world has ever drawn the sword so wantonly, with so little provocation.

June 19th

CAME THE NEWS ON MONDAY THAT THE FRENCH HAD ALMOST abandoned the fight. It was not unexpected. Already Paris had fallen. The cumulative effect of Leopold's defection, mass treason, vital blunders and the impact of this to the overwhelming purpose of the German Army shaped the course of events. Now, as the Prime Minister said, we must fight on alone, concentrating on the defence of our own island. To us falls the duty of defending democracy. It can only be worth defending if it doesn't fail us.

This is my leave week from the office. We arranged with the Esher Central Fire Station for a demonstration to my immediate neighbours on Saturday afternoon of fire fighting and incendiary-bomb fighting, stirrup-pump work, etc., so that all may know what to do in case of emergency. Ethel and Tom are with us for a few days so Pont and I took a day off together and had a quietly enjoyable time at Chessington Zoo, but wartime neglect is taking its toll on the gardens and ponds. Although the animals generally are in very good condition, the penguins were in a sorry state.

June 23rd

RESUMED OFFICIAL DUTIES TODAY, FEELING ALL THE BETTER FOR the change at home. Had our first meeting at Shieling of our neighbours and organized our fire-fighting squads and first-aid arrangements and planned intercommunications amongst ourselves in case of dire emergency. Significantly enough, in the night, commencing at 1.15 a.m. there came our first neighbourhood air-raid warning since September. We rose from sleep, dressed and proceeded to the most sheltered part of the house, but as no gunfire was heard, soon went back to bed, in our clothes, and there remained till the all-clear was given about 4 a.m., when we properly retired for what was left of the night. On the whole we lost little sleep. We afterwards learned that this was a large-scale raid with casualties reported from the west Midlands and north England.

June 26th

INSTRUCTED MY NEIGHBOURS THE ROBINSONS IN FIRE DRILL THIS evening and later rehearsed our second squad in Little Croft's garden. Everyone prefers the rotary pump to the stirrup pump as it is much less fatiguing to work, more certain in action and has a greater and more effective range.

July 1st

THE WEEKEND NOW GONE BY WITH NO FURTHER ALARMS, THE organization of our home ARP is now almost complete. On Sunday I distributed surgical dressings to my neighbours and inspected their house shelter portions. I also secured

Afflington's* consent to a fence gate in his garden, which gives emergency access to all houses without going into the street. My neighbour gave me *carte blanche* to do with Afflington's and the garden whatever was necessary for our common protection. I was very moved when he remarked, 'Don't risk your life for the sake of my home, just let it burn.' But we shall do our best all the same. With the Hooks and the Walkers with us on Saturday night and the Kenricks calling later, we had a merry evening with a fire rehearsal thrown in for everyone's instruction.

July 8th

ANOTHER WEEK PAST, AND ONE IS STILL ALIVE TO CONTINUE THE tale. One hears all sorts of stories about other districts, especially those remote from London in the SE, NE and SW of England where, by all accounts, there seems to be a good deal of enemy activity. Although it is always present in the mind that our own neighbourhood might at any time 'catch a packet', so far we have been lucky enough to escape the enemy's too close attention. Still, we go to bed prepared for the worst in a resigned sort of way, yet always hoping for the best, rising after a peaceful night to find the early-morning sun burning its way through the blackout curtains and all the birds of heaven singing at the top of their bent. All nature goes on in the same brave old way.

* Afflington, like Shieling, Xophil and Little Croft, was the name of a house.

July 22nd

MY WEEK'S LEAVE IS OVER. EXCEPT FOR A LITTLE SLEEP EVERY day after lunch, every hour almost to bedtime has been well and happily occupied. Seeing that a holiday away is out of the question these wartime days, I don't know what better alternative than some home occupation could have presented itself. The garden and greenhouse are now in very good shape and my garage workshop spick and span, ready for the many jobs coming along. I shall set up my handloom there. The kitchen garden is in fine form and will, I am sure, return to me in produce more than the equivalent of my outlay upon it. My tomatoes are quite the best in the neighbourhood. Yes, I've thoroughly enjoyed my week of home chores. Yet not once have I put pen to paper until today. Each day has been so full that the evenings have found me too drowsy to write. So drowsy that my thoughts seem to have had no beginning or ending, rather have they hazily trailed off into the nebulae of the outer spaces of the mind and eluded my grasp. The livelong week of fresh air and much activity had made me feel tired and the clean bed linen invited early repose.

July 28th

A LONG BRIGHT DAY OF USEFUL AND ENTERTAINING ACTIVITY. Having volunteered for service in the Esher war-salvage scheme with six others, including the dustman and his driver, I paraded for duty at the council yard at 8.30 a.m. for instructions. Arranging the fourteen roads on our list in topographical sequence we loaded the lorry then drove away to find the first and commence operations. So early on a Sunday morning many people were still asleep but it was the womenfolk, with a dressing-gown or coat thrown over their nightclothes, who appeared shyly at the doors to direct us to the cellars and outhouses where we found, in little heaps, the accumulated odds and ends of old iron which it was our job to collect. The response to the council appeal was remarkable and unexpectedly generous. In the first two roads we collected well over twenty old cycles and almost as many perambulators and push-chairs. Of old baths, buckets, fire-irons, flat-irons and stair-rods, there were plenty. From another road we collected copper preserving pans, much brass and aluminium ware and almost a ton of broken iron railings. Each of the four roads canvassed produced a load to capacity. Among the curious finds was a German cavalry sword of fine workmanship taken in the last war, a griddle plate over a century old and a set of old-fashioned servants' hall bells complete with springs and sprockets, which jingled merrily on their way to the lorry. In the afternoon two charming old ladies provided most welcome tea and entertained us with reminiscences of earlier years when the griddle plate was in daily use somewhere in the far north of Scotland. But perhaps no incident of the day was more indicative of willing sacrifice than when an elderly widow, having handed over her contribution to the junk, as an afterthought produced a bright shining brass and iron fender on which she said her husband loved to rest his slippered feet on winter evenings – he had been killed in action during the last war. 'But,' said she, 'you cannot have it whole.' She took a large hammer, shattered it with vengeful blows and, on her late husband's account, handed me the pieces – for Hitler.

July 31st

AT 10.15 P.M. YESTERDAY, JUST AFTER I GOT INTO BED, AN ENEMY raider, which could be heard overhead, dropped a bomb somewhere in the neighbourhood. It shook the house as might some momentary earth tremor. But there being no sign of its return I quickly went to sleep.

I broke into the fourth of a series of first-aid lectures and demonstrations at the office this afternoon. I was sorry to have missed the first three, which by reading I can catch up. I found it all very interesting and the course may prove to be very useful.

August 1st

AT 4.55 A.M. THIS MORNING ANOTHER RAID, AGAIN OVERHEAD, with the report two minutes later of the exploding bomb somewhere up-river. Almost simultaneously, like a challenge, came the pleasing notes of a thrush from our sycamore to herald the day.

August 4th

IN THE MORNING, AS A SUNBATHING OCCUPATION, I POTTED UP some 70 geranium cuttings ready for next season's use, and a few pelargonium and crassula, by way of relaxation this evening, it being still fine and warm. Alice Mary and I spent a leisurely couple of hours on the river in a punt. There were more people on the river than I have seen at any time these last few years. The south coast being denied them, the river comes into its own and was colourful with cheerful folk snatching some respite from the long day of war activities and the anxieties of the times.

August 13th

THIS MORNING'S REPORT OF THE GALLANT EXPLOITS OF OUR airmen against the enemy thrills me to the marrow. I feel I must write these words if only because the act of recording the event helps me to control my emotions. Over the whole weekend they have repelled, at great loss to the enemy, the mass air raids launched by the Germans over a three-hundred-mile-long front about our North Sea coastline. Captured enemy airmen speak with relief about the cessation, for them, of hostilities and by all accounts are gladly surprised at our humane treatment of them. In the last five days enemy plane losses total 168 against our own 54. To save some portion of a south-east coast town from disaster, Flying Officer Grice, his plane alight from prop to tail, with sheer pluck avoided crashing among houses by making for the sea, where he and his plane were lost. To him tonight be accorded the famous epitaph 'A very gallant gentleman'. According to the *DT* today the RAF profit and loss account from 3rd September to date is as follows: German AF losses = 2992 planes / RAF = 709. Gains to the RAF = 2283. Showing an average superiority for the RAF of 3 to 1, with promise of an increasing ratio in their favour.

August 14th

TODAY IT WAS OFFICIALLY ANNOUNCED THAT YESTERDAY 78 German planes and bombers were brought to disaster with no greater loss to our RAF than 13 fighter planes and only five pilots.

With the days so full of work at home, of neighbourhood jobs, and official duties that keep me absent from home for more than eleven hours daily, it has been pleasantly restful, after blackout, to turn to some light reading. For a collection of short stories Somerset Maugham's *The Round Dozen* provided interest enough to keep me up after my bedtime, several evenings. But I found Beverley Nichols's *Green Grows the City* not only interesting but informative as well. He waxes lightly satirical about Mrs Heckmondwyke, lyrically enthusiastic over his ferns and cacti and most inspiring when planning his triangular garden. He spent much more money on his domed greenhouse, rockery and leaden coalboxes than most of us could afford, but all gardeners can find worthwhile suggestions in his account of these achievements. But the last chapter is perhaps the most stimulating of all in his book. He expresses sentiments that cannot fail to find complete response in the heart of all decent folk, gardeners especially. One cannot intelligently tend a garden without sooner or later reflecting on the permanence of things of the earth, soil and their intrinsic timelessness. In them is a power of endurance that defies the threat of extinction. Let the scornful jeer, if jeer they must, but Beverley Nichols hits the nail squarely when he comments on the achievements of men which seem to him a little monotonous: 'Marching with bigger and better guns to louder and fiercer music . . . blind to the beauty that is around and above, deaf to all music save the snarl of the drum, marching to a destination that no man knows but all men dread. If these are the achievements of men, give me the achievements of geraniums . . . They at least have learned something with the passing of the years . . . If all men were gardeners, the world at last would be at peace.' Voltaire said much the same thing.

August 16th

A DAY OF WIDESPREAD EVENING AIR RAIDS INCLUDING TWO on London during which the office staff took cover in the well-equipped official shelter. The chatter of typists mingling with the droning buzz of the air-conditioning made it impossible to hear anything that was going on outside. Within the shelter there was no sign of panic. The majority of women were occupied in knitting and the men not standing by for ARP or first aid were playing cards. It struck me that office business could be easily carried on and thus save some loss of time. During these raids I wrote up some pages of my diary. Leaving on the all-clear at 6.15 p.m. after the second raid I found the home-going traffic for the SW district badly disorganized. The rush-hour was telescoped into a matter of minutes and there was much confusion at Waterloo from which, I quickly learned, only the Thames Valley loop could be operated. Platforms 1 to 15 were out of commission. Unable to get in touch with Shieling from the office I thought to do so from the station, but the queue outside each phone box made it impossible to approach nor could I telegraph. Not until I arrived home was I able to relieve Alice Mary's anxiety, or my own. At Waterloo the enormous crowd were calm and cheerful and waited with patience their turn to pass through the platform gates to the trains waiting to take them to Kingston en route for home, whence some had to continue by bus. After a long wait I boarded a crowded and very slow train to Kingston, having to insinuate myself into a carriage already packed with 21 people and finally finished my journey home by bus just 2¾ hours after leaving the office.

August 17th

ON THE WAY TO TOWN BY TRAIN THE REASON FOR YESTERDAY'S congestion and delay at Waterloo revealed itself in the state of partial ruin in which I found Malden station and immediate neighbourhood. High-explosive bombs had badly battered areas on both sides of the line. Several houses had collapsed, having skeleton timbers of their roofs grotesquely sagging in all directions, others had been damaged and many windows blown in. An air-raid shelter with a large hole in the roof told its own grim tale, as did telegraph wires broken and hanging in festoons by the railway. The approach to the station – where many people were injured – was wrecked. A group of greenhouses filled with tomato plants appeared to have lost every pane of glass. Later the owner told me that 4000 panes shattered in a moment. The damage to the line itself, which was slight, had been repaired, but a train waiting in the station at the time of the raid had all its windows blown out and damage was done to the driver's coach.

August 18th

A GLORIOUS SUMMER DAY, THE PEACE AND SERENITY OF WHICH was rudely interrupted by two raids, one at lunchtime, the other during tea, which obliged us to suspend our enjoyment of it and seek shelter in our 'hide' in the passage. Revelling in a nude sunbathe in a quiet spot in the garden when the second raid was announced, I had to dress hurriedly as I felt, curiously enough, that I didn't want to find myself in trouble, unclothed. Nevertheless, I had a good session of gardening in the morning and a quiet, restful afternoon. In spite of enemy attention the day was well and agreeably spent.

August 19th

NOT OFTEN DO I TRAVEL UP TO TOWN WITH NEIGHBOUR Edwards, but this morning, in the train, I found him a gloomy dog. He told me that he hated the work by which he earned a living. Seeing that so many of his waking hours, because of this, must be unhappy, I remarked that his choice of occupation was singularly unfortunate. But it appears that events for him just drifted that way and without gladness he accepted the conditions. Yet after most of a lifetime one would have thought that some measure of tolerant acceptance might have taken the chill off his hatred. But it is not so. I remember some time ago offering to introduce him to Frank Taylor. He declined on the grounds that he didn't think Taylor would be of any use to him in business! Without being caustic, there is little one can say in reply to such sentiments.

August 24th

I SUPPOSE ONE MUST EXPECT ENEMY RAIDS TO BECOME MORE frequent. This morning on the way to the station I had to take cover in Mr Nelson's cellar where five women in various stages of undress cheerfully chatted for the hour of its duration. I eventually reached the office at 10.15 a.m., instead of nine o'clock, and found that every member of my section was not less than an hour late and for the same reason. More raiding this afternoon, but I managed to get some gardening done and make an experimental batch of tomato soup for storing in an attempt to preserve for the winter, in a form most palatable to ourselves, the heavy crop of tomatoes which we could not possibly consume in the ordinary way.

August 25th

MORE ENEMY RAIDING IN THE NIGHT AND AGAIN TODAY. BOMBS seemed to drop all about us. Nevertheless, I carried on with the gardening and later affected some improvements in the house blackout. I thought it very kind of Bob Ayton to enquire by phone if we at Shieling were all safe. He informed me that Kingston had been rather badly hit.

August 26th

MY EXPERIMENTAL BATCH OF TOMATO SOUP WAS PRONOUNCED by my neighbours to be excellent, and close in flavour to the Heinz product.

August 27th

FROM 9.30 LAST NIGHT UNTIL 3.30 THIS MORNING CONTINUOUS enemy action, the longest and fiercest raid of the war so far. For six hours we remained in our hide. I'm thankful that Alice Mary remains so composed during these ordeals. The event had its lighter side too. Reclining in our deck-chairs with a cushion over our heads to avoid possible hurt from falling ceiling, we cut a funny figure for each other and when towards the end of the sitting the canvas of my chair, with a rending tear, sent me through the framework, our mirth bubbled over unrestrained as I awkwardly extracted myself from the ruins. Finally we undressed and turned into bed about 4 a.m. to be up again at seven for the day's chores.

August 29th

RAIDS EVERY NIGHT THIS WEEK OF SIX TO SEVEN HOURS' duration, without a break. Wearing my underclothes I sleep in a pair of old flannel bags, having handy my old tweed coat and shoes ready for any emergency, and wrapped in my dressing-gown, I camp out on a mattress on the floor of the passage leading to the bathroom. Here we judge ourselves to be reasonably safe from anything but a direct hit.

Last night deciding that a good sleep in her own bed was worth a risk, Pont retired shortly after the air raid, so I camped out with the dog for company and, on the whole, had a fairly good night, more restful, at least, than the preceding. Each of us started the day in good fettle. Tonight, however, passed peacefully for our district. Ethel, who spent the day at Shieling, loves to potter in my garden and has a passion for watering.

August 30th

AFTER A QUIET NIGHT WE HAD THREE AIR-RAID WARNINGS IN London, which lost for the office not less than two hours' work per head – for the entire staff, nearly a thousand hours. This is a very serious interference with output. In an elaborate shelter like ours at Millbank, I see no good reason why any portable work should be neglected. I suspect an over-eagerness on the part of many to hail the suspension of normal routine as a good opportunity for 'milking'. On completing the work I took with me to the shelter, I wrote up most of my notes for the 29th inst. It was satisfying to feel that my mind was ranging beyond the orbit of current political events, which earlier on threatened to deny me the intellectual freedom which is normally mine.

August 31st

ANOTHER NIGHT OF RAIDS AND BOMBING WITH LITTLE REST FOR anyone in my district and more this morning. One during my journey to town, another mid-morning and one at the midday rush-hour, which found me in the centre of Westminster Bridge en route for Waterloo. So I wrote these notes in a public air-raid shelter by St Thomas's hospital where, in an atmosphere of carbolic disinfectant, those occupants not dozing discussed last night's raids and, with grim gusto, sewed up the odds and ends of 'exclusive' news. All seemed to be stoically resigned to the situation and hopeful of better times. Leaving the shelter before the raid was over I made my way to the York Road entrance to Waterloo station beneath which in the vaults and passageways I found soldiers, sailors and all kinds of people taking cover. Subdued voices talking to while away time, some silently gazing before them, others sleeping. A few whose words tumbled out too fast to take proper shape obviously talking to relieve nervous tension. But everywhere it seemed there was a mutual acceptance of the quiet consolations of companionship in common adversity. Strangers became neighbours, neighbours friends. Under stress of nervous tension I have noticed that not a little private history finds expression these days, perhaps to steal a march on the teller, later.

September 3rd

TODAY COMPLETED OUR FIRST YEAR OF WAR WITH GERMANY. Two daylight raids each of about one hour duration and a thirteen-minute raid just before midnight marked this sinister anniversary as less eventful than many had thought probable. For this we have to thank our very gallant Air Force.

September 4th

LAST NIGHT WAS TRANQUIL AT LEAST IN OUR PART OF SURREY. I arose from my emergency bed refreshed by good sleep to a splendid dawn and enjoyed my early cup of tea and cigarette in the still dewy garden while the newly risen sun flooded with its warm radiance my whole body as I surrendered myself to its caresses. I'm glad the nuisance of taking cover at the first warning of a daylight raid is receiving attention from the authorities. Now it seems that 'watchers' are to be appointed to warn workers of the near approach of hostile aircraft to avoid the waste of time when, as so often happens, German raiders are driven back long before London is within range of attack.

September 7th

DO WORDS EVER CONVEY THE SYMPATHY THAT ONE FEELS FOR another's desolation? The more profound the emotion, the less articulate the tongue. Our feelings lie too deep for words, whether of ecstasy or grief. Some simple gesture, often the gentle presence of a hand, is unutterably more eloquent. So I thought this morning when on my way to town an elderly Scotsman whispered to me the reason for his visit to London. Joining the train at Surbiton with his wife he enquired if its destination was Waterloo. I replied yes, but seeing that a 'fast up' was standing on the other side of the platform, suggested that, if he was in a hurry, to transfer to it would save ten minutes on the journey, which might be important. So long as Euston was reached by 10 a.m. they were content to remain. His wife, on the verge of tears, seemed too distressed to be interested. They had come to London, he whispered, from

Glasgow to identify and arrange for the funeral of their pilot son who, having had his plane disabled in action during a raid, had tried to effect a forced landing in a local playing-field. In avoiding several children he had crashed to his death. I could but press the poor father's hand in mute sympathy, which his gentle grasp acknowledged, and wish them God speed as I left the train.

September 11th

THE NIGHT-LONG RAIDS IN LONDON CONTINUE WITH increasing fury and devastating effect. Daylight raids are now so frequent that I have lost count of them. The nights are nightmares, the days we spend scurrying into shelters. Railway communication with the office is greatly interrupted, especially between Clapham and Waterloo, and alternative routes have to be found. These other routes allow me to appreciate the extent of the damage. It is pitiful to observe the complete destruction of homes where not a vestige of treasured belongings remain, and the casualties and loss of life are appalling. The City itself is becoming a shambles. The sound near and far of exploding bombs and gunfire make a mockery of sleep. The drone of wandering night planes keeps nerves on the rack. Yet, in spite of all this, one slowly becomes accustomed to the changing conditions. To discover today a house in ruins that was whole yesterday is no matter for great surprise. That a bus is diverted because of a bomb crater in the road attracts no more than passing notice. We live from day to day, hour to hour. A high-class leather-worker whose factory was yesterday and is not today laughed grimly when he told me of trying to start up again quickly in order to keep his craftsmen employed. Surely that is the spirit.

September 16th

WHILE HARVESTING MY MAIN CROP OF POTATOES YESTERDAY and tending the kitchen garden, I dreamed as I watched the flights of Spitfires and Hurricanes passing overhead that a titanic struggle was going on in our south-eastern skies between the rival air forces. That Germany is making a terrific bid for the mastery of London is certain; that we are more than holding our own in the air is equally certain. True, Buckingham Palace was again bombed, wrecking the Queen's private apartments, as well as many other buildings, but this morning's announcement of the destruction by our grand RAF boys yesterday of no less than 185 planes out of some 400 launched against us, with a loss of no more than twenty-five, is the best evidence of the price Hitler is paying for his reckless disregard of our decencies. And on this Sabbath day at St Paul's cathedral an unexploded bomb weighing one ton, which had buried itself 27 feet below road level in stiff subsoil and was menacing the fabric of the old church as well as much property around, was lifted out, loaded on to a lorry and removed to Hackney Marshes, there to explode in safety. I cannot imagine any other act calling for such a rich degree of courage as the cool removal in the face of sudden death of this infernal machine. With the fourth raid of the day still in progress we have already spent five of our working hours in the office shelter. But I see no sign of any move by the authorities to turn this time to account or to devise some plan whereby the intentions of Hitler to paralyse production can be circumvented. The same difficulties in going home will confront London's workers tonight, as the nightmare of Friday. Then most of the terminus railway stations were closed, the buses were full to capacity, with queues at every stop patiently waiting in the drizzle. The majority of drivers of private cars appeared indifferent to the appeals of the anxious folk who hailed them. At Eccleston Bridge Green Line bus stop, where I waited over an hour, a riot occurred when a stampeding queue tried to board a bus that pulled up a couple of lengths in advance of its stand. The entrance became so jammed with struggling humanity that passengers could neither alight nor enter and the transport officials seemed powerless to help matters. On the other side of the road an objectionable bus conductor received a crack on the head which necessitated first-aid treatment.

September 18th

POOR OLD GRIMSHAW, SILENT AND UNSMILING, RECENTLY OF THE Admiralty, who refuses to acknowledge me as a neighbour and gazes through me with disapproval whenever we meet in the street. He had become more morose and disapproving since his retirement. A confirmed and well-regulated bachelor, living until recently with his spinster sister, aged mother and a few books in the big quiet old house opposite, he appeared merely to exist. But now I fear it is less than an existence for him. The old lady, a bathchair martinet of over 90, who ruled her son and daughter with inflexible determination, died a few weeks ago. On Monday, her daughter, a sweet, patient, enduring soul, bent with long service to the old lady, passed away suddenly of heart failure, following the shock of a nearby bomb explosion. She left her brother Grimshaw, to whom she appeared devoted, alone in that shambling old house with only silence for company. So far as I can ascertain, he has not a near relative in the world or even a visiting friend. Nevertheless Pont and I felt a very real sympathy for him in his desolation. And today I hear that Ethel's flat in Tulse Hill has been wrecked and that she and Tom have found sanctuary with a neighbour. I must enquire.

September 19th

A CROP OF GOODWILL LETTERS GREETED MY ARRIVAL HOME tonight. One from Maud Hoyle in Halifax expressing the family's concern for our welfare in much-bombed London and in particular pressing Pont to evacuate herself to Yorkshire, which enjoys relative immunity from raiding, and accept the hospitality of the Hoyles until enemy attacks on London have subsided. A sweet letter but Pont won't leave Shieling, although as I proposed I could shut the house and live at the office. I think she is unduly concerned about leaving me behind. And from my neighbour Mr Grimshaw a tender acknowledgement of our message of sympathy, which leaves me in no doubt as to the need for some revision of my early impression of him. We were both greatly heartened by our correspondence. It was a harvest of goodwill. Sorrow and danger make us all kin. Out of the welter of death and destruction are peeping already the little flowers of St Francis.

September 23rd

ALONG THE SHINING WATER OF THE MOLE AT ITS CONFLUENCE with the Thames, this morning a pair of leisurely swans leave an ever-widening wake. Hampton Court is bathed in sunshine. The little crowd at the station waiting for an uncertain train basks in it and neighbourly groups melt into cheerfulness after the anxious tension of another night-long raid. On so peaceful a morning the sight of shattered homes seen here and there from the carriage window as my train makes its slow way to town seems too macabre to be real. Except for mankind, all is well. But for man himself it is a diseased world, sick with the leprosy of political strife that takes toll of everybody within reach. Today we read that 600 miles from land, in darkness and gale, only 13 of 102 evacuee British children, bound for safer Canada, were rescued on Tuesday by a British warship from the waterlogged and battered lifeboats of the liner torpedoed by a German submarine. Many died of exposure in the boats. This act, if no other, confirms Germany's guilty record for sheer barbarism. Today, too, on the long platform of Wimbledon's emergency station I saw piles of stuffed mailbags, apparently in hopeless confusion, being sorted by postal officials who crawled like ants under the vast heaps. Out of this chaos emerges the orderly delivery of our long-delayed letters. Better late than never.

And as I passed along Lambeth Bridge to admire the Houses of Parliament and the majestic line of buildings sweeping along the northern causeway of the river beyond Westminster Bridge, now gleaming white in the sun, Big Ben with sonorous dignity boomed the hour of noon. It all seemed so richly English. And now at 9.30 p.m. I write up these notes by candlelight: ten minutes ago the electric light suddenly failed. Enemy planes droning overhead come and go to the sounds of the barrage guns whose triple bursting shells illuminate the sky like quick summer lightning. The muffled crunch of a distant bomb may account for the sudden extinction of the light. But my battery torch is in my pocket and the candle and matches handy.

September 26th

MY TRAIN IS RUNNING UP TO TOWN IN FINE STYLE. YESTERDAY the station was closed but today it is in service. Each night brings its renewed bombing of London, each morning a revision of transport and other services. We build to be destroyed. All is flux and change, hazard and adaptation. Like plants we thrive in adversity. The only certain event during all this upheaval is the timely arrival of the milk in the morning. That really is important. Our milkman is a miracle of punctuality and his horse of astuteness. The post brought me several letters from Yorkshire. Distant location doesn't seem to discount the neighbourliness of friends. Their concern for our welfare is the measure of their goodwill. It is pleasant to be in touch with these far-off neighbours.

September 27th

'THE RAILWAY ALWAYS SEEMS TO FIND A WAY OUT,' SAID A FELLOW passenger during a circuitous route from Hants en route for London via Weybridge, Staines and Kingston where I joined the train. The implied compliment was refreshing after the much grumbling I had been obliged to listen to. But he voiced a greater truth than he knew, for it applies equally to the Briton in trouble – the nation whole. With a network of railways in this small island such as no other country in the world possesses, exhaustion of alternatives should be well nigh impossible. Once again the line between Hampton Court and Waterloo was out of action. Only at the last moment did I find that I must contrive to get to the office via Kingston. And at Wimbledon, now a temporary terminus, I write these notes in an air-raid shelter crowded with town-going folk held up by a fierce overhead fight between our own and enemy planes, which for the second time since 5 a.m. have raided the metropolis. The sound of falling missiles crashing through the trees at 1 a.m. this morning brought me to the ready, to find in my neighbour's garden several incendiaries burning and setting fire to the latticework. They illuminated the garden as might so many bits of bright moon falling from the sky. Quickly I set to work to extinguish them and almost as quickly my neighbour Robinson joined me. By the time the AFS* arrived we had disposed of the danger and with them at once turned our attentions to a house on the next road, which we reached in time to save from serious fire damage. Altogether 8 bombs had dropped around us. As an introduction to the real business of fire-fighting, I counted ourselves lucky in getting experience at little more than the price of some trifling inconvenience. At 2 a.m. we celebrated our modest success with a glass of sherry and a chuckle at neighbouring fire squads, who remained asleep throughout the entire event. They never heard our SOS signal as all were out of their houses being entertained by the spectacle of other folk's fires! I didn't allow the incident to pass without comment.

September 30th

IN MY ENTRY OF THE 23RD INST., I WROTE OF THE VISTA DOWNSTREAM from Lambeth Bridge, of the perpendicular grace of the Houses of Parliament. Grandly they still stand, but seared and battered and almost windowless. Broken stone, glass and woodwork litter the pavement. The great Gothic window of St Stephen's Porch in Old Palace Yard received the full force of a bomb, which exploded in the road below near to the statue of Richard the Lionheart who, holding defiantly aloft his damaged sword, sits on his wounded horse proudly as ever, perhaps as a sign. But the great window is a sorry mess. Luckily Westminster Hall escaped, but the east wing of the old Abbey, only recently renovated at great expense, is seared and mutilated and almost all the windows gone. Nor has St Margaret's, another of Wren's churches and the scene of so

* Auxiliary Fire Service.

many fashionable weddings, escaped the vandal enemy. Under Westminster Bridge, still undamaged, the river runs black and evil-smelling, poisoned apparently by escaping effluent. At its southern end the nurses' wing of St Thomas's hospital, bombed into the roadway, is an obscene heap of broken rubble. All the waterfront windows of County Hall have been shattered. We listen every morning for Big Ben and breathe a sigh of relief for his friendly reverberations as the deep bass tolls the hour. Yet it has not altogether escaped the destructive hand. Each of its four faces bears the scars of flying debris. And so with the shops and offices in the vicinity. So much for the administrative heart of London. But what of its less spectacular sufferings? By the side of the railway between Clapham Junction and Queen's Road Station, acres, literally acres, of small houses of the poorer sort, old and ready for demolition, the homes of our workpeople, are in complete ruin. A melancholy scene of unutterable desolation, the terrible effect of a land-mine. It requires more philosophy than I can muster to view with stoic detachment this wanton destruction of lives and property which today is called total war.

October 1st

A BRIGHT, STILL MORNING WITH THE TANG OF AUTUMN IN THE air. An aura of glad peace invests the garden. In the greenhouse the arresting show of begonias is making its last glorious stand. The 'Paul Campbell' geraniums seem to bloom in perpetuity side by side with fuchsias, which extend their red and white skirts with graceful modesty. The faint perfume of a 'Cherry Pie' attests to its declining days. But the winter-flowering begonias and chrysanths daily grow from strength to strength and already take the lead in the promise of joy

this wanton destruction of lives and property which today is called total war.

for Christmastide. Nothing short of its destruction will interfere with the progress of events in the greenhouse. Long may it continue to flourish that we may have beauty and colour about us in the midst of all this beastliness of war.

October 4th

ON GLANCING AT BIG BEN ON MY WAY ACROSS WESTMINSTER Bridge this morning I noticed that all four of his damaged faces had already been repaired.

October 7th

ALREADY THE SCAFFOLDING IS ON COURSE FOR ERECTION FOR the repair of the House of Lords. The great crater beneath the south window is filled in and the road made ready. Richard I and his horse are in the hands of the renovators. It is a capital start for Monday morning.

Yesterday's dawn broke boisterously. The wind lashed the trees as squally rain burst upon them. Flinging off my nightclothes, into the garden I stepped naked under the scurrying clouds to know the cold sting of heavy rain on my body, to feel the rush of cool, clean air about me, to experience the surge of exhilaration within and proclaim, with the rest of shouting nature, the sheer joy that was mine this madcap morning. If this is madness, I prefer it to sanity. But I miss the sound of church bells these wartime Sundays. Without stopping for breakfast Alice Mary and I went forth into the wind and rain to enjoy the buffeting and for the best part of two hours wandered along the riverside sharing its wild exclusiveness and winning, in the process, a fine appetite for lunch.

October 11th

SAID A LITTLE CRIPPLED WOMAN TO ME, AS SHE HOBBLED across the crowded concourse at Waterloo on her way home this evening, 'Ah, well, with all our troubles I'm glad I live in England. It is so worthwhile. We shall win in the end and be the better for it.' I slackened my pace to accommodate her tortured steps as I piloted her to the Sunbury train and felt myself privileged to listen to these and other comments, so sane and brave, on the war. And from my carriage window I observed a Union Jack on an extemporized mast flying gaily over the rubble, which is all that remains of the homes of many of Battersea's working-class population. Several children scrambled over the ruins in search of such articles as might have escaped the shattering havoc of wrecking bombs.

October 14th

8. 30 P.M. I'VE JUST COME IN FROM MY NIGHTLY TOUR OF OUR back gardens to see that all is in readiness for possible events. Except for the barking of AA guns, the droning of nightly invaders and the hooting of protesting owls, all is silent and still. I've wound up the clock and set the alarm for 6.30 a.m. as usual, and now we, Alice Mary and I and the dog, sit quietly in the lounge enjoying its warmth from one element of the electric radiator.

I was lucky to get Saturday off, to harvest the last of my crops, plant some sixty young cabbages and a couple of dozen strawberry roots. All Sunday the garden refuse was burning. I have ample of last year's broken down with sulphate of ammonia to manure the soil for next year's crops so the ash from this with a bit of lime will suffice to sweeten the earth. After a good levelling up and some pruning of overgrown trees, the winter should put my land in good fettle for the spring sowing.

October 19th

THE GRIMMEST INCIDENT THAT HAS SO FAR COME TO MY NOTICE is the bombing, about a week ago, of the Morden–Hampstead tube railway near Balham where a considerable number of people were sheltering for the night. The bomb penetrated the road surface through to the shelter beneath killing many outright and, by its explosion, bursting a water main that drowned more. A motor-bus overhead, unable to pull up in time, fell into the crater on to the unhappy souls below to complete their destruction. The driver of the bus was able to jump clear in time to avoid disaster.

October 21st

WHILE WORKING IN MY LABORATORY THIS AFTERNOON TWO bombs fell whistling through the air, exploding one on either side of the office, shaking it to its very foundations. But nothing worse to No. 4 Millbank happened than a fierce rattling of doors and windows. Some already evacuated houses nearby were further shattered and two passers-by became ambulance cases. Whether dead or alive I know not.

October 22nd

I'M NOT IMPRESSED BY THE ARGUMENTS ADVANCED BY SOME, IN defence of Germany's territorial ambitions, that England herself is guilty of high-handedness in the pursuit of imperialism in the past or that weaker nations have been grossly exploited for tribute to the Empire. That not a few of her acts in the past were discreditable no one can deny but these in the main were due to misdirected private enterprise rather than to deliberate state policy. True, Britain has taken much of the world's wealth, but she has given more to mankind in return. By no other nation has so much been freely contributed to the well-being of man the world over, and if, in the nineteenth century, we enjoyed something like a monopoly of the world markets, to the first on the field are due the first rewards. If Britain was the marketplace for the world, it was an open market as well as a fair, for education and culture, invention and the exchange of ideas. All the world came and profited by these exchanges and no one was denied. Through British enterprise Earth's abundance has been made accessible to all, and because of these things the world is richer and life fuller. We have got to win this war to demonstrate the truth that evil doesn't pay and whatever sacrifices we have to make, whatever suffering and hardship is involved, however dark and chill the valley of shadows, I am convinced that right and decency will triumph in the end.

October 28th

THERE WAS SOMETHING LIKE A HOWL IN THE *SUNDAY EXPRESS* concerning delays in preparing crater-damaged roads and deploring the inconveniences caused to traffic recently by hold-ups and all that accompanies the overnight appearances of craters on traffic routes. Much of this criticism of the authorities appears to me to be quite unfair and ill informed. These services have all to be examined and, where necessary, repaired after the site is cleared and before the road is made good again. They call for the employment of expert craftsmen. Only the other day I saw the front wheels of a bus in a bomb crater, straddled across a whole series of electric cables. The following morning the bus had been removed and a gang was at work on the road and wire repairs. Two days later the work was completed, the road in full use. Growing up with these services, most of us take them for granted and give little or no heed to their machinery of operation.

November 1st

A SHERRY AND SANDWICH LUNCH WITH FRANK AT OUR ST Martin's Lane rendezvous today and some inconsequential talk about books, poetry, our diaries and letter-writing was thoroughly enjoyable. He remarked that he found it impossible to give more than vagrant attention to the fiction to which he turned, on his long and tedious railway journeys, for escape from the all too present events and topics. Living as we do in a period that itself is stranger than fiction, more ruthless, more incredible and wholly deplorable, maybe we have become a little scornful of imaginary situations and characters, of plots and counterplots. By the side of stark reality they are more anaemic than anaemia itself and as unsatisfying as too much vegetarianism. I think I understand his difficulty. While I appreciate the importance of mental and physical relaxation these days, the novel is not for me. So it comes about that I find myself rereading John Stuart Mill's *Essays on Liberty* with a new interest.

November 9th

MORE THAN A WEEK OF ALMOST CONTINUOUS NIGHT AND DAY enemy raiding since I made my last entry. Domestic and office duties go on just the same, affording no outstanding events to record. The journeys to town provide opportunities for quiet writing or some reading, but of late the morning journey is too crowded to give elbow room while evening journeys are made in almost total darkness and, during raids, with drawn blinds to the railway-carriage windows. One can only doze on the way home.

November 15th

MY FATHER'S 84TH BIRTHDAY. HALE AND HEARTY, HE CAN STILL tilt a lance in argument and admire a shapely leg. In my congratulatory letter I sent him the price of a modest celebration.

November 17th

SITTING ON THE SIDE OF MY WIFE'S BED WE HAVE OUR EARLY-morning tea and talk. For half an hour before she rises we indulge in this pleasant dalliance. It is the talk of the day. At this hour, with no better relief from the darkness than that of a small shaded reading lamp, which, while casting a halo over her silvery hair, intensifies the shadows, inspiration seems to inform our conversation. It is then that we exchange news and views. Never is tea more acceptable or a cigarette more agreeable on these dark days and never is she more lovable.

November 20th

THE FAST FADING LIGHT, WHICH I WAS STRAINING TO MAKE THE most of on my homeward journey this late afternoon, at last obliged me to close my book. Reluctantly I slipped it into my pocket, promising to finish my rereading of *A Christmas Carol* in the quiet half-hour before bed.

Except for myself and another, my railway carriage emptied itself of passengers at Surbiton and he, seeing that I was no longer reading, sidled up to me to ask, with a challenge, where this war, with its tit-for-tat night bombing, was leading us and when was it going to end. I replied, 'When we all return to sanity,' and remarked discouragingly that I was sick of all this war talk, that it had become an obsession with too many, that it spilled itself all over my office, tainted my food at the lunch table, spoiled my afternoon tea, invaded my precious leisure and would even invade my sleep, if I allowed it access. In this carnage everyone but myself, it seemed, gloated with ghoulish satisfaction over the sooty headlines that splashed themselves across his evening paper in contrast with which the reading of my frilly little book was a priceless relief. To dismiss the matter I added, 'While it looms large in our affairs war is not the whole of life, it is but a tragic incident,' sometime to pass. My companion, whom I knew slightly as a distant neighbour, threw back his leonine head and snorted. It was difficult to see the expression on his face in the darkness but I could sense the scorn as he held forth on the madness of war. That Chamberlain should plunge us into this fight with Germany on account of Poland, instead of acknowledging the 'new order' of things, was a wicked act. What were the Poles to us? There was nothing logical about it. We set too great a store by the past. We should cut ourselves adrift from history. And much more besides as we walked home from the station. Coming as all this did with such passion, I was not a little astounded and felt that such sentiments could not be allowed to pass without challenge. What was this new order if not the old order disastrously repeated by tyrants? That professing the sentiments of a free democratic people Mr Chamberlain had no option, in the matter of offering Poland what protection we could, quite apart from the prevention of our own subjugation. I reminded him that we could no more ignore the consequences of the past in the present than we could avoid its effect upon the future. And as for history, each of us is the evidence of its continuing vitality, history itself.

November 27th

FROM THE *DAILY TELEGRAPH*: 'A FLOOD OF CRITICISM FROM THE Government's failure to use its compulsory powers for war production was stemmed today by a blunt declaration from Mr Bevan, Minister of Labour, "I prefer to be a leader, not a dictator." ' That, it seems to me, is a typically English preference. The sanction of a free people affords the safest and most permanent foundation for all authority. I like to remember Disraeli's words, 'A people gets the government it deserves.' That is more true today than ever before.

December 25th

WITH ETHEL AND TOM AT SHIELING. WE SPENT THE DAY together with a quiet thought for our friends in the Army, RAF and Navy and a word with God.

December 31st

SAID A NEIGHBOUR'S WIFE TO HIM, IN HER FLAT, TONELESS drawl, in reference to the bombed-out area in York Road, Wandsworth, which we passed in his car on our way up to town together, 'I once thought it was nice to have houses all in a row, to save trailing about collecting rents, but when so many can be destroyed by one bomb, it isn't so good.' I was shocked by her outlook, and a further shock awaited me later when she remarked that it were better that the National Gallery had been bombed instead of Hampton Showrooms, as the destruction of all their beautiful furniture almost made her cry. And again, what did the wrecking of London's Guildhall matter? After all, it was an old building. Her chief regret at the end of the day's town shopping was the neglect, through her own indecision, of a bargain offer of a large lampshade, going cheap from a partly wrecked store, 'Oh, it was marvellous!'

Said her husband, 'You already have a good one in use at home, why want another?'

1941

January 1st

TWO YEARS AGO I COMMENCED THIS DIARY. LIKE OLD AND TRIED friends we speak to each other as and when the mood serves. It never has assumed the role of taskmaster; on the contrary it has played no inconsiderable part as a guide, talisman and friend. Of my various interests, this is the one that has brought the rest to a common focus. In it, more deeply etched, I begin to see myself more clearly than ever before. Let the walls of the world one knows and holds dear rock never so fearfully under the enemy's onslaught. Give us, O God, the courage to remain true to our best selves.

January 12th

PATHETICALLY OLD, BLIND AND INFIRM, OUR OLD DEAR DOG Nell, whom we rescued from abandonment some six years ago, today went to her last sleep. So passes a beloved and faithful friend.

May by St Rocco's grave she find
The paradise for the doggy kind.

It was no small tribute to her that our neighbours this morning came to Shieling to express regret at her passing. Little Croft will miss her hardly less than ourselves. This evening came a long-distance call from the Hoyles at Hippenholme, Halifax, and a renewal of their offer of shelter from London's blitzkrieg.

January 15th

MY SMALL LOOM IS A *FAIT ACCOMPLI*. THE WEAVING OF A TRIAL length of woollen material, except for a couple of trifling adjustments to the loom, and lack of skill in the art itself, is progressing satisfactorily. Faulty technique in warp winding is my chief trouble. This mastered, the rest is merely a matter of practice. Already I see ahead possibilities enough of employing in joyful experiment any creative faculty with which I may be endowed. With the war safely over and all well, I can envisage retirement in happy occupation.

January 19th

AFTER SPENDING THE BEST PART OF A LIFETIME – AS MOST OF US have in our corner – in establishing ourselves in our own little homes, we have to chance only those things which we must. So at last with my wife I settled down before our cosy fire to write only to discover that I had no cigarettes. Groping my way through the Stygian darkness along the icy road to the local pub, I restored the status quo and returned to my chair, when the sound of distant guns warned me of an approaching raid. Almost immediately the alert is sounded so the comparative immunity we have enjoyed these past few nights is ended. Or is it? Maybe it's just a lone raider. We hope so. Even so, I shall retire as usual dressed in my fire-fighting clothes with nothing more to put on than boots, coat and cap. War, like our baser selves, stalks with us, but it isn't the whole substance of our lives and, like life itself, is sometime to pass.

February 1st

AFTER A BUSY MORNING AT THE OFFICE, I ARRIVED AT WATERLOO with a few minutes to spare, so wandered into the station bar for a half-pint of beer during the drinking of which I took stock of the goodly crowd assembled there. Except in the faces of women present there were few smiles, yet there was no anxiety or gloom: rather, a certain preoccupation of mind was registered, serious rather than solemn. Feeling that our case must be worse before it is better and confessing for myself some measure of anxiety concerning coming events, notwithstanding my faith in the ultimate issue, I fell to thinking, as I quietly observed the crowd, that my interpretation of this mass attitude might take the colour of my own thoughts, that the crowd might be less serious than I imagined. With so powerful an enemy against us, to do anything else than look the facts squarely in the face would be imbecilic.

February 2nd

ROOSEVELT WAS ELECTED PRESIDENT FOR THE THIRD TIME IN succession, a unique event. His doughty opponent Wendell Wilkie visits this country to gather impressions of wartime England. In today's *Express* Hayden Talbot reports him as saying, 'At the end of a week in Britain I have discovered enough of fortitude, of neighbourliness, of self-reliance, of selfless devotion to the ancient faith of righteousness to convince me that British character will always be above par. British character – not the pound sterling – is the best security for the material aid which my country is sending.'*

February 4th

TODAY I WAS NOTIFIED OF MY APPOINTMENT TO OUR LOCAL FIRE Watchers and Fighters Committee formed at Sunday's general meeting at which I am informed that 61 persons were present. This evening we held our first meeting to discuss procedure and consider draft proposals, tabled by our chairman Mr Jones, for giving effect to the neighbourhood intentions. It was resolved that fire-fighting squads will be formed of eight persons under a committeeman leader, who shall be responsible for the efficient conduct of his squad, each to be on duty from 6 p.m. until 8 a.m. one night a week with two hours' active patrol for each of two watchers. Patrols are expected to commence on 10th February. The neighbourhood should be called upon to make a donation of 2/6*d.* per family to establish an initial fund for the purchase of necessary equipment. Finally, some distinguishing badge should be issued to identify members to the public. All this achieved with squads in action, our neighbours with reasonable confidence might sleep comfortably with both eyes closed.

* Wendell Wilkie failed to unseat Roosevelt in the presidential election of 1940 and later became his ally. He came to England at this time as Roosevelt's personal representative, and later urged the Americans to join Britain in the war against Germany.

February 7th

OUR FIRE MEETING LAST NIGHT WAS LIVELY. THERE WAS considerable opposition to aspects of the plan of action proposed. Objections were raised to a central HQ accommodating the resting patrols on the grounds that they could rest better in their own homes, yet be alert and ready for duty when called upon. I felt that there was something to be said for their view. Several other suggestions were advanced, the speakers vying with each other as to who could wander farthest from the matter in hand. Put to the vote we declared by 25 to 11 in favour of a central HQ. Nevertheless, the plan had to be abandoned for lack of numbers to make the rota of patrols workable. An old kite of predatory habits and Oriental ear-rings, blowing as the winds listed, greatly entertained me with her scatterbrained interjections, but being more hindrance than help she had to be silenced.

February 8th

AFTER A LITTLE INFORMAL TALK WITH ONE OR TWO LAST evening an alternative scheme was agreed upon tonight dispensing with street patrols (not encouraged by the local authorities) and which is being put into operation forthwith. We have split our designated area into five small zones, each under the leadership of a committeeman, Hansler Grove becoming my responsibility. This restores the elements of the plan I originally put into action with the rest of my neighbours last June. Amended slightly to bring it into line with the authorities' latest regulations, we are now ready for any emergency.

February 9th

SPENT MOST OF TODAY CANVASSING NEIGHBOURS AND ARRANGING squads. Being short of personnel, we shall just have to make the best of what we have, old and young together.

February 23rd

WITH FIRE-WATCHING ARRANGEMENTS AS COMPLETE AS I CAN make them, I was able to devote this weekend – which included my monthly half-day leave – to home affairs. Saturday morning for pressing maintenance jobs, Sunday with Tom McAward was spent in the kitchen garden and our own 'grow more food' campaign. The plot is now in good form, ready for planting and seeding. Potatoes are already sprouting in the greenhouse where, too, onions, leeks and radishes sown in boxes promise an early start. So the evening found me pleasantly tired and ready to sit before the fire and chat to Tom, whom I entertained at intervals with some excerpts from this diary. The absence of Alice Mary from our fireside – by reason of a sharp attack of bronchitis confining her to bed – directed my later reflections to more intimate matters. Not until domestic routine, by some mischance, is jolted out of gear do the majority of men realize how much their creature comforts depend upon efficient management and the smooth running of the household by their womenfolk. In the handkerchief box is the week's clean supply; in the airing cupboard are his lordship's shirts. Hardly noticed is the regular changing of the bed linen, or the never-failing supply of boot polish and toothpaste, of soap and matches. A late breakfast is generally of his own making. With little prospect of promotion, no annual increments, commission on sales, hours on turnover or other such inducements, domestic service runs quietly on without advertisement. For the majority of women marriage is still the career and motherhood the goal, housekeeping the occupation. Of the many female clerical workers I have met, most of whom eke out a thin 'bachelor' existence on their salaries, few there are of the older sort who have not impressed me with the notion that to them life has been something of a cheat. Sustained for a while by the precarious affection of nieces and nephews, these women pass pathetically on to retirement and unrecorded oblivion. And so I fear it is with the majority, for the simple, brutal truth is that few grow old gracefully and nobody wants to be bothered with them, not even their own kind.

March 10th

FIVE NIGHTS OF STEADY ENEMY RAIDING AND A LOT MORE OF London gone. Two of our pretty office girls, attending a party at Deptford on Saturday evening, were bombed into eternity, and of the rest of the young revellers, only one who had earlier slipped away escaped disaster. The crater in Abingdon Street, only recently repaired and into which a bus fell a few weeks ago, was reopened by another bomb during the same raid damaging all the below-ground public services for the second time. Once more our nightly rest is measured by the interval between raids. War is being accepted as a normal condition of life. By midwinter most of the Anderson shelters had been abandoned because they were too wet and cold to sleep in. The comfort of the home seems to be preferred to the somewhat doubtful protection they afford. Many people have a bed on the floor of the house and not a few resumed their regular sleeping habits in the traditional bedroom. The relative scarcity of food is assuming more importance than the matter of sleep. Certain commodities seem to have disappeared from the shops altogether. Onions have been unobtainable for weeks and leeks have soared to the fantastic price of 9*d.* each for large ones. Oranges are extremely scarce, and if we can procure as many as two eggs from our dairy, as a week's supply, we count ourselves lucky. While the supply of butter is better, jam, oatmeal and other cereals are very short, as are bacon and red meat. Poultry, especially chickens, are plentiful but price puts them out of reach for many. Still, there is enough to eat and drink if one pint of beer is made to do the service of three. Tobacco is short and expensive, but one can smoke less without undue hardship. And there is consolation, if not oblivion, in tea, which is not too restricted.

March 16th

PAYING A VISIT TO MY OLD FATHER WHO, FOR ALL HIS YEARS, IS still active and in good fettle, I found him grumbling because he couldn't get a job. I had to break it gently to him that even in wartime it was most unlikely that a man of 84 would secure paid employment. I advised him to cultivate his garden, and if that didn't give him occupation enough, to take on a small allotment as well.

March 23rd

TALKING TOGETHER OVER DOMESTIC MATTERS, MY WIFE commented on the grateful surprise with which the coalman – recently appointed – who delivered the last consignment of coal received the modest tip she offered as some acknowledgement of his good-natured service in trimming the coalbins to her liking. When, further, she produced a cup of coffee and a cigarette for his refreshment his delight was as transparent as it was comical – and perhaps a little moving too. Seldom a tradesman comes to our door who doesn't find himself in the possession of a token of our gratitude for services rendered. A hot drink on a cold day warms more than the stomach.

March 27th

THE 62ND ANNIVERSARY OF MY BIRTH. IT SEEMS INCREDIBLE TO me that so many years should have passed since my beginning. I remember it being said of me, as a lad, that I should 'never make old bones'. Well, I'm promisingly on the way.

April 17th

LAST NIGHT LONDON HAD ITS FIERCEST BLITZ OF THE WAR. WITH transport badly disorganized, by train I could travel no nearer the office than Clapham Junction and thence by tram only so far as Wandsworth Road station. For the rest the two-mile walk in bright spring sunshine would have been enjoyable but for the havoc caused by enemy bombing, which everywhere was a gruesome reminder of the horrors of war in this bitter struggle for mastery. For almost two miles a continuous line of hosepipes, fire brigades and ambulances, the scores of tired firemen attested to the intensity of the attack and its effects. So spent were the firemen, I found some asleep in doorways and corners amidst the ruins of burnt-out buildings. Pitifully the chattels of many a home lay exposed naked in doorless niches, or were still clinging to some blasted wall, for the curious to gape at. What could be rescued of the furniture was huddled together on the pavement. Perched on top of one pile a canary in its cage was singing lustily. Arriving two hours late I found that every window in front of the office had been blown out and even the heavy window frame shattered by the blast from a nearby bomb. Radiators had cracked and flooded some of the rooms. Equipment, files and papers covered in debris. Office routine was suspended while the staff cleared up the mess. Not until the following day did we resume normal duties; even so the draughty discomfort drove most of the women staff to the basement shelter to work.

April 19th

WITH THE LINE BOMBED IN TWO PLACES MY JOURNEY IS SADLY disorganized, taking sometimes upwards of three hours. Curiously enough, presence of the Wimbledon bomb, which had buried itself without exploding, was not suspected until two days later and put the line out of action. However, the broken journeys brought me an invitation to visit, tomorrow morning, a neighbourhood man whom I have long known only as a fellow passenger.

April 22nd

THERE IS SOMETHING SPECTRAL ABOUT THE SOUND THAT INVESTS the south side of Waterloo station on windy days. There is something macabre and haunting about it too, something that belongs to the supernatural, in the stories of Poe, at least so I felt as I stood and waited for my train. I heard it again this evening, indistinct, all about me. This curious noise is due in my mind to the shivering of countless fragments of shattered glass still loosely adhering as jagged margins to the hundreds of window-panes left after the bombing and audibly the fractured edges ride over each other in whispering protest.

May 7th

THESE ARE STRANGE DAYS. THE WINTER LINGERS ON LIKE AN unwanted guest and, like him, I'm tired too: having eaten after I got home tonight I couldn't keep my eyes open. I've just dragged myself into wakefulness and, Alice Mary having gone to bed, I felt I must do something positive to justify myself to myself, as it were. Reaching for some notepaper I jumped at the thought of writing the letter I owe Edmund Hoyle. What else better could I do at 10.15? So that when at last I make up and retire to my camp-bed, something will have been attempted, something done. So I thanked him for the indigo dye he sent me last week.

May 12th

DEAR OLD LONDON SUFFERED A FIERCE BLITZ ON SATURDAY night, during which the House of Commons debating chamber was wrecked and part of historic Westminster Hall. The Abbey was badly hit, including the partial destruction of both cloisters, and the church in Smith Square, damaged in a previous raid, has now only the outer walls standing. Its four towers – sometimes referred to as table legs, inverted, in reference to the story of its origin – even at 6 a.m. on Sunday still blazed like giant torches. A direct hit on the roof of Thames House shattered the upper floors of the south corner. The entry point of the bomb appears as a clean round hole through the sloping roof. Our own office suffered a few incendiary bombs which started two fires in the packing store and burnt a quantity of khaki drill clothing and much wastepaper ready for salvage. The prompt action of the night staff prevented more damage. Victoria station is partially closed on account of a delayed-action bomb falling into the approach yard. Waterloo is wholly out of action because of a time bomb buried in the permanent way between there and Vauxhall. The busy crossing is now deserted and silent since all traffic is diverted through back-streets. This morning I could only get as far as Clapham Junction. A thoroughly well organized service of buses carried us the rest of the way. I found the air, especially in the neighbourhood of the Abbey, still redolent of stale fire smoke. It's a mournful tale to be telling this best and sunniest day of our summer's beginning.

May 14th

THE ASTONISHING THING ABOUT THIS WRECKING OF LONDON – and I have seen much of it these past few months – is that one gets used to the sight of such wholesale destruction with all the grim tragedy it implies. In no sense am I indifferent, nor can it be said that I am callous. But there is a growing philosophical acceptance in the back of my mind that out of the welter of events a better London, more worthy of our times, will eventually arise from the ashes of the old.

May 23rd

AFTER WRITING SO MUCH ABOUT BOMBING IT IS PLEASANT TO recall the sight I had last evening, of a foster-mother cat suckling her one newborn kitten and four blind dachshund pups, whose mother died shortly after their birth, with an affectionate impartiality delightful to behold. Supplementing the foster-mother's efforts, my neighbour's wife gently detached each in turn from its warm paradise and, with deft fingers, parted the soft, toothless gums to receive the tiny teat of a small feeding bottle. Later, the mother cat and her mixed family, reunited in a warm furry mound, slept peacefully.

May 25th

ALICE MARY IS VERY POORLY AND OUR DOCTOR SEEMS UNABLE TO diagnose the trouble. His treatment doesn't arrest the steady decline of her health. In the circumstances I felt that loyalty to any patient/doctor relationship should not prevent me seeking other advice. Her indisposition has lasted too long. This morning I put my view to another doctor and he at once agreed to take up the case forthwith. I have a growing conviction that general practitioners are more concerned about their pay than their patients. Too often patients themselves, by unnecessary demands, have encouraged this attitude.

June 3rd

ANXIOUS TO GET THERE IN TIME FOR A GOOD LOOK ROUND AND anxious to get back to Alice Mary, whom I had left in bed enduring her malady with great fortitude, I travelled to Somerset through a countryside in mourning green under weeping skies with never a sign of summer this bleak cold day. A slow, comfortless journey, the train packed with women and children, soldiers and airmen, there was no food to be had and, but for that which I had taken with me, I should have gone hungry during the six-hour journey to Wells. Cigarettes were unobtainable en route. On enquiring for something to eat, the only offer I received from one of four shops was a small loaf of bread and a pat of margarine. From another a couple of slices of bread and a small tin of sardines or Marmite, but later, in a tiny general shop, I discovered some toffee sweets of which I was permitted to purchase four ounces, all that could be spared, to supplement what remained of my home-provided nosebag. Unless I am recalled to the office I now commence seven days' leave – my summer holiday. I had hoped to spend a few days away with Alice Mary but she is not fit to be in any other but our very own Shieling. A recent examination disclosed some obstruction in the lower bowel, which appears to be the cause of the involuntary looseness during the past few months. With all my heart I hope the doctors' next step will provc succcssful in arresting her malady and to our anxiety bring relief. At least during these few days of leave I can look after her. And on 1st June, her 69th birthday, following the distressing examination, one conspired with neighbours and friends to make it a specially happy day for her. May it please God that there are many other, not less happy, occasions ahead for her and me.

June 10th

DAY BREAKS, STILL GLOOMY AND WET. FOLLOWING FRIDAY'S examination of Alice Mary, the diagnosis foreshadowed by the gynaecologist was, unhappily, confirmed. The growth on the lower bowel, believed to be in its early stages at the moment, must be removed to prevent the inevitable stoppage if allowed by time to develop. After a week of watching her grow pathetically weaker, I took her yesterday to our local cottage hospital where preparations had been made for the operation tomorrow. She had been dreading the thought of hospital, but her reception by the smiling nurses, the comfort of the bright ward allotted her, and our dainty tête-à-tête tea cheered her. Finally, as if to lend official sanction to the festive atmosphere, the matron introduced herself and assured us of the comfort of patient and visitor alike. She replied, in a Scots accent, to my appreciative comments, that if I cared to remain she would quickly find something the matter with me to justify detention in the male ward. And so, relieved at Pont's response, I plodded homewards through the heavy rain, unmindful of my wet clobber and waterlogged shoes.

Stripping off my soaked garments, a good rub down before the fire put me in good fettle to attend to what must be done in Pont's absence. This bachelor existence must not debase our Shieling standard.

June 11th

A DAY OF ANXIOUS WAITING AND PONT RESTORED TO HER BED at 5.15 with the major part of the operation over. A peep at her a few minutes later filled me with pity. A talk with the surgeon, whom I invited to be unreservedly frank, disclosed that the trouble was more deep-seated than at first anticipated.

June 21st

JUST AFTER SIX O'CLOCK THE SUN ASCENDED LIKE A BALL OF molten copper. Still glowing it was soon reaching up into the quiet blue of morning, promising another to the tally of torrid days this week. To the hospital for a peep at Alice Mary.

June 22nd

AFTER A NIGHT OF HOT BEGINNING, I FELT MOST REFRESHED when I awoke to the cool air of early morning, for it was not yet six o'clock. Maybe the relief I felt at Alice Mary's progress added much to the buoyancy of my spirits. I was wholly and vigorously awake. To fling off the bedsheets, to let in air through all doors and windows, to step naked into the garden was the occupation of moments. Comfortably cool in my birthday suit, by 9.30 a.m. I had trimmed the hedges, shrubs and bushes, weeded the borders, watered the pot plants and finally cleaned up the rubbish ready for burning. With only the birds to witness my abandon, I flit as free and happy as they. And then to breakfast, frugal tho' satisfying, taken sitting in the now sunlit veranda while I surveyed my handiwork, glad of the respite. Nothing human disturbed my quiet save the milkman on his round in the street beyond. Clothing myself only for the visits to hospital the day moved peacefully on. Of frugal appetite and not unduly interested in my stomach, nevertheless the longing for an eating of good red meat occasionally descends on me out of the blue: with luck, and by the grace of our butcher, I was able to indulge it liberally today. The hoardings of Saturday's marketing made for Sunday a banquet. Rubbing into my rare cut of steak, both sides, a little salt and pepper, a trifle of grated onion and a spoonful of olive oil, I grilled it to that perfection which I felt the occasion demanded. To prepare a garnish of mashed potatoes and a picking of home-grown spinach entertainingly filled in the intervals between turning and basting the meat. To eat meditatively as I viewed the garden was to extract from my repast sustenance and content for both mind and body.

Comfortably cool in my birthday suit...

Not until my evening visit to hospital did I don my clothes. Some neighbours dropping in on my return to Shieling for a short space rounded off the day with pleasant talk, and while twilight lingered, I tumbled sleepily into bed well content.

July 9th

THE FIRST RAIN LAST EVENING, AFTER A MONTH OF ALMOST overpowering heat day and night. The steady patter on the trees was sweet music; no less sweet was the smell of good earth responding to the timely downpour. And this morning the vegetation stood crisply confident in its green vigour. And I, too, seemed to respond with it for Alice Mary displayed welcome signs of returning strength, which this morning's sight of her confirmed. The healing rain had come for her and me, too, and if our anxieties are not yet over at least, like the plants, we register a renewed confidence in things to come.

Still in our cottage hospital she is now looking forward to her first spell out of bed to enjoy the light airs of the garden, under the trees. From then on we may begin to count the days to her homecoming. And now I am on the way to Portals Mill, at Overton, to examine a large making of security paper. The rains of last night have freshened the air and tempered the heat, and everywhere objects sparkle in the sun. The news of Russia's continued resistance to Germany's invading hordes, our own ever-increasing bombing from the air by night and day of the enemy's vulnerable production and military centres, our expanding occupation of the Near East, America's action in the garrisoning of Greenland and Iceland for the protection of Atlantic sea lanes, our own relative freedom, at home, from enemy night raiders and Mr Churchill's new note of confidence all help to brighten the general outlook and strengthen our belief in the ultimate issue. Japan as yet makes no sign of active belligerency on either front, and Italy, it seems, is slowly crumbling. My last letter from Frank makes reference to Nostradamus and his book *Centuries*, condemned in the eighteenth century on the grounds of its prediction of the extinction of the papacy. Now extremely rare, this remarkable book foretells war in the air and England's ultimate victory over Germany through the aid of America. Is it coincidence that the name given to the betrayer of Europe is Hitler, and his warning to Italy that her dictator will be completely crushed? Russia and Germany will practically exhaust themselves by the destruction of each other. And to lend seeming authority to the rest, the month of May is actually given for the fall of Belgium.

The train takes me home through the peaceful countrysides of Hampshire and Surrey. All along the line stand fields of ripening oats, barley and wheat, which seemed to have suffered little from the drought. And waiting at Woking for my home connection, the news sheets announce Germany's retreat before the Russians. I wonder. But war seems remote at the moment.

July 18th

DISCUSSING WITH MY WIFE THE QUESTION OF SECURING HELP against her homecoming and convalescence, she remarked that if her sister Anne would take over the duties of home management, not only would that problem be solved but, Anne being a laughter-provoking woman, they could laugh freely together. Laughter is a tonic. Probably I don't laugh enough, at least about the house. Not being a laughter-maker I need the provocation that others give; not that I am habitually gloomy, on the contrary, I am said to be of cheerful habit, to possess a lively sense of humour, moreover I like a good laugh, but it doesn't often come my way. But my wife is a laughter-loving woman. God knows, she has little to laugh about just now.

July 26th

LONDON'S WARTIME BUS CONDUCTRESSES ARE TAKING SPLENdidly to their new job. Many of them are pretty and as charming as they are cheerful and almost all of them smartly groomed. Their courtesy leaves nothing to be desired. Active and resourceful, they are expeditious in the discharge of their duties to both passengers and employers. An obviously friendly understanding with the male driver leaves efficient co-operation in no doubt. I should say that the majority of them are young married women, possibly with husbands in the services. From all to whom I have spoken I felt a cheery response, and without exception they have declared themselves happy in the job. Taking stock of her passengers, the conductress signals the driver to move on and, cool and confident, threads her way about the bus demanding, 'Fares, please.'

July 30th

IN A LETTER TO THE *DT* CHAMPIONING THE CAUSE OF THE unskilled labourer, the essayist Morley Roberts rightly condemns the too free use of the term 'unskilled'. He reminds us that use of the shovel is not to be learned in a day. And the navvy of the railway, the highway, all skilled men who have known the growing pains of learning the proper use of the pick and shovel, the axe and sledge, and all the rest of the tools to be found grouped at night about any watchman's shelter. And what of the nightwatchman himself, usually a navvy, too old for laborious work, finding light employment in the not entirely unskilled job of cleaning, oiling and placing his lamps and generally assuring the safety of tools as well as of the highway for the public? How many of us could get a fire going in his brazier? Study well the men at work in some bomb crater. No mere puddles in the mud these days when every hole is a duck run. For the many onlookers, not all idlers, that gather round the navvy at work, there is a fascination in watching. As with farm labourers, deckhands and all doers of menial tasks, man's world would be a sorry habitation without them.

August 14th

A MORNING OF GLOOM AND PERSISTENTLY HEAVY RAIN SHED BY blue-black cloudbanks as they drifted solidly and sullenly across the sky. Yet there is brightness for Alice Mary and me. Today she returns to Shieling after some ten weeks away. Although still weak and ill she expressed a desire to leave the ward and come home. The need for a sight of our pretty home was within her and not to be denied. But my gladness is tempered by a new anxiety at the thought of an instinctive awareness within her of some imminent crisis. Hospital staffs entertain the superstition that, in such cases, the end is approaching – the patient wants to be with familiar faces and things at the last.

All preparations are complete for her reception. I accompanied her to Shieling in the ambulance and arriving at 3 p.m. I put her straight to bed.

August 28th

WITH THE SHORTENING DAYS BRINGING A PROGRESSIVE intrusion of the blackout, opportunities for evening work in the garden dwindle as the prospect of indoor recreation advances. And this last night or two, with an hour or so to spare after drawing the curtains, it has been pleasant, while sitting with Alice Mary, to browse about the colourful bookshelves in contemplation of a reunion with patient old friends.

September 3rd

THIS MORNING CAME ANOTHER LITTLE GIFT PARCEL BY POST from the Brackenridges for Alice Mary. Briefly to thank them conveys little of our warmth of appreciation. They cannot know her tender smile as she displayed to me the dainty bed cap, and the pretty blue and white cravat. I wish they could.

October 4th

MAUD HOYLE'S LETTER OF 14TH SEPTEMBER CONCERNING MY domestic anxieties was encouraging and altogether matey. A week ago, just after dawn, fighting for her very breath, Alice Mary nearly died in my arms of heart failure, the third and worst attack she has sustained since she came home to Shieling. The prospect of others is not remote and lest, in my absence, they recur I have made arrangements for immediate help as she is beyond one person's strength to handle during a crisis. Returning home that afternoon, I found her after a wonderful rally smiling bravely on. I wanted to gather her frail body in my arms to afford her the security I cannot give. Sitting quietly with her these blackout evenings her little sleeps provide me with an opportunity to read. Elsewhere in my diary I have it that if private motives could be written down honestly and without reserve, many of us would be horrified at the reading. But it is comforting to reflect that for most of us few of the baser sort survive to become operative; they are mostly stillborn.

October 9th

UNAWARE THAT THE RAILWAY BETWEEN WIMBLEDON AND Putney Bridge stations was closed and calling for a ticket to the latter the surly-looking clerk with devastating sarcasm replied, 'Can't you see the noticeboard?' Pointing to the three women standing directly in front of it I retorted, 'I can barely see through the woman I do know and not at all through three I don't.' Arriving by bus at Putney and booking to Westminster, the booking clerk, observing my unlit cigarette, offered me a light and smilingly informed me that his small service was inclusive in the price of the ticket – and a famine in matches too!

October 15th

QUOTED BY ARTHUR STANLEY IN HIS *THE BEDTIME BOOK*, THIS anonymous translation from the Gaelic is especially entitled to a place in my diary:

From the lone Shieling of the misty island
Mountains divide us and the waste of seas
Yet still the blood is strong, the heart is Highland,
And we in dreams behold the Hebrides.

Well, we all have our misty island, if only the isle of our dreams. Though mountains divide us and the waste of seas, still might our dreams come true and make of our Shielings a reality indeed. We are such stuff as dreams are made on.

October 26th

WRITES 'J O'L' IN HIS LETTER OF THE 24TH, 'IT OCCURS TO ME that a man who wishes to know himself well enough to write about himself would be greatly helped if he could relive his most striking and most haunting encounters with books. Those which in his journey from childhood to age have hit him most in the reading and which have become not so much the furniture of the mind as its fixtures.' In my early teens I read little, except for the kind of thriller popular with boys in late-Victorian days. *Chums*, a boys' pictorial of the better sort, was a favourite of mine. Looking back I now see that it appealed to the spirit of adventure within me. With small change scraped together from part-time employment, I wheedled from my friend the local chemist his much-used students' box of tricks and set up my lab in a corner of the spare room. Attendance at evening classes first in electricity and physics and later in chemistry gave directions to my gropings and finally, at the age of 20, rewarded me with a junior demonstrator's post in the chemical department at Battersea Poly.

Thanks to the encouragement I received from the Head and the opportunities afforded by my later appointment, I was enabled to follow a definite course of study and, in effect, was launched upon a career concerning which I can record nothing of regret. A season of Shakespeare and Grand Opera at the Old Vic immediately after the Great War gave me a zest for Shakespeare and folklore and brought me closer to the classics of which, until then, I was almost entirely ignorant. Of my book memories *Marius the Epicurean*, next to *Modern Science and Modern Thought*, is the most outstanding, most haunting. From Marius I radiated in all directions. These and many others, together with something of the Old and New Testament, constitute my book of life from the collected writings of which I feel to have formulated a satisfying creed that leaves faith unshaken.

Regarded as the outward expression of my musings these notes afford some measure of my inner resources and in these dreadful days of world strife, beset as I am with anxiety for my wife, provide me with a means of escape from the world of men that is too much with us.

November 15th

MY FATHER'S 85TH BIRTHDAY, WHICH, WITH HIM AT HIS HOME, I quietly celebrated. Not in good fettle just now – a temporary indisposition I think. He still wears well and is wonderfully active and if he dwells a little in the past he is still mentally alert.

November 23rd

IT IS SUNDAY EVENING. THE BLACKOUT CURTAINS ARE DRAWN and the house is quiet and still. Its very stillness presages the end, which, for my Alice Mary, is now very near. My heart is full to overflowing. The few chrysanthemums in the bowl on my table seem to bow their heads with mine in sympathy. I strive not to weep in my devastation.

November 26th

BY ALL THE RULES OF MEDICINE MY ALICE MARY SHOULD HAVE passed over this day but, thank God, she rallied wonderfully and we spent a quietly happy afternoon together and a peaceful night followed.

December 2nd

IN SPITE OF MY ANXIETIES, FOR MY ALICE MARY IS DRIFTING slowly away, I have pinned myself down, during the quiet watches, to some solid reading and in Ruskin's *The Crown of Wild Olive* find plenty in which to sink my teeth. Nor have I neglected my physical needs, for Sunday found me in the garden. Seeing me in my agricultural disguise the doctor remarked, 'You look like a farm labourer,' to which I replied, 'Well, it's an honourable craft and who wiser than the intelligent farm labourer? Is he not a doctor, too?'

December 5th

THIS MORNING I SAW A WOMAN SEATED ON AN UPTURNED BALE on the tailboard of a passing railway van, as unconcernedly knitting as if during her spare half-hour at home. Not a little was added to my general amusement as the van jogged past, when our bus conductor facetiously observed that an official issue of wool he thought would shortly be made to bus conductresses for knitting between stops. Anyway, it was heartening to reflect that women 'van boys' had so easily made themselves at home in the job.

December 6th

HOW OFTEN IT IS THAT THE ACHE TO SERVE THOSE WE LOVE hurts most when service is least capable of benefit. Never so closely has it come home to me as during these recent dark days and nights, which for Alice Mary carry little distinction, when love reveals in adversity its abiding qualities – capacity for pain for another, recognition of its emotional responsibilities and consequences, and the precious gold of quiet joys shared in other days. At 7.30 this morning putting her dear wasted arms about my neck and feebly drawing me to her she whispered uncertainly, 'Take me away somewhere, dear, and hide me.' Limpid with vague comprehension, her eyes looked into mine filling me with impotence as I suffered the agony of an abysmal pity. Heeding her appeal, I felt that I too wanted to hide.

December 7th

FIRST RUSSIA AND NOW ENGLAND ARE FORMALLY AT WAR WITH Finland, Romania and Bulgaria, as well as with Germany and Italy. And today Japan threw in her lot with the Axis Powers and declared war against the United States of America and Great Britain. Thus is involved on the side of democracy the whole British Empire, the United States and her dependants. With Japan already at war with China, the stage is now set for all the violence and tragedy of a world war, or is it a world revolution between the lawful and lawless? And such is the ironic confusion in this contest for political supremacy that often enough old friends are now foes and old foes friends. Well, man has no one but himself to blame. Refusing peacefully to accept Creation's kindly offer of Earth's abundance, each squabbles with his neighbour about his share like a pickpocket.

December 8th – Monday

MY ALICE MARY PASSED PEACEFULLY AWAY THIS EARLY EVENING at 5.30. God preserve her dear kindly soul. May her whole spirit watch over me and be with me for the rest of my days. And now:

I am left alone in the sitting
With no one to sit beside.

And if for me there can be no second spring, the rosemary of her unseen presence will remain for me always fragrant and sweet. Amen.

December 9th

AND GAZING ON HER DEAR FACE THIS MORNING, A SMILING tranquillity shone through her still features. Never so poignantly did I know my grief and loss as then; never so certain was my conviction of her safe Gathering In.

December 12th

TODAY WE TAKE MY ALICE MARY TO HER LAST VISITING PLACE where, in God's good time, I hope to join her, a place of gentle green peace in our village cemetery. Her cherished holly decked with scarlet fruit in the form of a cross was the floral tribute of my choice as being most tenderly appropriate to her memory.

And hallowed by a God-given interval of sunshine in an otherwise gloomy day, as if momently all nature smiled through its tears at the homecoming, I with my little party of mourners accompanied her to the very gates of sleep where shall she find 'A safe lodging and a holy rest and peace at the last'.

December 23rd

TONIGHT THE HOUSE SEEMS VERY STILL. IN THE ROOM, IN THE presence of this silence, I felt remote, and strangely, unemotionally alone. The reaction no doubt from the year-long anxieties over my Alice Mary's declining. From Christmas to Christmas seems the sequence of events; last winter's illness, the gradual weakening, the fruitless operation and the months in hospital until the wheat ripened and was golden; her eager homecoming, when the begonias bloomed, and her final twelve weeks at Shieling where, to the last, she knew the benefit of tender service gladly given day and night finding in her own room a quiet joy in familiar faces until at last she has drifted peacefully and unaware into the Great Unknown. The sudden cessation for me of the long vigil, the void that is mine with her passing, the curious strangeness to me of familiar things in this silent room, the stillness of all things so lately animated by her presence seem at this hour to impart a feeling of unreality. Yet Christmas must not be a time of lamentation. Others there are to whom I owe the better part. Since Alice Mary would have it so, the spirit of Christmas present must be invoked for their sakes as well as for my own. Presence innumerable shall memory supply and in quiet gladness will her spirit be with us to consecrate the day.

December 25th

ANNE, CLIFFORD AND DORIS – WITH CASUALLY VISITING neighbours – made Christmas Day for me quietly happy, and for themselves.

December 29th

MY FIRST JOURNEY NORTH SINCE MAY 1940 – AND THE COLDEST day of the season. Even the windows of the carriage were coated in frost. Later, to reach the lavatory at the corridor, either end, was rather like being in a rugger scrum. Still, by common consent priority was good-naturedly accorded the most pressing cases.

1942

January 11th

I HAD ALMOST COMMENCED THE NEW YEAR ON A FALSE NOTE by writing on January 1st that the death of my wife had left me much to readjust. But has it? Wrestling for days with a stubborn bronchial cold and feeling generally under the weather doesn't make for clarity of mind, so I drifted into a mental lethargy, glad to relax, and, in the evenings, doze fitfully in front of my fire before turning in. I know that any diary notes would, in such circumstances, be forced and unworthy. And now, this evening, returning to a more normal state of mind and reviewing these introductory weeks of this my widower life, I can see that little or no adjustment is necessary. The mechanics of domestic routine continue along much the same lines under my sister-in-law's management.

The loss of my wife is an event that must in the nature of things live on with me. I would not have it otherwise. I seem to hear her voice, as often of late I have, reminding me of the lateness of the hour and gently summoning me to bed. Yes, there is truth in tragedy and gold in grief. Thus is my night hung with stars that I may hope to journey through it, without stumbling, to the dawn.

January 12th

TODAY IS FRANK'S BIRTHDAY, WHICH WE QUIETLY CELEBRATED over a glass of wine, then lunch. Two hours of delightful companionship for our heart's ease. I only wish that all men had such understanding of each other, yet it is denied to none.

January 14th

AND BY THIS MORNING'S POST A LETTER INFORMED ME OF Frank's son Matthew's reported death, 'Killed In Action'. On my journey to town I wrote him as follows, 'What shall a man say to his friend for a comforting? Except that words dewed with the sweet rains of understanding are fresh gathered from the garden of sorrow shall they bring to him balm for the healing and to his house of mourning the bitter sweet of consolation.'

January 30th

ARRIVING AT KING'S X AFTER A SIX-HOUR JOURNEY FROM LEEDS I wandered along to Lyons for a refreshing cup of tea and waited for a waitress. Observing people in single file progressing along the service counter it dawned on me that here the cafeteria system was in operation and that if I wanted my tea I must fetch it myself. Observing my patient waiting, some few amused glances in my direction confirmed my thoughts and joining the moving queue I was soon on my way to tea. Here, a marcelled maiden was dispensing cups of tea with luminous dexterity. Collecting the 3½*d.* change from my tendered silver sixpence and slipping across to the table from which I had started, I sipped the golden tea and watched the procession at the counter while I reflected on the events that had made necessary, in the interests of man and woman power economy, this excellent co-operative effort in our popular catering service. And to the disposal squad who removed the time bomb threatening St Paul's cathedral, this tribute by Gordon Bushell of the *Daily Mail*: 'They scorned the menace of an ambushed death, that future eyes might share the dream of Wren.'

February 5th

AN SOS FROM MY FATHER'S WIFE LAST NIGHT TOOK ME TO Tolworth to see my old dad who, I fear, is approaching the end. I found that he had rallied and was cheerful, although somewhat ailing. Occasional fits of the touchiness of earlier days, if something did not please him, were manifested by his quick frown, but he was pleased to see me. He spoke of the possibility of his sudden end and in anticipation discussed intimate affairs without embarrassment, expressing the wish that I should see his wife through the difficult time. It being already in my mind to do so, the promise was no sooner asked than given. For Agnes, at 61, to marry a man twenty years her senior had appeared rather to invite disaster even in the very few years left to them together, but they seem to have rubbed along happily enough. In her care of him she has been a good wife. Her arrival solved the problem of what to do with him when my mother died, when he was so very lonely. If for no better reason than that of her loyalty to him will I do all I can to help her when the need arises. Looking through his papers in search of some document he wished to hand over to me I lighted upon the certificate of his marriage to my dear mother, dated March 3rd 1879, and was amused to find that only by the narrow margin of twenty-four days did I achieve respectability on my entry into this world. Yet I can well imagine that for my blessed mother there was little amusement in the anxious waiting for a marriage ceremony so long delayed when, in those Victorian times, the social whispering gallery was alive with tongues more maliciously devastating than now. And knowing well my mother, I have no doubt that she was not less concerned for my legitimate birth than for her own honourable motherhood. Maybe to me as an unborn babe she transmitted, in the esoteric manner of mothers, some measure of her own anxieties in the quality of her affections. But for these things I bless her memory. It is one of the tragedies of life that complete understanding so often comes too late.

After leaving my father, I groped my way through the darkness along the icy streets to the bus stop and found myself the only passenger on the last service to Surbiton. I sensed that the conductress wanted someone to talk to and quickly we were engaged in conversation. She bemoaned the indifference of London Transport to the welfare of its female employees, who, after duty, had to walk home for lack of alternative transport when ordinary services had ceased. I wished her luck, departed, and was soon sitting by my own good fireside.

April 2nd

SMILING ALL OVER HIS FACE, THE YOUNG NAVAL OFFICER, SON OF a neighbour, whom I met on my way to the station this morning, looking manly and alert in his uniform, told me, over a genial handshake, that he was never so happy in his life as now, that with all its hazards he enjoyed it better in wartime than in peace. In the spring sunlight of this wonderful morning his eyes shone merrily, his van Dyck beard, which waggled as he talked, was luminous with chestnut hues, his fine broad shoulders seemed square set to the world, his voice had the richness that belonged to an ample chest. In fact, his whole demeanour was one of vast confidence and easy grace. It did me good to see him, to sense his complete accord with the living of life. Continuing my walk to the station, I surrendered myself to the emotional thrill that was mine at the thought of what we older ones owe to the good-humoured acceptance by the countless thousands of young men like him of the high adventure of war. Perhaps, too, I felt something of the exhilaration of spring, for earlier in the morning, digging over the last of my potato patch, I enjoyed a sight of the first pink of almond blooms. And the other side of the story, another neighbour's only son in Libya, so I hear, has made the supreme sacrifice.

April 20th

I'M NOT SORRY TO BE BACK AT WORK TODAY. MY WEEK'S LEAVE was marred by an acute depression, rare with me. Morose and irritable, I found it difficult to be more than civil to others, and to avoid inflicting my churlishness on those about me occupied myself early and late with the garden. In work I found some relief. With my old father, who was spending the week at Shieling, I found it difficult to restrain my impatience at his rambling repetitions. In his 85th year he lives much in the past and is now inclined to be infantile. Myself in the doldrums, I found it hard to bear. For lack of proper training the young dog his wife brought with her rooted unrestrained over my herbaceous borders and rockery and played havoc with choice plants. In the house it was a pest and fouled my carpets, as if to the manor born, without check. To avoid hostilities I retired to the garden and busied myself when otherwise we might have entertained each other round the fire. I was a stranger in my own home, missing my wife horribly. Like a sick dog, I wanted to be alone. The anticipated three days of country tramping with Frank fell through but my week with Claude Yearsley and his family did much to help me out. Free to brew myself early-morning tea I found myself enjoying the quiet beauty of a new day beginning while others slept.

May 3rd

FOR THE FIRST TIME THIS YEAR I ENJOYED, IN MY GREENHOUSE, an afternoon sunbathing. At the comfortable temperature within of 80 degrees it was pleasant to abandon myself to complete relaxation and doze in the warmth of gently moving air from the open door. Tea and a cigarette rounded off my afternoon.

May 9th

THE BLITZING OF BATH BY ENEMY BOMBERS LASTED FROM 11.10 p.m. to 5.50 a.m. on the first night, and on the second from 1.20 a.m. to 4.45 a.m. In his letter to Frank, T. B. Donovan has nothing but praise for the fortitude displayed by all with whom he came into contact and most of all for the bombed-out families, whose practical concern for others in distress was a feature of the tragic hours. Donovan writes, 'An unforgettable night dragged to its weary close and we lay exhausted on the floor to try and rest, unsuccessfully I fear, as vivid images chased each other through our minds.' Bath looked a sorry sight with all its churches gone, except the abbey, preserved by a miracle except for its windows. The famous assembly rooms restored to their eighteenth-century beauty some years ago at a cost of £90,000 were completely gutted. The official list of dead up to the time of writing is 391 persons with many still to be added. Enormous damage was done and great fires fanned by a chill night completed the misery. The public services were well organized, despite the wrecking of so many essential shops, smashed water supplies to the city; communal restaurants were opened and milk, eggs and other rationed foods were made freely available, as were emergency homes for the homeless. And to his word of sympathy for the Countess of Berkeley, whom he found, worn out, sitting on the kerb dissecting the removal of what remained of her shattered £3,500 home, she replied, 'Gosh, but I'm tired,' and in allusion to the disaster that had befallen her she remarked, 'But that's nothing, I've lost my husband, which means much more to me,' and later, on meeting her parading sandwich boards advertising, 'Information! Please ask me,' she said, 'I'm so thrilled! I've just met the King and Queen and talked to them for ten minutes. His lip was trembling as he saw the damage.'

'A grand woman,' says TBD, 'but her spirit was equalled by the poor whom I met on my tour today.' And Lord Haw-Haw, so I am informed by a neighbour, announced over the air recently that among other show places for bombing is Hampton Court. Well, well.

May 26th

ONLY BY A SUPREME EFFORT COULD I GIVE MYSELF AN EXTRA hour in bed over this Whitsun. With my body at rest I found it difficult to relax my mind. My thoughts chased each other and disturbed the primeval sedimentation in some age-old pool, and in the mist Alice Mary seemed to take shape and we were alone, as so often we now are. I could never hope or desire to be with another.* I seem at her near presence, to experience a sense of savage satisfaction in physical exertion as if my unwonted energy was an act of defiance of that fate which had taken her from me and a tenderness floods my soul to shake me with an emotion too profound for words.

Today, I planted out two dozen tomato plants of my own raising from last year's crop and, tying them to their stakes, was caught in the evening deluge of rain, but this gave me little concern. To strip, enjoy a brisk rub-down and change my clothes put me in good fettle to tackle the evening meal awaiting me and to enjoy also the conversation on educational problems that followed with a friendly neighbour who had called, as he explained, to take me away from too much gardening. Feeling that he himself had done enough gardening for the day he conceived the notion of buying me a pint of the best bitter ale he could find in the village. Meeting at the Old Inn with another familiar, we talked gardening unto closing time and not until we parted at my gate did we cease. I must remember that Tarbut promised me some chives for the planting! And now here I am in a tram crowded with somnolent servicemen, approaching Peterborough, en route for Leeds.

June 6th

MY NEIGHBOUR NICHOLS, THE DENTIST, CALLED FOR ME THIS evening to rescue me, as he proclaimed, from too much work.

* Walter later developed a deep friendship with his old friend Mrs Sheard, and invited her to live with him as housekeeper and companion, though they never married. His feelings here may explain why Walter never asked Mrs Sheard to be his wife.

With him and his family I was to attend a tennis party at Whiteley, between Surrey and Weybridge. Gladly I went there to find that a racquet had been reserved for my use. But first a tour of the estate, which delighted me. Meandering thus, I gathered dandelions and docks enough to keep my rabbits in green stuff for half a week. Then tennis. Not for twenty years had I wielded a racquet and, playing two moderately fast sets, I was not a little pleased to find how quickly my old form came back to me.

June 10th

LIKE A SLOW RENDERING OF THE STRANDS OF SOME WELL-TRIED rope the ties of life sever one by one to leave me poised on the threshold of another beginning, uncertain and wondering, feeling rather more alone and stranger, perhaps a little, to myself. Such were my thoughts as I shaved this morning and reflected on the passing, yesterday, in his 85th year, of my dear old father. After a tedious declining he quietly slipped away in the morning sun with his arms outstretched calling softly for my mother, to tell her that he was coming. It was a peaceful going, for him perhaps the most peaceful and real moment of his long life.

June 16th

AT THE SIGHT ON THE PLATFORM OF THE STYLISH PORTRESS whose flax-like gold hair in shining splendour literally cascaded over her well-moulded shoulders, into my mind as my train stood at Huddersfield this evening came the old music-hall refrain 'And her golden hair was hanging down her back.' And to hear this uniformed, trim-ankled blonde shrilly pipe, 'Stand away there,' to the two venturesome passengers as she finally signalled the train out excited admiration as well as amusement. And in the evening at Leeds I saw a wisp of a girl in dungaree trousers and a jacket with a white collar stoop to inspect, as she passed along the side of the train, the axle bores, while from the guard's van a buxom lass in dungaree slacks and sleeveless scarlet jumper with the help of another of her kind was hurling with rare gusto hefty bags of Canadian mail on to the platform. And in Yorkshire, as elsewhere, I noticed that tram and bus conductresses generally display a kindly thoughtfulness for children, the elderly and infirm and in the main are responsive to the casual courtesy of passengers. Their attitude leaves me with the impression that for them this wartime occupation is something more than a job of work for a wage. To the business of collecting fares many of them bring something of neighbourliness, which it should not be beyond the wit of their opposites to emulate.

July 20th

AT THE BACK OF THE MIND OF ENGLISH PEOPLE THERE RESIDES, I think, an uneasy feeling that in our hesitation to provide a second front in aid of Russia, against the common enemy, it might be thought that we are not putting forth our whole strength and that to correct this impression we should do something spectacular and by land invasion force the enemy to face us in the west. But it seems that the same North Sea, which is the barrier to Germany's land invasion of England with all Europe's western seaboard in her occupation, in turn prevents us attempting a big-scale land invasion of Germany, at least, just yet. That so little is known of the Allies' help to Russia in other respects does not mean that she is not getting the utmost assistance in matériel that we in England can give her.

...to hear this uniformed, trim ankled blonde shrilly pipe 'Stand away there'...

Rather is it that for such information to become public property here it must be equally well known to the enemy. That our air raids increasing in magnitude over Germany's vital production centres and our Air Force help on the Russian fronts must be having a cumulative effect on the enemy goes without saying, even if the results are not appreciated by the man in the street. Trusting Mr Churchill, we must have also faith in his wisdom and leave to the better-informed the care of events. The voice that cried in the wilderness before the war has proved to be right in its warning forecast of events. Let us listen to it now. With Russia conquered and England starved into submission, Germany's world ambitions would be well on the way to fulfilment. Then it might be expected that the nationals of enemy-occupied countries, giving up all hope of rescue, would, for a time at least, accept the inevitable and settle down as subject peoples under the direction of the *Herrenvolk*. America would then be in the position that England now is as a besieged nation and, China being denied supplies of munitions of war, would be obliged to make some partial surrender to Japan who, no doubt, is waiting for the propitious moment to give the *coup de grâce* to Russia from the rear before making her onslaught on Australia and India. The war is entering a critical stage and it is vital to our existence that no ill-timed large-scale operation should jeopardize the issue. All the more necessary to proceed boldly, yet warily, to our appointed end of winning the war for democracy.

August 9th

MY DEAR OLD FRIEND AND NEIGHBOUR THOMAS HOOK PASSED over at 4 a.m. today after two strokes in quick succession in his 82nd year. Another of my fine landmarks gone. At business as usual on Thursday, and dead today, after 66 years in the City of London. Accepted at sight by the Almighty, I do not have to pray for him. Rather will he be putting in a good word to God for me.

August 14th

CHALLENGING THE STATEMENT BY A WRITER THAT 'IT IS impossible to go on living the life of the people unless you have developed an intellect of your own', the critic Robert Lynd questions the right of the intellectual to regard himself as a human being superior to his neighbours. 'After all,' he says, 'there are more points in which the intellectual resembles other people than in which he differs from them. Intellect is only one of the talents that may fall to the fortunate man, it is no more to be praised than is self-denial without charity.' Allied to moral and spiritual greatness, it produced Milton. Divorced from these attitudes it gives us Hitler.

September 13th

IT IS EARLY EVENING, MY WEEK'S LEAVE IS ALL BUT OVER. Tomorrow I resume official chores. In certain respects, this taste of home for the few consecutive days has given me a desire for more, as a quiet haven of retirement. Perhaps it is that I am feeling that way after a strenuous week, for now it seems agreeable to my need to sit quietly by the open veranda and, overlooking my garden, catch up arrears of correspondence. Not for days have I touched my pen. To come back, as it were, after a few days and have a word with my diary is like coming home to familiar and tried things.

With the help of my neighbour Mr Mason, this morning I

stripped my well-laden pear tree and in addition picked a few good eating apples overhanging from another neighbour's garden. And during a resting interval amidst the pears, over my last half-bottle of real sherry, I entertained my neighbour's brother, Captain Douglas Mason, hero of the oil tanker *Ohio*, which he recently got safely through to Malta during the Mediterranean sea battle. The largest tanker afloat, twice hit by torpedoes, bombed, burned and harried by a veritable hornets' nest of enemy planes, two of which crashed on her deck, one in flames, her skipper got his crippled ship into Malta and discharged his vitally important cargo intact. Covered with sandfly sores from head to foot but otherwise uninjured, he sat quietly in my garden and with us enjoyed a sherry and smoke while narrating these terrible events. The George Cross, bestowed upon him, was well and truly earned and I felt just a little humble in the presence of so much fine manhood. Yet I counted it a privilege to be able to afford him the hospitality of my peaceful garden on this morning of harvest. Commenting on the worldwide publicity the event had brought him, he declared he found it very embarrassing. A pint of beer with a pal in some quiet corner would have been more to his taste. Measuring the man, I know he spoke from the heart.

September 24th

IN THESE DAYS OF SEVERE RUBBER SHORTAGE, SO ACUTE IN FACT that such articles as rubber gumboots, ground sheets and mackintosh garments, even for priority purposes, are now obtainable only with the greatest difficulty, it is not a little distressing to find that over the years no adequate substitute for the natural product has been invented. Forty years ago, as a works chemist, I was engaged in the preparation of rubber-substitute compounds which, during the interval, it seems have been little improved upon. So it was with great interest, concerned as I am officially with the provision overseas of alternative supplies of these commodities, that I visited in Burnley today the works of a firm engaged in the production of substitute materials, with a view to reporting on their possible utility overseas. To walk into the spreading shop was to take the forty years in a stride, and made the old days seem but yesterday.

While there is no substitute for an article endowed with such peculiar properties as natural rubber, and while it is to be deplored that so little has been done to effect an alternative against the rainy day now upon us, still, the best not the worst must be made of what a few enterprising industrialists have done in this direction, hoping that events will further stimulate research in a matter so important.

September 26th

STILL VIVID IN MY MEMORY AS I WRITE ON THE TRAIN, STILL insistent in its wonderful effect of uplift, I experienced in the early hours of this morning what I then felt and now believe was a revelation. I felt that I had my dear wife in my arms. So real, so intense was her presence that it seemed actually physical and brought with it for me a great peace.

September 27th

WE ARE CURIOUSLY INCONSISTENT: MY FELLOW PASSENGER opposite, yesterday, addressing another in reference to a pronouncement in the *Yorkshire Post* by Lord Woolton foreshadowing further food economies during the coming winter, himself audibly professed a rigid economy in food, declaring with a certain unction that for a whole year he had denied himself the delights of cake eating. Of Hebrew persuasion, this abstention probably cost him no little effort and, anyway, judging by his complexion it was possibly offset by over-indulgence in other directions. But it seemed never to occur to him, as for half an hour or so he compiled in note form from the *Sporting Pink* data from the racing columns, that he was indulging in a multiple form of wasteful extravagance.

Still, the frail elderly woman who so politely endured his exposition of virtue, herself chaste, could not know the real significance of his activities, imagining that, as she afterwards told me, 'He was engaged in a crossword puzzle.' I didn't undeceive her.

October 10th

WRITING TO THE *DT* TODAY MR A. MACHIN OF BATH SAYS, 'My son, a pilot officer, has recently been posted missing, "believed killed", in the Middle East. A little before his final crash he wrote a letter to be posted only in the event of his not returning. This has just reached me. He says,

'Please do not think I have not enjoyed this life of suspense. I think it is great never to know from one day to the next where you will be – anywhere on earth or elsewhere. I have actually liked it all – being bombed in Malta and Africa; being 500 miles from the nearest friendly soil, your life hanging on two British-built engines and two British wings; fighting a Heinkel 50 miles from land; hunting for trouble 300 miles over hostile territory. Believe it or not, I have enjoyed it all. And when that last action comes, I shall enjoy that too. Well, don't worry about me, Dad.

If there is one iota of a chance, I will be back and if not, well, I'll see you later.'

Well, such letters are their own comment.

October 14th

IN A RECENT ENTRY I COMMENT ON THE CLEARANCE AROUND ST Paul's cathedral forced upon us after the destruction by enemy action of so many neighbourhood buildings and of the possibilities now presented by this clearance for a scheme of replanning, which would enable our national shrine to be viewed in its proper setting. And now in yesterday's *Times* is announced the publication shortly of the interim report of the Royal Academy Planning Committee, formed in 1940 under the chairmanship of Sir Edwin Lutyens, 'to consider and plan a scheme for the architectural redevelopment of London . . . Making use of the additional opportunities offered by areas devastated by air raids . . . To give clearer expression to the leading motives of London's vast and varied activities.' As reported, the salient features of the proposed replanning are:

A ring road connecting all main-line terminal stations, some of which are moved to new positions. A new circular electric railway underground, connecting all terminal stations. Within the circle of the ring road all railway lines electrified and underground. The canals treated as amenities as well as means of transport. Parks and open spaces provided for the east and south side of London on the same scale as for the West End. River front to be developed with embankments and gardens from Putney to Tower Bridge. Markets removed from the central positions they now occupy, to positions on the ring road as may be found convenient. Pedestrians given opportunities of gathering in relative safety and quiet in squares closed to wheeled traffic. Streets paved over as shopping centres, free from road traffic. Access to public buildings planned to give the maximum dignity and convenience in the means of approach. Relief roads provided to supplement the main traffic routes. Better building sites on important road fronts and the opening of street vistas.

Among plans for St Paul's, now on view at the Royal Academy, there are provisions for a green open space about the cathedral, flagged in front of the main entrance, in which will stand the deanery and chapter house. A tree-lined avenue with steps leading up to it from a reconstructed riverfront is designed to afford a magnificent view of the great building. From it, spacious thoroughfares will radiate to important centres and finally give access to ring roads connecting London's terminal railway stations, themselves to be rebuilt, some in new sites. At least, so far as the cathedral is concerned, it is comforting to reflect that my dream of 'simple unenclosed lawns' seems not unlikely to come true. Such bold planning as officially contemplated augurs well for the revival of Wren's earlier scheme, abandoned for lack of support; and at long last the emergence of a new and noble city, literally from the ashes of the old, is in sight.

November 3rd

IN THE LATE NEWS COLUMN OF THE *DT* TODAY, 'MOSCOW RADIO stated last night that when a large coal barge sank in Dortmund canal, Gestapo arrested 60 Polish stevedores. Port workers, including Italians, French and Poles, struck in protest. Two days later Gestapo released arrested men.' If not yet a gale is blowing, the drifting straw shows the direction of the wind.

November 6th

NOW COMES GOOD NEWS FROM THE AFRICAN FRONT. THE Eighth Army under Gen. Montgomery, with adequate co-operation from the Navy and Air Force, is putting the enemy to flight. At least the Axis Army under Rommel is retreating; one hundred miles of ground has been regained and the flight continues with substantial loss to the enemy of men and materials. Important enemy supplies have been sunk in the Mediterranean. To make good the losses the Germans are withdrawing several divisions from the Russian front. But not until North Africa is clear of the enemy can we say our success on this front is complete.

November 13th

ANOTHER MATTER OF URGENCY: IF THE WHEELS OF INDUSTRY are not to be retarded at the very onset of their moving, mention must be made by some authority of the manner of disposal of the accumulated surplus government stores after the war is over. Profiting by experience from the last war, this material should not be allowed to fall into the hands of not over-scrupulous dealers who, paying little for their purchases, not only made the ultimate consumer pay handsomely a second time what he had paid for once, but so effectively did they flood the market that the spate of stores seriously retarded new production and had no little effect on the incidence of the post-war slump, which added still more to the price. Surplus stores should therefore not be made available for predators with self-enrichment at heart over the nation. But what shall be done with these surplus stores which, when the war is over, will be immense in quantity and variety? To burn them would be a crime. To sell them, however judiciously, would dislocate world markets and create unemployment. But they might be given away. To our Chinese and Russian allies and the more devastated of the German-occupied territories they might prove a godsend in helping their unhappy peoples over the initial stages in the reconstruction of their ravished lands. As an earnest of our post-war intentions towards our world neighbours, who better deserves our magnanimity? And, having been paid for in blood and cash, the cost of this could then be written off the War Account as some small part of the price we must pay for that freedom.

November 15th

AS I SWEPT THE LAWN OF ITS LITTER OF LEAVES THIS GREY Sabbath morning, the church bells in clamorous competition for the first time in three years suddenly filled the quiet air with their vibrant music. Halting in my work, I stood still and with feelings of restrained gladness suffered the occasion to evoke memories of quiet home joys belonging to happier Sundays now, alas, gone. Moved to prayer I remained leaning over my broom on the dewy grass and gave thanks to God.

November 28th

NOT SO LONG AGO A HALIFAX FRIEND, OPENING THE GULLET with a sharp penknife of a cropbound hen, removed the offending ball of grass that was choking it out of existence and, with a needle and thread, sewed together the edges of the wound, to enjoy the satisfaction forty-eight hours later of seeing the bird, along with the rest of its kind, eating as though it had never before had a meal in its life. It has since paid for the operation by producing many eggs!

December 5th

SOME FIRESIDE THOUGHTS THIS EVENING INCLINE ME TO WRITE to Frank Taylor. My afternoon talk with the vicar, who called to share with me a cup of tea, may have given direction to my musings, although discussions about the Beveridge Report occupied most of the time.

My Alice Mary is dead only in a mortal sense; on occasion I am so intensely aware of her presence that it seems physical. Only this morning as she lay so otherworldly remote on her palliasse bed in the lounge without surprise I watched a flush slowly invest her pallid, still features, as when I last looked upon them all but a year ago. She stirred and looked around wonderingly, patiently, as life returned, and I gently raised her in my arms. Lying there in my own little bedroom, in the darkness of the blackout, with the experience still vivid to my senses, I found myself asking, with Keats, 'Was it a vision or a waking dream? Do I wake or sleep?' I started these notes soon after, at the breakfast table, and such was the intensity of my vision and its persistence that I just had to finish them later in the deserted public bar of a bomb-blasted pub while I steadily munched my way through a meal of bread and cheese, garnished with pickled cabbage and a few shreds of celery; my usual Saturday lunchtime place and fare nowadays, when lunch at home is no more. And all that reached me clearly from the muffled hubbub of the crowded saloon bar – where one or two brazen young women, swaying gently to their gins, giggled inanely – was the penetrating voice of the barman, calling back in the vernacular the confused orders for 'cough and sneeze', local slang for bread and cheese. But I would not like Frank to imagine that, because of such experiences, I am becoming morbid or melancholy. On the contrary, I am curiously happy, a little remote perhaps but exclusive and apart and invested with a strange quality of independence which suffices, a sort of finality of acceptance. And afterwards strolling leisurely along to Waterloo, I paused for a few lovely minutes on Westminster Bridge to enjoy the play of sunlight through the gathering mist, the broad track of its reflection indicating the rippling water with the fierce glow of silver, new minted, which, by contrast, made the rectangular mass of Thames House to appear in dark silhouette against a rain-washed sky.

December 8th

ON THIS DAY, WHICH MARKS THE FIRST ANNIVERSARY OF THE passing of my Alice Mary, I feel that I may be forgiven the conversion to my own aching need of Tennyson's lovely lines from 'In Memoriam'.

Whatever way my days decline
I seem to feel tho' left alone
Thy being working in mine own,
Thy footsteps in this life of mine.

Thus do I speak to her at the graveside, and in the speaking find comfort.

December 10th

IN ITS LEADER COLUMN, DEVOTED SOLELY TO THE GENTLE rebuking of Mr Claude Mullins, Metropolitan Magistrate, the *Evening Standard* of tonight says of his attitude to press reporters, 'He seems to liken them all to the great Espinasse, who heard half of what went on in court and reported the other half.' The magistrate's tilt at the press over the housekeeper case raised a storm in a teacup which, no doubt, will subside as quickly as it began, but the aspects of the case more related to domestic affairs afford other material for reflection. Reported as criticizing the morals of housekeepers the magistrate stated that appearing in his court 'there are numbers of women who describe themselves as housekeepers who, in fact, are living with their men, sometimes having children by them. I have repeatedly rebuked such women for using the honourable name of housekeeper.' Being neither married wives nor harlots, by what other name shall they be known? But I imagine his stricture was intended to stress the distinction between the many decent, companionable housekeepers and the others, the harpies and the vampires who, with less compunction than the professional prostitute, inveigle their men into all sorts of unsavoury tangles. One knows perfectly well from observation that, not uncommonly, quite nice women serving as housekeepers to decent lone men are generous in their interpretation of home needs. Benefits are mutual when there is loyalty, sympathy and understanding.

Men and women brought into this relationship – one under stress of economic necessity to service the home for another – in most cases with the first fruits of love already gathered, tend, by their very propinquity, to approach that stage which conditions the beginnings of more intimate relations. Surely it is pharisaical to condemn in others that which concerns nobody but themselves. At least such couples are not living the lie that not a few others, by a miserable show of respectability in falsely declaring themselves man and wife, prefer to act.

December 18th

HIS CURIOSITY BEING AROUSED, THE OLD MAN AT LAST SAID TO the elderly visitor from Leeds at work in some old corner at Heysham, 'And what may be the purpose of your seeking with that hammer and chisel?' 'Well,' came the reply, 'I am interested in geology and there are some good fossil remains here which I intend to secure.' 'Oh,' said the old man, 'then you'll know Mr —— of Bradford who himself was a geologist?' 'I've known him all my life,' came the reply. 'Well, then, perhaps you can give me news of him?' asked the old man. 'Yes, I can,' was the response. 'I received a letter from him only a few days ago, but maybe he is not now alive. Seeing that you, too, knew him, perhaps you would like to read his letter . . .'

Sixty years earlier two Bradford boys set out for a holiday at New Brighton. Eager for their first bathe in the sea, no sooner were they on the beach than, stripping off their clothes, they were enjoying themselves in the water. Returning later to dress, one remembered the golden sovereign – his holiday money – which he had secreted for safety in a certain pocket but, alas, it had vanished. Although their efforts were devoted to a frantic search in clothing, sand and all other hiding places in the vicinity, it could not be found. Baffled and crestfallen, the lads returned home. And presently, as the old man read the shaky handwriting, came the passage, 'My end is near, I know it, and, while there is yet time, confess that it was I who stole your sovereign sixty years ago at New Brighton. Through all these years the thought has brought a recurrent canker of remorse and now, at long last, I ask your forgiveness.' 'The sovereign was mine,' remarked the elderly geologist, a little sadly, as he took back the letter. Calling today on Walter Marsden, to leave with him my good wishes before returning to London, he told me this story of his geologist neighbour.

December 25th

WITH DORIS SPENDING THE SHORT HOLIDAY WITH US, CHRISTMAS was a happy event of visitors and visiting, and it was pleasant to be admitted into the family circle of so many friendly neighbours and as pleasant to admit them to ours. With no lack of good cheer I felt we were privileged.

December 31st

AND SO STANDING THOUGHTFULLY ON THE THRESHOLD OF another New Year, one looks back with mixed feelings. And forward we must go as we have come, a step at a time, with a growing faith in the goodness of all things.

Inspired by the concluding essay 'Ripeness is All' in Max Plowman's thoughtful book *The Right To Live*, Frank in his letter today asks if we had known any of the authors whose writings we admire, whether as men we should like them, or be able to regard them as good companions. I am aware that in my diary I put on record the best that is in me. In it I consciously and deliberately express myself while striving always to achieve some improvement in character and judgement. These entries enable me to look at myself more objectively.

This New Year's Eve, in the quiet of my home, from that

inner sanctuary which is mine, I again thank the Creator of all things for the blessings of consolation that my thoughts – and the unseen presence – bring me.

1943

January 13th

WALKING TO THE STATION THIS MORNING UNDER A STAR-LIT SKY, the strains of martial music coming from a neighbourhood machine-tool factory brisked my steps to its rhythm and I railed a little at the seeming incongruity of radio music invading so early the still dark street. Then I thought of the cheer it brought to workers on lathes and drilling machines, which, as I passed the screened door, hummed in unison with the accompanying chorus of singing voices within. I am not aware that I stepped with less care but somehow the music seemed to lighten the darkness, and the yellow pools of reflection from the approaching bus lights on the wet road had in them the friendliness of a harvest. There was something sprightly, too, in the sound of quick steps, as dim shapes hurried. At last, groping my way to the platform, even the carriage seemed to offer welcome as I opened the door to its dimly lit interior. For a moment, standing, I gathered in the beauty of the faint lilac halo that suffused the darkness about the pea-green light of the station signal, unwinking bright. Projecting my cheerfulness onto all things, all things to me were cheerful.

Changing over to a fast at Surbiton I stood for the rest of

the journey to Waterloo in the corridor and watched the dawn spreading. The solid black mass of the tower rising above the general level of Carter's seed warehouses at Raynes Park against the pale of the eastern horizon took on the grim significance of some Moroccan port from which one could fancy anything sinister might emerge. Half-screened lights shone from the bedroom windows as suburbia tumbled out of bed and here and there from drawn curtains shot a beam like a beacon across the streets while electric trains emitted a discourteous fire of golden rain from their pickup shoes as they rattled past. Groping my way to the Underground, I reached Paddington and, with some minutes to spare before my Bristol train backed in, wandered about the station. Never before have I found the station so unhurried; there was little noise and no bustle. A leisured resignation seemed to invest the majority of people waiting about the platforms. Not so, however, with the crates of geese being loaded on to the Cardiff train. A chorus of raucous honks made known their protest against the indignity of the ungentle handling they received during shipment; nor were they content when at last they were stored safely aboard. Fierce-eyed and still chuntering, their protest reached me on the next platform. At least they made themselves heard, I thought, as I stepped on to my train.

And now I am on the way to Bristol, my first West Country trip for over three years. A cheerful sun shines warmly through the carriage windows suffusing with a soft radiance the grey-haired lady asleep in the opposite corner. The tender green of winter wheat pushes its way through the black soil and the rich brown of newly turned earth describes dark lanes through the lately ploughed stubble. In the hollows, still water left by swollen streams gleams against bare hedgerows while beyond, in a shadowy fold of the Wiltshire Downs, the White Horse endures, patiently on.

January 15th

WILFRED WHITTEN, OR JOHN O'LONDON, DIED A FEW DAYS AGO at the age of 86. A literary landmark in journalism is gone. No more shall I be able to look in his weekly paper for his letters to 'Gog & Magog', nor for his 'Passing Remarks' by Jack Daw, which I imagine were a joy to many who, like myself, were striving to achieve some discrimination in literary taste. He was a journalistic bookman. As he himself averred, literature is life, and long years ago the current of his writings gave direction to my own confused imaginings and with Walter Pater's example share responsibility for guiding my efforts. The extent to which I have profited by this tutelage, I have my diary to speak for itself.

January 17th

LISTENING TO SOME GRAMOPHONE RECORDING AT A NEIGHbour's house last evening, it occurred to me that this war so far has produced nothing in the way of songs so popular, of such universal acceptance in expressing national sentiment, as did the war years 1914–1918. There are no generally accepted equivalents of 'Tipperary', 'Keep The Home Fires Burning', 'The Little Grey Home In The West', etc., and, to go back further to the Boer War years, 'Tommy Atkins' and 'Soldiers Of The Queen'. So far there are no popular captions like 'Killing Kruger with your Mouth' or 'Hang the Kaiser'. Yet it cannot be said that, as a nation, we are bankrupt of sentiment or wit. The battle of Britain and the miracle of Dunkirk raised us to a pitch of intense national excitement but left unborn their story in song. It is still a long way to Tipperary, but for these reasons and because of our worldwide obligations, because of the global magnitude of the war, its technical nature and soullessness, and perhaps because of a better and more general understanding of its graver implications, because of our preoccupation with post-war affairs and the signs and portents of the fiercer struggle yet to come – in the face of such catastrophic events our songsters and bards, as well as ourselves, have become a little chastened and mute and, anyway, 'Roll Out The Barrel' is a poor substitute for the real thing.

January 22nd

AFTER COMING OFF MY LEEDS TRAIN, WHICH ITSELF WAS LATE arriving at King's X, here I am at Waterloo with nearly an hour to wait in the black and gloom. So I find sanctuary in the station buffet where I sit before a mug of tea smoking a Woodbine – all I could get – feeling a little tired and hungry and with just a touch of lumbago, leisurely taking stock of the uniformed crowds thronging the long bar, besieging the tables, standing in groups in the big room, quietly enriching myself at their expense yet leaving them none the poorer. Heavy with tobacco smoke and the smell of beer, the air buzzes with their chatter. The poor old waiter shuffles around collecting glasses like an automaton and shoulders his way through the unyielding ranks to the counter to collect fresh supplies to order. English, Scots and Irish, too, Poles and Czechs; sailors, soldiers and airmen; the women, some in khaki, some in Air Force blue, others in the rough indigo serge of the Navy, and all seemingly purposeful, going their several ways, but for a few brief moments casually thrown together here before passing on.

March 4th

AFTER A SHORT RAID LAST EVENING AT 10 P.M., THE ENEMY IS treating us to another this morning at 4.30 a.m. Fingers of light feel their way restlessly beneath the canopy of stars while quick flashes in the east announce gunfire too distant to be heard. Soon a low rumble rising to a crescendo marks the approach of enemy planes, and the tinkle of falling shrapnel lends a comfortable feeling to the chilly and unyielding steel helmet, which lets in through the gaps in its clumsy fittings, little blasts, on my bald head, from the nor'-easter, which makes it cold this morning. Warmly wrapped in woollies, neighbour Ward, faithful to duty on all these occasions, greeted me through the darkness as I joined the group and with me returned to our respective fire-watching posts until the all-clear sent us back home to bed about 5.30 a.m. But a cup or two of hot tea persuaded me to remain up for the day, and in the quiet of the kitchen with the boiler fire crackling cheerfully, I jot down these notes.

Having given Berlin a thoroughly bad time a couple of nights ago, reprisals were not unexpected but they were not severe and the interval of six hours between raids afforded reasonable time for sleep. But there is something queer in sitting down to write. More queer is it to have to undress to perform these duties when one is already dressed for the day. So ingrained do habits become that any sudden departure from these makes the event seem a little unreal. But it is now 6.30 a.m., Anne has appeared and tells me, without words, that she wants the use of the kitchen table. The day has commenced.

March 5th

ONLY THE OTHER DAY I SAW IN A STATIONER'S WINDOW A writing pad, priced at 2*s*., containing not more than 4 ounces of paper of indifferent quality which, at mill selling price, would not exceed 6*d*. per lb. Purchased in my village recently a very inferior toilet roll weighing 6 ounces cost 1/3*d*., which works out at 3/4*d*. per lb. Present-day mill price for the grade of paper is round about 6*d*. per lb – pre-war price, tuppence ha'penny. The retail price of such articles as blotting-paper, wrapping-paper, labels, string, tape, etc., nowadays bears no real relation to production cost, and trading at these prices, in effect, is almost as unscrupulous as was trading gin for ivory in slave-running days. This state of affairs is only possible with a public ignorant of values and can only be remedied when not only the worth but the worthwhileness of an article is known.

April 12th

THE QUEEN'S RADIO TALK TO WOMEN OF THE EMPIRE LAST night, reaching to the core of things belonging to our common life, clearly and sympathetically given, was moving in its simple sincerity. 'Most of us,' she said, 'at one time or another in our lives have read some fine book that has given us courage and strength and fresh hope; and when we lay it down, we have wished that we could meet the author and tell him how much we admire his work, and how grateful we are for it. Something of the same kind makes me feel that I would like to meet you this Sunday night. For you, though you may not realize it, have done work as great as any book that was ever written.' And later, speaking of women workers generally, 'Their courage is reinforced too, by one of the strongest weapons in our

National Armoury – a sense of humour that nothing can daunt. With this weapon of amazing temper, our people keep guard over their sanity and their souls. I have seen that weapon in action many, many times over the last few years, and know how much it can help through the really bad times.' And lastly, 'That it is in the strength of our spiritual life that the right rebuilding of our national life depends . . . It is the creative and dynamic power of Christianity that can help us to carry the moral responsibilities which history is placing upon our shoulders, and our homes, the very place where it should start. Then the influence of that spirit will assuredly spread like leaven through all aspects of our common life, industrial, social and political.' I pray that it may be so.

April 15th

WANDERING ON FOOT FROM LONDON BRIDGE TO MILLBANK THE other day I dallied for a few leisurely minutes to have a look at Southwark Church of St George, damaged in the blitz, and afterwards stepped across the once narrow lane to its burial ground, a quiet little oasis of green but a short distance from the noisy Boro Market, now laid out as a tiny park affording rest and repose for the living as well as the dead in its sunny enclosure hard by the armoured walls of the old Marshalsea Prison. To these in those bad old days as well as to the dead might equally apply the epitaph deeply carved in the stone of the weathered and overgrown sepulchre by the main gate –

How loved, how valued once avails thee not
To whom related or by whom begot.
A heap of dust alone remains of thee
Tis all thou art, and all the proud shall be.

And reading this I thought of Omar's lines –

And those who husbanded the golden grain,
And those who flung it to the wind like rain,
Alike to no such Aureate earth are turned,
As, buried once, men want dug up again.

And so for us all.

May 20th

DISCUSSING IDENTITY OF INTERESTS WITH A YORKSHIRE FRIEND of mine today, he related that sitting one quiet evening with his wife, in a surge of poetic enthusiasm and thinking to share it with her, he commenced to read aloud some of the lovely lines from Tennyson's 'The Lady of Shallot' [sic]. With a far-off look in her eyes she presently exclaimed, 'That reminds me, I must get the pickling vinegar for my onions!'

May 25th

A SHABBILY DRESSED OLD MAN RECENTLY WALKED INTO THE RED Cross HQ at Halifax and, fumbling through his pockets, drew from them a miscellaneous assortment of cursory notes, postal orders and cash, which he proceeded to spread over the counter. Not a little astounded, my young friend Wendy Hoyle, then in attendance, inquiring the reason for this display was told that after a lapse of many months he had at last received news from his son, a prisoner-of-war in Germany, that the parcels of comforts which he had sent to him had duly arrived. In gratitude to the Red Cross for their care of the matter, he wished them to accept all the spare cash he had to offer as a contribution to their funds. Declining to reveal his identity, he departed as he came. Very different was the attitude and temper of a drunken seaman who later entered the office and, declaring that he was penniless, demanded the price of his fare to some distant town and was grossly abusive when he was told that he must apply to the appropriate authority nearby. Eventually declaring that they could keep their money as he had plenty anyway, he lurched out of the office with the truculent threat that he would 'show the Red Cross up as a fraud in every newspaper in the kingdom'.

June 1st

THE SEVENTY-FIRST ANNIVERSARY OF MY ALICE MARY'S BIRTH, which I celebrated quietly with her by a new planting on her garden grave, and felt comforted.

June 15th

SHIELING COMES TO LIFE. MY SISTER-IN-LAW ANNE DEPARTED ON 2nd June and my old friend Mrs Sheard arrived from Leeds the same day to take over the management of my domestic affairs, since when the atmosphere of subdued hostility, which for so long has invested my home, has given way to a friendly homeliness. If for Bobby Sheard and me the tally of years has left spring behind, at least there is a comforting warmth in the quiet glow of autumn when sympathy and understanding live together in harmony to enrich the hearth. After eighteen months, little differing from some place of gloomy seclusion, Shieling is again a meeting place for friendly neighbours who, it seems, have been waiting for the atmosphere to change before restoring it to its former condition of open house. With this I am well content.

June 22nd

A NATIVE CHARM OF MANNER AND AN EAGER AIR OF ENQUIRY, which seemed to tally with his youthful figure, characterized the Duke of Devonshire's attitude to me when, for half an hour this morning, he peered into the mysteries of testing and chemical examinations as I conducted him round my office lab. Introduced to him during an official tour of the Crown Agents' office, as 'our chemist' by my Dept. Chief, I found him at once genial and eager. He followed with interest all I could display for him and I was not a little amused by the tactful disregard with which he parried the efforts of the official retinue to hurry him through his visit. Nor was I invisible to the compliment implied by his enthusiasm for such matters of technical interest with which, I felt, it would not have been difficult to sustain the day long. But he was duly whisked away, and instead of the genial talk with him that I would have much liked, the few crumbs had to suffice.

July 26th

I'VE NEVER SEEN A CHARGING RHINOCEROS, BUT THE FAT, elderly man with the pale, puffy, wobbly face I saw from the bus this morning charging, head bowed, up the incline to Lambeth Bridge with the set, purposeful look of one determined to do or die made me think of such an animal. Too fat and old to run easily, he seemed to gallop flat-footed, with a loose, shambling

I've never seen a charging rhinoceros...

action, the numerous creasings of his dark trousers much resembling the folds in the hide of some pachyderm. He needed no more than a horn between his two small eyes to complete the illusion. And the idea so tickled me that I badly wanted to share it with my neighbouring passenger. But one glance at his uncompromising stance convinced me that any attempt to share my fancy with him would assuredly leave him with the impression that I was dotty and, anyway, the moment for the telling passed as quickly as it came. So I kept a little gurgle to myself.

August 14th

LAST NIGHT AT HENLEY-ON-THAMES BETWEEN 8 P.M. AND 11 o'clock while Frank and I combed the town looking for a night's lodgings, a steady stream of four-engined bombers overhead droned their way south to Milan on their mission of destruction. Viewed from this peaceful town there was something portentous in the sight of these enormous engines of war flying, irregular formation, silhouetted against the evening skies, and our good wishes for their safe return were not less earnest because of our tiresome search for a bed. At the eighth time of asking we found sanctuary at the Old White Horse at the Northfield end of the town, glad to relieve ourselves of our rucksacks, refresh, and finally turn in to our comfortable beds to sleep a sleep made generous by leisured hours in the open air. Where, in peacetime, tourist traffic from the river steamers was solicited by the many local residents with accommodation to offer, the casual visitor must now seek diligently for his bed and be not dismayed at the frequent curt refusals. Eight o'clock yesterday morning found us at the Kingston landing stage for the Oxford steamer. Due to sail at 9 a.m. a queue had already formed and by sailing time the boat was full to capacity, but so chilly the morning that not for a couple of hours did the air become warm enough to stimulate that observant curiosity which is so essential to the complete enjoyment of a river holiday.

There are many indications of wartime activities on either bank to arrest attention and of the more obvious the building of many little ships of strange design and purpose on which a host of men and women are engaged provide much for interested comment and speculation. But beyond Weybridge the voyager settles down to the enjoyment of this clear old waterway and highway of our ancient forebears, as the steamer threads its way round the bends and along the reaches, avoiding here the shallows, there a laden barge, slowing up for the camping points moored to the bank and, at intervals, nosing into a lock, there to exchange a few passengers and with the lock-keeper a trifle of banter. But the stepping up from one level to another is a brief business to which, because of wartime lack of staff, all ratings from the skipper down lend a hand. Not infrequently the lock-keeper's womenfolk preside over the sluice gates and generally some Sea Scouts or Girl Guides are at hand, seriously and solemnly to do their good deed for the day. With but a few inches to spare, no little refinement in steering is called for to avoid bumping but, with confidence born of long experience and a fine nonchalance, the helmsman holds his course and, passing safely through the lower gates, we glide gently between the enclosing walls. A turn or two of the engine at full speed astern brings us to a stop within a yard or two of the upper gates and, with a throw of the hawser over the bollards, we warp into the side as the water rushes through the sluices, shutting with a thud the already half-closed lower gates. Rising gently in the flood tide the flowered lock garden comes into full view. Then, in the quiet of the brimming lock, the exchange of voyagers begins. The upper gates open, revealing a glimpse of still water beyond, the bell tinkles and with a gurgling thrust of the propeller, we slowly move out of the lock into the upper reach. The loveliest of the Thames locks is Sonning, to which for the third year in succession has been awarded the first prize for lock gardens. Such a wonderful display of begonias I have never elsewhere seen. Not outside a professional show have I found such variety of form and colour and with lilies coming into bloom these beds, I thought, expressed in perfection the gardener's craft at its best. And from his friendly smile and general bearing I judged the keeper to be of a piece with his garden, with his pretty flower-endowed cottage. I could well imagine it to be the ideal setting for a June honeymoon.

Friday morning, grey and cloudy, found us in the boat resuming our journey to Oxford, partly shielded from the chilly head wind, which persisted most of the day, by the ample proportions of the lady immediately in front of us, who seemed to be impervious to its searching buffets. Tuning up for a song as we idly looked about, we heard her chiming in to some of the old Victorian ballads we were quietly warbling. She turned to us to express her enjoyment of the impromptu concert and remarked that, providentially it seemed, the occasion had restored to her something that she had given up as lost to her for ever. She had lived through Coventry's worst blitz, had remained buried for hours in a demolished shelter with her dead husband until rescued, only a little bruised, to find that her home was no more. 'Not even a needle and thread to mend my tattered garments,' she said. Not until later when she discovered a complete blank relating to things musical did she realize the effect of the bombing upon her. Naturally musical, she had not since then been able to recall a single song formerly familiar to her until this sudden revival of her memory when, apparently taken at the flood, a recollection of forgotten songs surged into her mind. And so the morning passed into the afternoon, with occasional dips into nosebags and talks with the skipper, a benevolent man of 76 with a record of 45 years' railway service and 16 with the Oxford steamers. Approaching Oxford in the cool of the early evening we steamed past the college houseboats to Salter's landing stage at Folly Bridge. Lacking paint the moored craft looked very worn, for here war has also taken its toll and the normal activities of the river have practically ceased. Nevertheless there are some bright spots surviving the war and a few fine old mansions, which seem to have escaped the deterioration and lend a venerable dignity to their respective reaches where 'sweet Thames runs softly' and herds of fine cattle graze ruminatively in the lush meadows.

All the same, war has obliged many to turn to the river for recreation who, in days of peace, knew it only from one of London's great bridges. Because of it, these and many from the distant corners of the British Isles and overseas comrades-in-arms, now on service duties in and around the metropolis, may for themselves discover something of the rare peace and gentle beauty abiding along the upper reaches and, through this discovery, sense that tradition which, through their forebears, has brought to this green and pleasant land that dignity and calm serenity so characteristic of all that is best in England. At Oxford Salter's brother's agent gave us comfortable lodgings in his house and Saturday morning, sunny and warm, found us again on the steamer bound for Reading, entertained en route by a RQMS of the Canadian Armoured Corps who, returning from a short vacation course of lectures, was eager to talk of his experiences there. Discussing books and sociology and something of the New Order, with an interval for an altogether satisfactory lunch at Wallingford's British Restaurant, the day passed pleasantly enough and after some friendly goodbyes at Reading, we caught the six o'clock train for Waterloo and home.

August 15th

A SUNNY SUNDAY MORNING, SUCH AS THIS, SEEMS TO INVEST THE hour for breakfast in the garden with a calm serenity peculiar to the event. The peace of this Sabbath in Shieling's green and sunlit retreat has in it something of the transcendental, and when comes the summons to the faithful for early service to tune the emotions to a deeper pitch, more is felt than the mind takes cognisance of and I feel not less responsive because of my environment. Reflecting thus, my eye wandered to the breakfast table and, absently ranging over the refreshment placed before me, I began to realize that of the eight items of food and drink, no less than four were from my garden and one from a neighbour's. Here, I thought, in this quiet corner of mine, are answers enough for most prayers and, if work and worship are the same thing, reward enough too.

August 23rd

REPORTED MISSING RECENTLY, MY COLLEAGUE'S NEIGHBOUR'S LAD was given up for lost. Their airman son had lately set out on a bombing mission to Milan. Approaching the Alps one of his crew mentioned that he felt a little sick, due, he thought, to the hearty meal of fish and chips he had taken with the rest before the trip. Soon, another of the crew became sick, and another. Then the pilot, a Norwegian, complained of nausea. One of them, checking on the oxygen supply, found that it had exhausted itself through a leak in the apparatus, just when most needed. Already above the safety limit of 9000 feet it was decided, on consultation with the pilot, who declared his intention of attaining his objective, if at all possible, that they would severally transfer to him their personal emergency oxygen supplies to enable him safely to ascend the

16,000 feet required to clear the mountain range in the hope that all would eventually survive the ordeal of impaired respiration and all its attendant evils. Getting safely over and the crew restored, the pilot descended to 9000 feet which, at Milan, exposed him to attack by flak from below and the hazard of falling bombs from our own aircraft above. He duly released his bombs on the target. Turning away he reflected that, without oxygen, he couldn't return via the Alps as briefed, and without charts for an alternative route they were in a quandary. But, rising to the occasion, the navigator declared that they might make the 700 miles to North Africa. Arriving safely at Tripoli they decided to go on to Algiers, finally to land at Gibraltar. There, they reported to HQ and were given two days' leave with a fortnight's pay in advance. Off the chain for a couple of days while the plane was reserviced they were made much of and thoroughly enjoyed the visit. Meanwhile, London had been advised of the safe arrival of the missing plane and its crew. Laden with bananas and lemons, the crew returned to the airfield for take-off to find the plane contained eight passengers for London, a large parcel and mail which, together with the quantities of fruit stowed on board, exceeded their original payload by a thousand pounds in weight. And so a cheerful party started off with a still-leaking oxygen apparatus and, never rising above 9000 feet, they crossed the Bay of Biscay and home to England. Whistling loudly along the home road at 11.30 p.m. the following evening, to the inexpressible delight of his parents, came the son and later, telling his story, he placed in his mother's hand – a lemon!

August 31st

AND NOW FROM AN OPERATIONAL FLIGHT TO ATTACK München and Gladbach in the Ruhr Valley last night my fine nephew Clifford, with his plane, is reported missing. Telling me in his letter today that my nephew was an efficient member of a good crew in which he was navigator, the Wing Commander, Red Squadron, RAF, said, 'There is a fair chance that the whole of the crew may be reported as PoWs.' But it is sad news, and one can only hope that if he is dead the death was merciful; if alive that he is not maimed; if a PoW that he may successfully escape.

Most of all does one hope that he may return to his wife. Without children of my own my dead brother's son was son to me and my wife. For his mother, whose only chick he was, one can only pray, and praying, remember countless other bereaved mothers and wait.

September 3rd

THIS MORNING I SAW BOBBY SHEARD COMFORTABLY SETTLED with her blind sister in the train at King's X for her journey to Leeds to wind up her own affairs as a preliminary to making her home with me at Shieling. Coming to me on 2 June for a month's holiday she busied herself with domestic affairs to such good effect that she seemed naturally to fit into a scheme of things at once and, for all her seventy years, supported cheerfully her self-imposed task. For me Shieling had come to life. One sunny morning over breakfast in the garden together, following a frank exchange of views on our respective individual needs, I suggested that by making her home with me at Shieling we might be able to solve each other's domestic problems through the satisfaction of each other's needs. On the basis of companion-housekeeper, and on level terms sharing with me my home, she might care to consider a permanent transfer from Leeds to London. Later, interrupting her stay with me during a short visit to Leeds, I wrote her as follows.

Out of that affection and understanding which has grown up between us has sprung, during these lonesome days, a very real need of each other, and if I cannot now, in the forbidding circumstances of my widowhood, offer you marriage, my dear, all is there in my house for our mutual comfort that a wife might need and a husband offer for a loyal and happy sharing to make, God willing, pleasant and secure the road to the end for us both. Related to these ties of affection that unite us you have personal problems in respect of your own home which, sooner or later, will call for solution. With these, no doubt, I can help you when, after due consideration, you may have decided to throw in your lot with mine. For the rest, dear, I am content to wait, happy with you in the present, grateful to God for a precious friend and, with him, I confidently leave the future.

Returning to London after an interval of three weeks, she announced that, having given my proposal careful consideration, she had decided to dispose of her Yorkshire home and settle down with me. With the known prospects of companionship and service, and congenial occupation at Shieling she was content and, like the 'Snow Goose', of her own free will, gladly would come to live with me. For thirty years a loyal friend, with loyalty I must pay and give her no cause for regret.

September 12th

ON THURSDAY MORNING WITHIN A FEW STEPS OF HOME, tripping over my neighbour's shallow kerb and awkwardly falling on my foot, I severely damaged my right ankle and had to be carried home by a few kindly neighbours. Later the doctor diagnosed a broken fibula and possibly tibia, and a fracture of one of the tarsus bones and bandaged accordingly – all subsequently confirmed by X-ray at hospital. Unable to put the leg in plaster because of a large blister, which appeared overnight thro' the rupture of some small blood vessel in the foot, from the knee down the injured member was encased in a wooden cradle and with it in bed I must remain until the bones knit.

Alone, with Bobby in Leeds winding up her own affairs, and dismissing all suggestions of hospital treatment, I felt that I should be putting an undue strain on the neighbours if I tried to continue without resident help so, writing to tell her of my predicament, she wired to say she was returning at once. Reflections on my immunity for a matter of 65 years from such accidents as broken bones brought to me in this stroke of ill luck no little consolation. The doctor asked me if I had heard any sound of bones cracking. The sound resembled the crushing together of a handful of sugar cubes, and if I was not conscious of any well-defined cracking, quite apart from the queer distortion of the foot, I knew that I had sustained something more serious than a simple sprain. Moreover I at once realized that here was an end to all my immediate plans, official and private. Yet I did not feel unduly concerned. It could have been much worse. And at 7 a.m. this morning Bobby appeared at the kitchen door, to which I had painfully hobbled while brewing myself a pot of tea. It is said that the wise man turns opposition into opportunity – well, here is mine.

September 23rd

VISITORS I HAVE APLENTY DURING MY ENFORCED LIE-IN, FRIENDLY neighbours abounding. I am embarrassingly bankrupt of thanks enough for their cheerfully solicitous concern and the many little gifts and rewards by which they express it. They 'do' sympathy as well as 'say' it, and I sometimes feel that this neighbourhood demonstration of goodwill is compensation for a broken bone or two.

October 1st

IN AN ILLUMINATING ARTICLE ON GERMANY'S MANIPULATORS OF the home front in today's *DT*, the Swedish journalist Gunnar T. Pihl, in his skilfully drawn thumbnail sketches of leading Nazis, with reference to the attitude of the Church to the war, writes, 'But the Catholic Church is an international power; Catholic bishops in Berlin and Cologne have not hesitated in their sermons to speak out openly against the Nazis. A story long current in Berlin tells of a sermon preached by Bishop Schultz of Cologne against "The lie that limps through Germany". Called to account by the Gestapo for insulting Propaganda Minister Goebbels, the Bishop replied indignantly, "But I was referring to the devil.." ' A very adroit parry, I thought, and subtly sardonic, which pickles in brine a lash for the wounding.

October 18th

I'M TOLD THAT I SOMETIMES TALK IN MY SLEEP, BUT BEYOND THE telling I know nothing of it and when I dream I do so seldom remembering my dream except for some vague outline. In my early years, to dream that I could fly was not an uncommon experience. I remember my anguish when at Speak's Mouth, in N. Devon, my wife and dog descended the precipitous path to the little rocky cove 70 feet below. Needlessly afraid for them, I was even more afraid for myself and in a welter of conflicting emotions despised myself for being craven. Not until a week had passed did I summon courage enough to attempt the descent and felt, when at last I arrived on the beach, that I had achieved a great victory, but a secret victory. But each succeeding day the path became easier as use dissipated my fears and, in the end, instead of following my wife like some scared rabbit, I took the lead – if not boldly at least with the comforting thought that I was keeping my end up. But my recent dream, since lying on my bed with a fractured ankle, is of a different quality. For three nights I have wandered about a warehouse loft – which I recognize as a certain Yorkshire woollen mill – surprising myself with the discovery that, with my crutch well out of reach downstairs, I was walking quite normally, my injured foot stepping with no more discomfort than my uninjured, suddenly to realize that I had no business to be about on it, that I was risking further trouble and proceeded in haste to return to my room. But before I could reach it the dream faded completely. So vivid these three dreams, as vivid my next morning's recollections of them; nor do I seem able to dismiss them from my mind. It is said that superstition is the religion of the weak-minded. Despite the psychoanalyst's plausible relation of cause to effect, I wonder a little at their possible significance.

October 25th

MAYBE I'M SLIPPING, ONE NOTCH PERHAPS. THIS MORNING brewing my early tea I found myself fitting the kettle lid to the teapot! Sign of the times, I suppose, happily not to be ascribed, as I feared, to any worrying preoccupations but rather to lack of method. Clearly I'm out of my element as an invalid. With Bobby in Leeds to resume the winding up of her affairs, it occurs to me that a whole range of degrees of loneliness seems possible; a state that, these tragic days, is the lot of many caught up in this overwhelming tidal wave of war; late-evening moments of reverie when loved ones have gone to bed and, in the still cosy room, the last coal is burning itself out in the grate, those personal moments when the falling embers and the ticking clock lend movement to stillness and wrap us in tranquillizing folds ere sleep.

October 29th

THE COURT OF APPEAL YESTERDAY, VINDICATING THE LAW ON the subject, decided that money which a wife is able to save from her husband's housekeeping allowance is the property of her husband. The appeal was brought by a Mrs Blackwell for a reversal of the decision given by the Oxford County Court awarding the husband's claim for the return of her surplus housekeeping money – some £103 – which she had banked in her own name. The case excited considerable interest in the press and was the subject of some lively discussion this afternoon during my tea party.

The ladies without exception declared that no wife could count herself honest who failed to disclose to her husband the amount of her allowance surplus. Conversely the husband who demanded its return was a self-confessed cad. It was agreed that not only should a husband make himself acquainted with housekeeping expenses but he should keep his wife informed of his true income. An earning wife too, in fairness, should declare her income to her husband. Any legislation concerning these regulations should have reference to the new equal status of the contracting parties and be drafted only in general terms. But so often one or other of the parties is improvident that it is difficult to conceive how such differences can be adjusted outside the home concerned. The risk of adding fuel to the fire is ever present where animosity inspires contention.

The ventilation of such grievances in the courts and press little differs from the washing in public of soiled underwear, stained and rent, and as such offends good taste as the suction kisses of Hollywood.

November 2nd

WITH DORIS STAYING AT SHIELING TO HELP ME OVER THE weekend, time passed happily in her company. With Clifford still missing, I discussed with her matters I had been turning over in my mind in respect of redrafting my will and its provisions concerning Bobby Sheard. It is little enough I have to leave but to them both it is a matter of importance. For one, it ensures a reasonably comfortable old age; for the other, in the event of Clifford's death, it provides for a helpful start in any new life she may have to contemplate.

November 5th

<u>Missing – For Doris</u>

To them the call to action, fitting,
Daring alone those hostile skies,
Not less alone their loved ones sitting
Braving a dread the heart defies.
And we whose thoughts with theirs are mingled
To silent prayer await reply
That theirs the faith undying kindled
Lest chill despair their hopes bely.

The loom of time, like shuttle throwing,
Building a web of patterned years,
Weaving to plan, for all our knowing,
With warp and woof of joy and tears.
Then come, let faith his sole supporter
The touchstone of those joys to be
Signpost the way for you, O daughter,
The path that leads to Sovereignty.

November 16th

MY DOMINA, AFTER TRAVELLING ALL NIGHT FROM LEEDS, turned up this morning at 6.50 a.m., enveloped in a huge woolly travelling rug, but as cold as a frog after waiting at Wimbledon forty minutes for the Hampton Court connection. But I had stoked up the fire at 5 a.m. so Shieling was comfortably warm for her reception, and a hot cup of tea with a lashing of whisky, so rare a commodity that it is only used on very special occasions. The winding up of her Leeds affairs being satisfactorily accomplished, she was as glad to be back as I was to see her after three weeks of camping out in the lounge with a gammy foot. Cutting herself adrift from the incubus of a too-lonely home, we now make our real start together at Shieling, where neither of us needs be lonely. And as we talk, a slow dawn suffuses the sky with the palest of rosy hues, the light of enchantment for the day's beginning; and a sign, maybe, for our own.

November 18th

MY FOOT MENDS BUT SLOWLY. MY LEG IS STILL ENCASED IN ITS chimney-pot of plaster. I still hobble about with the aid of two walking-sticks but with progressive ease. It seems unlikely that I shall be back at the office this side of Christmas. But I'm not unduly distressed on this account. For the past three years I have been training my only remaining junior as to the way he should go in matters technical. And with Bobby home looking after the chores which, during her absence, occupied much of my time, I am free, in my lameness, to tackle jobs about the house which, a month ago, seemed unlikely ever to have a beginning.

November 26th

I RECENTLY READ THE REPORT OF THE INTERNATIONAL JEWISH Convention on the Huns' treatment of the Jews in German-occupied Europe and Hitler's policy of extermination, partly by shootings and hangings, by torture in the many Jewish prison camps but chiefly by starvation in the ghettos. It was grim reading. According to statistics collected from enemy sources, it seems that a cold-blooded calculated adjustment of food supplies to human needs leaves for Jewish consumption only 20 per cent of the nutritious value considered by German food experts necessary to maintain the German people in reasonably good health.

A deficit in ration value for the Jews must eventually result in their extermination by slow starvation, which is perhaps the most torturing of all deaths. But this is no new experience for the Jews. Ever since their dispersal by the Romans from the Mediterranean basin at the beginning of the Christian era – until when they were a normally constituted people – and their scattering over the then known world, they have suffered agonies of persecution wherever they settled, even in England. Instead of remaining international pariahs surely somewhere on the face of this earth there is space enough to spare – a bit no larger than England, perhaps – in which 17 million Jews could achieve redemption and political unity, there to live and call home, standing four square as a nation to take with proper pride their place in the world community. With the goodwill of the rest of the world they could, I believe, do much towards this end for themselves. This, it seems to me, is the real solution for the Jewish problem.

November 27th

MY *BONNE FEMME* TRANSFERRED MY BEDROOM FROM THE LOUNGE to its proper habitat today and it is right pleasant to contemplate the restored spaciousness of my most pleasant room and, as it were, renew its acquaintance, at long last.

November 29th

MY NEPHEW CLIFFORD, REPORTED MISSING ON 31 AUGUST, IS now reported dead. I gather from information passed to his wife from the RAF that his plane crashed in Germany and presumably was burnt out as only one of the crew of five had anything left about him that gave any clue to their identity. One can only hope that death was mercifully swift, and grieve that a fine young man was so early cut off. With us this weekend Doris endures bravely the final loss of her husband and the bleak prospect of that awful aloneness which for her is inevitable in the tragic circumstances. She is young, energetic and intelligent, and eager to come to grips with some creative work. This need satisfied, time and her activities will soften the blow.

December 10th

IT IS THREE MONTHS SINCE I FRACTURED MY ANKLE AND THIS evening, with the doctor's consent, I removed the plaster. This little job took the best part of two hours and at times called for the acrobatics of a contortionist. However, it was a great relief to get it off. But I noticed that my calf had shrunk considerably and the muscles had become flabby and poor. The ankle and foot were still appreciably distorted and somewhat discoloured too. The foot itself was numb and stiff but a night's rest restored it to something less remote from normal. But I must put on record that it was agreeable to go to bed unencumbered. The doctor, examining the foot afterwards, gave me the comforting support of a crêpe bandage and told me to continue with the aid of my two walking-sticks when, perhaps, at the end of another two months the foot might be restored to normal. I hope so.

December 18th

IN SPITE OF THE DECLARED INTENTION OF SO MANY THIS FIFTH Christmas of war to dispense with the customary greeting card, already I have received a considerable number of the traditional tokens of remembrance from widely scattered friends who, because of my immobility, I have not seen for so long. And one is grateful.

December 23rd

YESTERDAY THE STATION CAB TOOK ME TO THE CEMETERY where, with the help of my always courteous old cab man, I paid a seasonal tribute to the memory of my dear wife.

Unknown to me a kindly neighbour, since my accident, had been keeping her grave in order for me. I was well pleased to find it, instead of a wilderness of neglect, well cared for, trim and tidy. And this afternoon Rosamund Carter called, and from the depths of her capacious basket produced two small bottles of champagne, a bag of walnuts from her garden and a large cigar from her father, by way of contribution from the house of Carter to Shieling's Christmas festivities, and for Bobby, a kettle-holder. After an hour or so of merry talk, she departed to dish up the meal she had left slowly cooking in a casserole – a kindly and lovable neighbour of vigorous mind and generous outlook, whose conversation is always stimulating and refreshing. And now this evening, looking across to the coffee table in the big room, I see it littered with cards and letters of greeting, warm friendly letters of old friends. The piano, every available inch of it covered with cards, is a riot of colour, vying with the gaudy green and crimson plumage of the entertaining parrot, which for a few days I am minding for a neighbour, who is spending Christmas in Brighton.

December 24th

FROM THE OFFICE THIS MORNING CAME A TELEGRAM OF greeting from one of our packers who, because of his many gratuitous services and attention and to distinguish him from two other Bill Smiths in the same employ, I had long dubbed my 'Man Friday'. A little shrunken deformed man, shattered in White Russia during the last war, he has a shrewd, penetrating mind, but a heart of gold. Of all the greetings I have received this season, there is none I treasure more. An early visitor, my brother-in-law, brought with him a jar of preserves and, incidentally, cut my hair, which after four months of neglect had begun to look like an ill-formed haystack in a gale. If I don't now look as if I had recently been released from a German prison camp, it is only because he excels as an amateur barber. Edith, my across-the-road neighbour, who, insisting on anonymity, has during the war years made for me from odds and ends of material some hundred small garments of all kinds for distribution among refugees and evacuee children, this afternoon presented me with a generous supply of cigarettes. My old friend Frank Hook's widow later came along with a basket of very fine apples, a quantity of currants and some cooking fats, together with news of her American officer guests who, from all accounts, count themselves lucky to be admitted to her beautiful home on such friendly terms. But she is a generous soul whom adversity, in the loss of her grand husband, has made more generous still. And while we were all having tea together, over which Bobby presided with her usual grace, the Nichols children arrived with arms full of holly and Shieling made merry. It is nearly midnight and a happy Christmas is drawing to a close. This evening has passed without an air-raid alert. The turkey, a nice young bird of about 12 lbs, is ready for tomorrow's cooking. Bobby and I are having a quiet half-hour before the dwindling fire. The parrot has already gone to bed and the dog waits on the hearth for us to move. And looking at the mistletoe, a tiny sprig with only two berries, all I could get, I reflect that it is symbolic of the abundance of all the good things for which I traditionally stand and know full well that, in spite of this warring world of men, I possess all that is worth the wearing and am gratefully content.

December 25th

AND SO AT SHIELING THIS DAY WE KEEP OUR TRYST WITH DORIS and our Dear Dead, my Alice Mary and her Clifford, not unhappily. To all in this world conflict who have made the supreme sacrifice, quietly and with reverential gratitude, we stand to; to all absent friends and those we love, in affection and regard, we raise our glasses. To God, we give our humble thanks for His many blessings. Amen. It has been a day of quiet happiness. Rising early this morn of open weather, culinary matters got well started. And during intervals between phone calls of greetings to Frank and others, all was made ready for the reception of the stream of friendly callers who not too boisterously occupied the forenoon. Our Christmas dinner was a festival of quiet joy appropriately rounded off by my neighbour's gift of champagne and, leaving the ravaged table for the cosy big room, for a space, we rested. Later friend Nichols arrived with a wheelchair and out into the sunlit afternoon I was taken to his house to attend the family tea party, there to spend some three hilarious hours beneath the festive paper chains and bells and mistletoe and eat ice-cream with the children young and old; afterwards, with Bobby in tow, to bump along home in the blackout, supporting gaily the good-natured railing about my bathchair existence. And so with a quiet hour before the fire with Bobby, the happy day came to an end.

December 31st

TURNING THE PAGES OF MY DIARY WITH ITS RECORD OF endeavour, of achievements and failures, of quiet joys and heartache and bereavement, of stress and strain, of observation and reflection, of friends and felicities, of life's slow ripening and generally looking over the few recorded years of my logged journeyings, whatever the weather, my strayings from the set course do not seem greatly to have imperilled my progress. After four years of war, friendships have been formed and now from our local fire-watchers comes the whispered beginnings of a neighbourhood social circle, born of the fire-watchers' rota. Living comfortably together, no neighbourhood activity could be more agreeable to my sentiments than an extension of this wartime good fellowship to the days of peace when it may be even more necessary to our collective welfare.

1944

January 16th

BY THIS MORNING'S POST COMES A LETTER FROM A COLLEAGUE asking if I have 'yet made up my mind whether I want to remain in harness at the office after reaching the venerable age of 65, or whether I want to shake off the dust'. Which brings me face to face with an important decision I can no longer defer, but I must confess to mixed feelings.

January 17th

SLEEPING ON IT OVERNIGHT, I REPLIED AS FOLLOWS: 'YOU HAVE done me the service of bringing to the forefront of my mind thoughts which now, at close range, incline me to retirement before, as an ancient monument of 65, I begin to show signs of crumbling. I take it this means that I go on pension round about the date of my 65th birthday, viz 27th March next, but if for a month or two longer my services would materially help matters at the office, I offer them gladly.'

And to Fred Walker: 'And now about myself. I have arrived at a decision concerning official chores and by this post have indicated to the office my wish to retire at 65, that is in March, although I'm not particular to a month or two if, by carrying on, I can be of any special help. Whilst I am yet in possession of my faculties, I feel that the time has come when I would like to employ them in a more leisurely and pedestrian manner and, in my own way, so far as I may, gather in what is left to me of the slow harvest of my dreams.'

January 22nd

AND NOW COMES A LETTER FROM THE CHIEF CLERK, WHO writes, 'Dear Musto, Rae has given me your letter of the 17th inst., so that I can note your remarks as to retirement, and I have conveyed the gist of it to Ranson and the Crown Agents confidentially. I hope you will soon be quite fit again. Yours Sincerely, H. K. Purcell. P.S. Barkis is willing.'

January 24th

IT IS DUSK. I HAVE JUST BEEN OUT IN THE WIND AND RAIN, ostensibly to buy cigarettes, but primarily to get a blow of weather after a surfeit of fireside idling. The urge to recapture quietly exultant joys in the sting of cold rain and the buffeting of wind was strong within me. To lend my head to the sudden squalls and observe the shininess of glistening pavements in the half-light and trace through its long, pencilled reflection the half-screened parent light on the car in the bend of the road in the nursing home and, to give my lame foot a little rest, stand and listen to the hollow gurgle of water as it cascaded over the manhole grating to the drain below. But for a mad half-hour I turned myself inside out that every bit of me might revel with the riotous elements, as in fancy I raced with the stormy clouds, in the enjoyment of complete abandon.

It is dark, the curtains are drawn and, seated comfortably by the fire, I enjoy the booming of the wind without, the metallic whirring of Harry, the revolving chimney cowl, as it speeds up in the sudden gusts ready to fly off at any moment. And the slash and stir of rain on the greenhouse roof as much as when, three hours ago, out in the street, I gladly shared with the elements their rebellious mood. But no longer a hero, I now prefer the fireside and the shelter of home, and the small sounds of domestic activities from the kitchen that lend animation to quietude, and for occupation employ myself with plans for the gardening season, now opening. Already seeds are ordered, and half of my vegetable plot is in trim for the spring sowing and preparations are made for the rest. The ornamental garden is cleared for the spring show, the lawns back and front lined and trimmed, the borders forked and manured and, in the greenhouse, my pensioners are stirring into vigorous life, with geraniums, rock carnations and winter-flowering begonias in bloom. And again my thoughts turn to retirement and the unhurried employment of my leisure in gardening and weaving and other home and neighbourhood activities. And arising out of them, I recall the sharp enemy raid in the dark hours of Saturday morning last, when one of our AA shells, crashing unspent through a neighbour's roof, exploded and blew out the back of his house, took his leg off from below the knee and deprived his aged mother of her lower jaw. I wondered whether, in the circumstances, I had not after all considered unduly my intimations to the office of my intention to retire just now. With my opposite number, Watkins, in the Home Guard, any assault by the madman of Europe would necessarily mean a call to my colleague for active service in the country's defence, leaving my old department without a leader. Such a contingency might be provided for by offering myself at call to maintain continuity of service, in the event of an emergency of that kind arising. I imagine from the tone of Purcell's letter that such a proposal would be acceptable to the office, moreover it would release me of the uncomfortable feeling of abandoning the ring while the fight is still on.

Just before turning in for the night, neighbour Tindle called and handed to me a small book which, with a mischievous grin, he described as a good bedtime story, *The Specialist*, by Chic Sale,* concerning the professional activities of Lem Putt, specialist in elementary sanitation, described by the publisher as 'innocently Rabelaisian'. Anyway, I went chuckling to bed, thinking about the privy expert and contemplating from a new angle the mighty restful joy that is mine at each new day's beginning.

January 26th

RETIREMENT, LIKE SOME INFECTING BACILLUS, SEEMS TO BE IN THE air. Frank's letter this morning tells me that newly elected members of NZ Parliament are insisting on the retirement, at the proper age, of the NZ Civil Service, to make way for more promising and younger men. Except that the war and its manpower needs necessarily alter the gearing of routine in these matters, this is as it should be. As I have sometimes noticed, many older men of the barnacle type, who hang on to their jobs, are merely slothfully greedy and, from a strictly economic point of view, are not worth their pay. With a pompous gravity

* Published in 1930, this is a satirical American novel about a character named Lem Putt who built privies for a living.

they somehow succeed in making a show at their more competent juniors' expense, generally without acknowledgement, and bar the way to promotion. But his reference to 'Dockside conditions and the New Order' is not encouraging. He writes, 'I came home from Liverpool with a sad feeling. The comments of dock overseers on the selfish attitude of dock workers and the careless handling of produce shows how impossible it would be to allow these folk to hold the reins of government. Some pay envelopes there were for men of over £105 for a fortnight's work, and the produce thrown in such disorder on the wharves that it will require re-sorting. The government allows these wages in order to get ships away, but what will happen after the war when these rates of pay have to be passed on to the public?' Of course the public now pays through taxation. But how can such men who, by their showing, are neither Communists, socialists nor democrats, be other than unscrupulous dictators and traitors to boot? A law unto themselves, with a low cunning, they keep within the law yet succeed in blackmailing the community with impunity. With equality as an ideal, he goes on, 'We begin to breed that stunted and envious sort of mind which hates all superiority. That mind is the special disease of Democracy. It will kill us all if it grows unchecked.'

February 4th

IT IS 5.30 A.M. AS I WRITE, THE NUMBER OF AA GUNS STEADILY rises to a fierce cannonade all about us. Overhead I hear the drone of enemy planes, occasionally the doors and windows rattle as the nearby batteries have their turn. But here in the warm kitchen the kettle quietly sings on a peep of gas in readiness for my second cup of tea and, during the interval, I thought the time could not better be employed than in writing friend Goldstein to thank him for his gift of a pint of orange juice, which he sent to me two mornings since.

It's a grand, beautiful world we live in, if only man would let it remain so. But it seems man must fight, and too often, to preserve his place in it. Maybe he will achieve sanity before it eventually becomes dark and cold and uninhabitable. The all-clear has just sounded, at 6.50 a.m. and my two visitors have just departed. It's an unusual hour to receive callers, but at 6 a.m. Nichols and McDonald groped their way along the garden path to my door to see that all was well with Shieling. Friendly neighbours doing a spot of fire-watching, carrying on with duties which, in other circumstances, would be mine. And for a cold, dark, windy morning nothing is more appropriate than a cup or two of good hot tea, reinforced with a lashing of whisky. The morning wears on. I think it hardly worthwhile returning to bed, so perhaps I'll make a start on one or two little jobs I have in mind regarding the greenhouse, and watch the first flakes of snow that come with the dawn, beating down from the north, from within. This is the most wintry day of the year.

February 6th

AND NOW I LEARN WITH REGRET THAT MY CHARMING OLD lady neighbour Rosamund Carter, sister of the art critic A. C. R. Carter, is in hospital recovering from an operation for abdominal cancer. Lady Bonham Carter – I don't know if she is related to my neighbour – once wrote that the secret of life is to grow old gracefully.

February 15th

I HARDLY THINK THAT DESMOND McCARTHY* CAN FAIRLY APPLY his critical faculty to another's attitude to old age with any reasonable prospect of agreement. Although for all life ageing carries the same inevitability, yet I cannot imagine for man any standard attitude to growing old. It is therefore no matter for surprise that in his review of Mr J. Cowper Powys' book *Art of Growing Old* he finds himself in conflict with the septuagenarian author. Expressing his disappointment concerning the advice he seeks in the book for his own case, he proceeds to air his personal views on the subject and, reading both, I find myself disinclined to agree with either. And with my 65th birthday near at hand, how do I feel about old age or its approach? The mirror presents a little man of five foot four, slim, even of boyish build, without being skinny, a little stooping at the shoulders, with a dome-like bald head fringed with thin grey hair; a wide somewhat furrowed brow, black eyebrows over medium-set grey-green heavy-lidded eyes, clear of bagginess beneath, moderately high cheekbones, a somewhat prominent nose with generous nostrils and long upper lip leading to a fairly full mouth, which in repose is firm set, and a smallish chin that is neither weak nor strong. The close-set ears of good shape have rounded lobes. And if the neck is a trifle scraggy, the face, which inclines to pear shape rather than oval, is less spare and healthy of colour, has few lines and generally is a fairly reliable index of the mood of its owner. Hands and feet are small and of good shape, the former expressive and sensitive but now with tell-tale hints of swelling at certain finger joints. The body, by nature active, is nimble in movement with quick responses. An all-weather body for the open

* Desmond McCarthy was the drama critic of the *New Statesman*.

air, it is healthy and trim. And what does it tell me about myself and growing old which might be disentangled from illusion? No. On reflection, it seems that I am my own best critic. In a matter of six weeks I am due to retire. The five months of enforced absence from duty due to my fractured ankle I now look upon as a period of easy transition from active service to occupied leisure, and in thought, I have been mainly concerned with plans for giving effect to a more extended cultivation of those interests which, for long, have been my chief recreation. Yet, growing older, I have seldom considered old age in prospect, even, and not until now have I begun to think about my attitude to it.

As a corollary, old age brings one to thoughts of death, the end of it, but that is merely the finale, not an attitude. Living little in the past, but eagerly in the present and the future, a kind of perpetual restoration of youthfulness seems to have made old age recede at my approach, but of late, perhaps, with a diminishing recession. As I see it, this is the beginning time of leisurely harvest when quality matters rather than speed or quantity. A harvest for happy sharing, and in the sharing achieve a long lease for my capacity for wonder in this beautiful world about us. I take comfort from the growing conviction that the helm is set for the sunrise, 'when night shall be no more'.

February 21st

TODAY I FORMALLY RESUMED OFFICIAL DUTIES ON A SHORTENED day to avoid further risk of injury to my ankle during the rush-hours. I seemed to take my place in the general scheme of things as if the sequence had never been broken. The rhythm of work came easily, and with an added zest I plumped myself into the bench left by another who himself had gone sick and was glad to feel that my return was opportune.

February 24th

FOR AN HOUR OR SO LAST NIGHT ALL HELL SEEMED TO BE LET loose over our village to remind us of the 1941 raids. The fourth raid in five nights this week, although of relatively short duration, it was more intense and vicious than the earlier all-night raids during the Battle of Britain and with the enemy's new technique of illuminating the target and our own for his destruction, the night air is full of light and sound which, because of its sinister import, is not a little terrifying. The red and green lights from tracer bullets soar towards the outer spaces of darkness, the comet-like rocket shells trailing plumes of fire in their wake, the light in the heavens as scores and scores of AA shells burst, the drone and zooming of planes. The whine and shuddering crump of earth-rocking bombs, the blaze of incendiaries, the clink of falling shrapnel. The sound of crashing glass and the clatter of one's own dancing house tiles, a window shattering here and there, all add to the confusion and alarm of these mad, murderous moments. With every minute lived tensely, the experience for most is a nerve-racking strain. Alert and fearful with anticipation, the fear of being afraid is hardly less than the fear of being bombed out of existence, and to sit and wait is perhaps the greatest trial of all.

For my own part, only by occupation is the mind relieved during the terrifying imminence of events, and a word or two over the fence with my neighbour as we fire-watched through this moonlit inferno brought as much comfort to him as it did me; our desultory talk lent a warmth to the spirit that not even the icy north-east wind could chill as we stood in the Arctic air. And looking round next morning before leaving for the office,

I found that he had already replaced, with old sheets of corrugated iron, the shattered glass of his greenhouse roof.

March 2nd

YESTERDAY I FORMALLY TOOK UP MY DUTIES AS SECTOR CAPTAIN 308 under the revised fire-watching regulations, which came into force on the 1st inst. An enemy raid in the small hours following came along to inaugurate the proceedings and supply a touch of reality to the event. At 2.55 a.m., awakened from my catnap by the sound of distant gunfire, I hopped out of my warm bed and, donning the outer garments of my fire-fighting kit, scrambled downstairs in the dim light to my office and, taking out my official log sheet and mobilization board, opened shop almost as soon as the last alert signal sounded. Within a minute or so my good neighbour Ward appeared to take up his duties with me. But there was no local intensity of gunfire and, except for the whirring of falling bombs twice heard in the distance, the event for us was without incident. After looking around outside once or twice we settled down to enjoy cups of tea, and almost before we had finished drinking, the all-clear signal released us for what was left of the night, and bed. Of the small number of enemy planes invading us, the railway official told me that five had been destroyed.

March 15th

NO LAST-MINUTE AFFAIR, SHAVING WITH ME IS A LEISURELY process. My mind, freshly alert, is generally well occupied, and in the mirror I seem to watch myself thinking. My thoughts, as it were, are on parade. A pleasant rhythm attends the process of their ordering not unrelated to the day's orderly beginning. So it seemed this morning when in retrospect I surveyed the 51 years of my working life with never an interruption of employment, and thought of the wealth that my first whole pound a week – paid as a golden sovereign – represented to me, and of the joy of the job as lab assis. and junior demonstrator in the Chemistry Dept of Battersea Poly, which crowned my earlier part-time student years. And I recall with gratitude the fatherly interest of its head, who appointed me his private research assistant. Taking full advantage of the two and a half years of free study this post and an evening scholarship offered, I plunged into industry as assistant work chemist at a textile factory at 30*s.* a week – when I brought into existence the composition for coating Bowden brake wire, still in use – to become in five years its works manager. Another five years of this and I entered into agreement, on a salary and profit-sharing basis, with a Yorkshire mill owner, and for three years managed a subsidiary mill in Leeds. But of business or any other morals I found that my principal had none. Very soon we were at loggerheads and, on the completion of those unhappy years, with the appointment to the Crown Agents already confirmed, I joined their staff as assistant inspector in the clothing-inspection branch.

During the old days in Upper Thames Street the activities of G7 were confined mainly to the inspection of clothing. Its transfer to Millbank and my release from the Army in 1919 pulled the trigger for their extension to include paper and stationery, rope and twine, leather, hardware, surgical instruments, chemicals and drugs and even gunpowder and foodstuffs.

Later, with the help of my old chief, H. M. J. Warde, the only departmental head who displayed any interest in G7 affairs, our section was reorganized, inspectorate grades established, salaries improved and provision made for the appointment of technicians and craftsmen more appropriate to the range and scope of its needs. Now I am retiring, and if for me this chapter is finished, I feel I cannot put the book away without marking the page. Learning, as they say, is ever in the freshness of its youth, even for the old.

March 24th

THREE SPECIAL AND PECULIAR JOYS WERE MINE THIS MORNING. The feel and sparkle of early spring in the sunlit air. The sight of massed almond bloom through the haze of buttercup yellow of riotous forsythia in my garden. The sound of drumming overhead as a woodpecker sought its breakfast. And speaking of these things to the lady at the station kiosk, she said, 'Why, you put me in the country at a bound.' And to my companion on the train, who said, 'I suppose all this will be spoiled by the invasion,' 'All the same,' I replied, 'let us make the best of things while it is good.'

March 26th

VALEDICTION. WITH YOUR EDITOR'S KIND OFFER OF SPACE IN Sub Corona *I am able more generally to address my colleagues of the Crown Agents' office on the occasion of my retirement. It is in the nature of things that to some my greeting must be hail and farewell; to others I say with a full heart goodbye and good luck; to my old establishment friends it is merely au revoir. I am glad to be able to put on record my grateful thanks to my colleagues for their contribution to the goodwill, which over the years has grown up between us – as much through happy service as through personal regard – that it has been my prolonged portion to enjoy. From my thirty years among you I carry with me into retirement the happy recollection of a large part of my working life to which I look back with no regrets and from which I look forward with a serene expectation of joyfully occupied leisure, leavened with the comforting thought that, because of it, I shall be no deserter from the ring while the fight is still on. And to these thirty years, and the opportunities they have offered me, do I owe the quiet harvest which, under providence, is at hand for my gathering, where the validity of spiritual independence is freely and tacitly acknowledged and, say with Robt. Browning, 'Grow old along with me, the best is yet to be. The last of life, for which the first was made.' I take leave of you to continue the journey in my own pedestrian way. WJRM, Deputy Inspector, General Stores Dept, Crown Agents for the Colonies.*

March 27th

THE DOUBLE EVENT OF MY 65TH BIRTHDAY AND RETIREMENT from the office passed off today without undue excitement. My morning post brought me good wishes from those I most regard, my last journey to town was a quietly enjoyable festival of congratulations and good-natured banter from my town-going neighbours. My last official day was occupied mainly with routine duties, interrupted by informal visits from one or other of my colleagues whose handclasps were more eloquent than their words. The Senior Crown Agent sent for me to have a talk about the future of inspection, graciously wishing me a happy retirement. I departed. For both of us it was hail and farewell. During the afternoon the Chief Clerk came to the lab to present me with my last official pay cheque and a banker's draft for my gratuity, which usefully augments my cash reserves, and after a little pleasant conversation left me to my penultimate visitor, friend Metcalfe of the Staff Dept, to whom I returned my official steel helmet, office pass and spare travelling vouchers. Finally my old colleague Fred Watkins, with whom I had worked closely for thirty years, came to enquire my wishes concerning the disposal of a sum of money contributed by my old colleagues for the purchase of some memorial to my liking to our long and friendly association. I shall purchase with it a spinning wheel and a new hand loom for the congenial occupation of some of my leisure in the promotion, locally, of handicraft interests.

And, last but not least, as I passed by his workshop I had a word or two with our friendly old carpenter 'Chips', who was waiting unobtrusively to say goodbye. And so with my parcel of personal belongings, for the last time I passed quietly between the big mahogany front doors and stepped out into the sunlit air of Millbank for my bus to Vauxhall and home. An important day in my life was coming to a close, almost imperceptibly, as a train moves out of a station, but without the fuss of the platform. And arriving at my village, I found Shieling just where I left it in the morning, with a smiling welcome from Bobby.

April 4th

AND TO CONCLUDE THE STORY OF MY RETIREMENT I RECEIVED today a memorial dated 1st April, signed by some thirty of my old colleagues, inclusive of a handsome cheque.

April 20th

'GRIM TALES WERE TOLD OF CHILDREN KILLED BY BLOOD transfusion. Children have been running through our streets begging to be taken in, saying, "I won't eat much and I haven't lost any blood"!' So writes the Odessa correspondent in today's *DT*. A more pitiful or tragically poignant story I have never heard. Of all the evils of the war, for me, it doubly shames the Germans against whom I felt I must vent my indignation.

<u>*Travail of Odessa's Children*</u>

Can we bear the cry of children,
Children of Odessa's dead,
Orphaned lost and hungry children,
Mother Russia's little children,
Begging bread.
Wand'ring homeless, little children
Roam Odessa's streets at dawn,
Fearful yet heroic children,
Mother Russia's little children,
Soldiers born.
Mother Russia's little children,
Yours and mine they might have been,
Seared their souls with nameless horrors,
Which their frightened eyes have seen.
Mother Russia's little children,
Not in vain to passers-by,
Lisp a plea for friendly shelter,
Too stunned and over-worn to cry.
Mother Russia's little children,
Despairing not with naïve appeal,
'My blood is strong I eat not much, sir,'
Still a childish faith reveal.
Let all men avenge these children,
Children of Odessa's dead,
Brave unhappy little children,
Mother Russia's little children,

Begging bread.
The flaming sword of retribution,
Merciless its work begun,
For Mother Russia's little children,
Yours and mine these little children,
Smoking red with blood shall run,
The blood of every monster Hun.
WJRM 20/4/44

May 28th

SINCE I MADE MY LAST ENTRY SPRING SEEMS SUDDENLY TO HAVE leaped into midsummer. May's beginning seems to have flung itself at a bound into the middle of June. The greenhouse thermometer registers 112 degrees, and out here even in this shady corner, notwithstanding my scanty attire, it feels at least 212 degrees! Under the veranda are some hundred tomato plants in pots, and marrow and cucumber plants jostling with boxes of celery and celeriac, kale, thyme, sage and basil, all robust, healthy little fellows waiting for transfer to my own soil, now resembling desert dust. But I console myself with the reflection that the farmer cannot water his acres and, anyway, the hoe is a truly venerable tool. After all, gardening is a specialized form of farming on a small scale, and we must follow the rules. But rain would be most welcome now.

May 31st

A QUIET DAY UNDER A SHADY LIME TREE ON A GENTLE SLOPE overlooking the lake at Kew Gardens. Shadows of leaves dance in the dappled sunlight on the outer fringes of our encampment and long rush blades glisten as they wave lazily to the soft breeze from over the water.

And now as I write the sky becomes overcast and a cooler breeze springs up to silver the foliage of the heat-tired trees and lend a mystical gloom to the lake shadows and a paleness to the highlights. But I have enjoyed this interval of aloneness, in charge of bags and baskets and all that remains of our picnic, while Bobby and her niece Doris and the elfin Maureen are strolling abroad in search of the azaleas, which this season are an unforgettable blaze of colour. But perhaps the most amusing incident of the day occurred this morning, during our bus ride from Kingston to Kew, when a good-natured elderly passenger made room for our little maid that she might get a good view from his top front seat. Assuming from her Yorkshire accent that we were all visitors to London, he proceeded to point out to me various features of interest en route and, finally indicating at which stop we should alight for the Gardens, wished us a happy day. Abandoning my similar programme of entertainment as guide to my guests I hadn't the heart not to play up to the part of a provincial visitor with the rest of my party, and realizing that we were in good hands, was content to remain a spellbound listener. But of Maureen, acutely observant, intelligent, forthright and bewitching, she is an elfin Puck with all the grace and charm that can belong to an innocent little rogue of nine years. She will return to her Yorkshire home with such stories 'as never was' to spellbind her listeners and, from what I know of her, the telling will lack nothing of conviction, and her prestige with her schoolfellows will mount to the skies.

June 6th

TO FRANK, ON INVASION EVE, 1944. THIS IS THE DAY AND THE HOUR is not less dramatic because of its slow unfolding. Heroes in the making during the lagging years at home; heroes on land and sea; winged heroes of the skies; heroes of the Battle of Britain, the Blitz; heroes of the railroad, the merchantmen and tankers, mill and factory; of office and shop, of the farms and mines, of quiet homes, old and young alike; heroes and potential heroes all, are our people of the town and countryside, the man in the street and overseas kinsman, all kinsmen in the cause, in this vast incalculable crusade for the defence of the rightness of right things.

And now as I write, Big Ben, steadfast as ever through these momentous years, calls us to national prayer, and to listen to the King. Tonight we waited expectantly for its tolling. Not so long ago there was in our waiting something of anxiety, of fearfulness, lest in the agony of war it failed us. But, as with St Paul's, it stood, amidst all the desolation, a symbol of the indestructibility of symbols, a steadfast inspirer of hope and faith as enduring, it seemed, as time itself. It is, with all its associations, a National Prayer.

June 7th

I AWOKE THIS MORNING AT DAWN, SOME EXTRA SENSE ALIVE AND responsive to the impact of events across the Channel, but without any ability to give expression to my thoughts. A vague picture of strong men, tired but resolute in a hostile country, where the dull sky is blowing apart, carrying the sword of retribution in the great cause for which they offer and hazard all they have and are in its defence. And in spirit I find myself with them, humbly proud to be of their number, yet curiously ineffective to do aught but pray for the success of their arms and myself carry on with the daily grind. It seems to me that nothing else now matters. All the rest, the petty trivial things of life, are but the unsubstantial vapourings of its conceits. Only the soul remains. Affectionately thine, Walter.

June 22nd

YESTERDAY WAS THE LONGEST DAY OF THE YEAR, AND THE NIGHT the longest ever, or so it seemed. The playful German, grimly amusing, entertained us for twelve hours with a continuous service of his robot planes which, the night through, kept us all tensely preoccupied, destroying all possibility of rest. There were explosions throughout the sombre hours as the doodle-bugs crashed to earth. We remained in helpless suspense until with an all too brief feeling of relief the sinister tail-light of each succeeding horror passed over our village, an omen of evil for the less fortunate beyond. The enemy's flying bomb is a soulless diabolical instrument of war, carrying death and destruction by the violence of its mechanized disintegration when its fuel supply runs out and the 2000 lbs of high explosive detonate at the impact of its crash. For six days and nights in succession have we lived under this Damoclean threat which, to every individual, is a personal anxiety not lightly to be dismissed. The strain of last night's especially heavy going has brought many to the point of confessing their nervousness.

All neighbourhood pettiness dissolves in the fellowship of fear, which not only equates our various emotions but sustains hope. My neighbour, to whom with her two small boys Shieling affords sanctuary these fierce nights, remarked as she disappeared with them through the fence gate into her own garden this morning, 'Thank goodness the Germans have only another fortnight's supply of these dreadful robots.' I hope so, but greatly

...have we lived under this Damoclean threat.

doubt it. And now, internationally outlawed by their own devilish devices of destruction, it seems no qualms of conscience will restrain the Nazis from carrying to a logical conclusion their evil intentions to achieve a final conclusive effort. We must be prepared for their horrible worst. And, for a token, at dawn the thrushes sang as blithely as ever their challenge to the despairing.

July 13th

IT IS STRANGE THAT I SHOULD OMIT FROM MY EARLIER ENTRIES Captain F. J. Walker's* gracious reply to my verses to him on 20 March. Under cover of an Admiralty service envelope came the following verses from him:

Our thanks for your verse are too humble,
And o'er them we have spent quite a time,
We feel though we may take a tumble,
We would like to express them in rhyme.
The metre's all right, so's the rhythm,
I assure you we'll do all we can,
We know of the right stuff to gi'e them
But the trouble is making it scan.
The pen so we've heard has much might
When it's compared to the sword,
But oh, for a poet who with us would fight
And help us to find the right word.
All our efforts at sea have been crowned,

* Captain F. J. Walker, RN, was a hero of the Battle of the Atlantic. Walter had sent him a hero's accolade in doggerel verse: 'Of valiant men and strong. Who with game breeds of the feather, In the fellowship of the free, Care not for the Hun or the weather, When our convoys tramp the sea.'

With more success than on paper we fear,
And our thanks, though in print, so futile may sound,
Are, nonetheless, most sincere.

Capt. F. J. Walker, HMS *Starling*

I can well imagine Captain Walker with a few of his brother officers in the smoke-laden wardroom of one of their little ships, perhaps with a drink or two, scratching their heads over this little problem in versification, and getting not a little fun out of it too, maybe. Whatever its literary merits, their kindly acknowledgement gave me much pleasure and not a little gratification. And now this fine man is dead. He died in hospital on the 11th just after a heart-attack and was buried at sea after a service in Liverpool Cathedral. Only 47 years of age, he was responsible with the ships and aircraft under his control for the destruction of more German submarines than any other officer in the British Navy, being credited with an official tally of twenty U-Boats. Acknowledging his services to the nation, Admiral Sir Max Horton said, 'Victory has been won and should be won by such as he. May there never be wanting in the realm a succession of men of like spirit and discipline, imagination and valour, humble and unafraid. Not dust or the light weight of a stone, but all the sea of the Western Approaches shall be his tomb. His spirit returns unto God who gave it.' Throughout the service on board HMS *Hesperus* in Liverpool Bay, Captain Walker's ensign, tattered and torn from many actions, flew at half mast.

July 24th

SATURDAY LAST BROUGHT US TO THE END OF OUR LOCAL 'SALUTE a Soldier Week'. The area target was £1 million. Occasionally doing duty at the courts for the issue of stamps, I was mostly concerned with publicity matters and had a thoroughly enjoyable time. Drafting the slogans for window display I discovered in myself an aptitude for display writing, so with Indian ink and a poster pen I set to work and soon had an arresting series pasted in the windows and on walls for all to read as they ran:

1. *War Bonds are shares in the best firm in the world – Old England. Buy till you're broke.*
2. *Your front line is here at the war savings counter. You cannot in decency retreat; nor can our lads.*
3. *You are lending money at interest when buying British Bonds, the Germans have to give at a loss. That's not so good, is it?*
4. *Interest on war savings buys things for the bottom drawer. Now, girls, step in and make sure of your dowry.*
5. *Let your bonds pay for the rainy day, that's better than cold comfort.*
6. *There's no man in the Doodle Bug, let not that be said of you.*
7. *To say thank you to our lads at the Front isn't enough.* DO *a thank you here and now.*
8. *War savings certificates are endowment policies in British freedom and the heritage of your children. Take yours out here and now.*
9. *War savings require no coupon – nor do they ladder!*
10. *This war is being won by men and money, not magic.*
11. *The Pharisee passed by on the other side. Let not that be said of you.*

The slogans, which seem to have been much appreciated, have since been used elsewhere.

Among other devices used to attract money from the pockets of the more reluctant was a series of raffles; the gift of a shilling to the Soldiers, Sailors and Airmen Benevolent Fund secured a numbered acknowledgement, the duplicate of which was deported for drawing later, the lucky number entitling the holder to a gift. Of the several prizes – a hand-woven woolly scarf was my contribution to the event – a very useful basket of dairy produce, preserves, etc., and a voucher entitling the winner to a portrait of himself in oils by a very promising local artist were never claimed. Probably the holders lost their tickets or, being casual visitors, had never returned, or seeing that quite a number of local people were temporarily evacuating themselves because of the flying-bomb menace, the tickets went with them, but whatever the reason, it seemed curious that some quite useful prizes should remain unclaimed. Anyway, my scarf having fetched the sum of 53*s*. for the good cause remained unclaimed and in due course was returned to me almost immediately to be offered for sale in support of a relative good cause, held in the village, and found a buyer at 40*s*., realizing altogether 93*s*. for war funds, which I felt was reward enough for my trifling weaving effort. The week was a great success. The target of £1 million was exceeded by £300,000, and per head of population for the area, Esher's was the highest in all England.

July 26th

THIS WEEK COMPLETES FOR ME A TERM AT THE KINGSTON School of Art where I took up a course of hand spinning and weaving. But I was not a little amused during my first interview at the school when its principal, with a twinkle in his eye, gently reminded me that, in entering the class, I might experience something of the embarrassment of a Rip van Winkle among so many very young students. However, the curiosity they at first evinced soon subsided and I early found myself accepted by them on level terms and, sharing with them their difficulties, the sooner I mastered my own.

Altogether it was a very pleasant few weeks I spent with the class and I brought away with me some five yards of a check tweed of my own weaving, which, when milled and finished, I shall have made into a 'lumber' jacket for winter use in the garden.

August 8th

TO ENTERTAIN VISITORS FROM MORE PEACEFUL PARTS OF THE country just now is a responsibility not lightly to be undertaken, and this morning I knew that I had done well to advise Bobby's brother at Muirfield to postpone his holiday with us at Shieling and the agreeable prospects it offered for us all. The relative immunity of our immediate neighbourhood of East Molesey from the Flying Bomb came to an end this morning just after dawn with a reverberating crash that seemed to shake the whole district when one of these horrors fell nearby. Already partly dressed, I sprang from my mattress-bed first to do the rounds of the house – which had suffered nothing worse than the flinging open of already unlatched doors – and admit my opposite number, neighbour Ward, himself still in his pyjamas, who had called for emergency instructions. However, in the absence of any immediate call for help from the adjoining sector, we could only stand by until the all-clear released us from our own. By 6 a.m. I was at the scene of the action, less than ten minutes' walk from home, the trail blazed by the steady mounting numbers of dislodged tiles, shattered windows, burst doors and piles of ceiling plaster and, presently, the wreckage of whole houses with the stricken occupants already sorting from the indescribable confusion of debris such articles of clothing and furniture as were still recognizable. US soldiers from their nearby Hurst Park Camp were first on the scene with every sort of rescue appliance for the succour of victims, closely followed by the regular wardens, WVS, and first-aid parties. It was indeed a sorry spectacle, which, to me, seemed the more grimly ironic because of the bright sunshine of a perfect summer morning as the rescue squads moved slowly to waiting ambulances with the dead and injured. Not the least inconspicuous and useful of the rescue equipment from the camp was a large mobile canteen, which introduced a specially welcome and friendly note into the story with its inscription 'Presented to the US Army by the town of Honolulu, Hawaii', and was supplying much-needed refreshment to helpers and victims alike. Falling between two streets direct on to a double Anderson shelter full of people, it devastated these and wrecked many of the houses in two other streets, turning into a heap of rubble the adjacent homes and making uninhabitable many more. Partly dressed, unwashed and still a little dazed, men, women and children were trying to make something of the wreckage, not moaning about their calamitous experience, and I was proud of my countryfolk's fine spirit. Of two tousled, elderly, half-dressed women in a front garden standing almost knee deep in ceiling plaster, broken furniture, torn bedding, curtains, etc., one, as I passed, said to the other, 'I wouldn't care a damn if only I could find my other skirt.' Later, on my way home to breakfast, I took particulars of damaged roofs, windows and doors in my own sector, to pass on to the authorities for attention when the more urgent matters had been dealt with, myself doing certain small neighbourhood repairs later in the day.

August 25th

THESE ARE GREAT DAYS. HALF OF FRANCE RESTORED TO THE French with de Gaulle as leader. Romania breaks with the Nazis and declares war on Germany. All Italy except the far north freed from the Germans, Poland coming to life as Poland, and Russia on the borders of East Prussia. Yet assailed from almost every cardinal point of the compass Germany fights on in support of what now seems to be Hitler's personal and private war.

September 3rd

FIFTH ANNIVERSARY OF THE WAR, WITH, I THINK, A NOT UNLIKELY prospect of a sixth. Our successful military operations in Normandy have inclined not a few people to anticipate a speedy collapse of Germany, to think that hostilities are almost over, but cornered rats don't surrender and I fear a tough time is ahead – at least on the Continent – before the Germans give up the struggle, however superior the odds against them. The continuing visits of the Flying Bombs, now carried and released by pick-a-back planes, are evidence enough of the enemy's intention of fighting on to the bitter end without regard to unavoidable losses on either side. I think that the final clean-up will be the most difficult and unpleasant of all our operations against them. And I think, too, that the vicar did well at this morning's special service to remind his congregation that the war is not yet won, that if light is at last coming to us in this valley of shadows, we must not relax our efforts until we actually stand upon the broad sunlit uplands of peace only now becoming visible. We have some way to go.

October 8th

REPLYING TO A *SUNDAY TIMES* INTERVIEWER, BERNARD SHAW IS reported as saying, 'Do not deceive yourself, the world is not going to be a new world, you will have to put up with the old one with occasional spring cleanings in which a good deal of the dirt will be swept under the furniture instead of being removed.' Yes, I fear it may be so. In the occasional turn-out and tidy-up of my writing desk, old letters for the most part merely find new hiding places. We are hoarders of habit as well as jailers of junk. And, with regard to post-war Germany, he scornfully remarks, 'All this talk of governing Germany when we cannot even govern ourselves is childish nonsense . . . When a horse is down you may have to sit on his head for a minute or two before helping him up.

'Both horse and man must get up on their own legs pretty quickly if they are to survive . . . Leave Germany to itself and there will be a reaction against Hitlerism as surely as there was a reaction after Cromwell's Major Generals.' All the same, I cannot imagine that this war is being fought in vain, surely two such experiences in a lifetime will not be fruitless?

October 15th

THE SMALL LOOM IS BUSY, THESE DAYS. I HAVE JUST FINISHED light colour schemes with a check design in herringbone tweed, just pattern specimens about a foot square, which are my conception of the 'Liberty' tradition. At least they have secured the approval of several of my neighbours who, perhaps, are less critical than flattering. However, I am posting them to Edmund Hoyle with the suggestion that he might find them suitable for the better end of his business of cloth-making. Anyway, I have achieved a good deal of quiet joy in their creation.

October 20th

SHIELING HAS ABOUT COME TO THE END OF ITS WINE-MAKING. Each of the three brewings has turned out very well and except for 'just a spot' set aside for current use, they are now stowed away for maturing. Already christened, their names are Nocturne, Invernadine Lady and Amber Delight. The first is a full-bodied wine, looks like stout, is pleasant and round to the palate and intriguingly potent. The colour is derived from toasted malted barley of pre-war origin. The second resembles Madeira in colour and flavour and is very moreish and stimulating. It is the vicar's favourite as an after-dinner wine. The last is a sherry-like wine in colour and flavour, with a delicate aroma. Although with less body than the others it is agreeably enticing and, leaving no after-tang, is cleansing to the palate. It is an excellent aperitif. Certainly Shieling vintage has acquired some popularity with my friends and neighbours, even so early in the making. On fully maturing we may expect something really good. It has been a profitable conclusion of a great deal of surplus fruit of all sorts, supplied from my own and neighbours' gardens, and well worth the considerable sacrifice of much of our sugar rations to the brewing. At least we shall have something to offer for the Christmas celebrations.

October 21st

IN HIS WEEKLY *DT* SERMON THE REV. L. B. ASHBY, UNDER THE heading 'Can We Forgive the Germans?', refers to Christ's doctrine 'Love Your Enemies', so frequently quoted by the too-forgiving. How then shall we answer those who would let the enemy off so lightly? To assume a kindly moral superiority over them is not enough. Christ Himself condemned the oppression of the weak by the strong and strongly denounced tyranny. For ourselves to forgive what might be done to us personally is one thing, but to pass by on the other side while a bully beats up a fellow creature is quite another and would condemn us for unchristian indifference.

November 4th

NATTY IN HER OFFICER'S RED CROSS UNIFORM OF SERGE BLUE AND charmingly naïve and natural, Wendy Hoyle, having handed over her five sick evacuee charges at King's X, arrived at Shieling from Halifax last week for a couple of days bringing to it something of the brisk happy freshness of 21 years. Infected by her eager mirthful youthfulness, we recaptured something of our own, which not a little added to the gaiety of the event. There was something in it for Shieling of the joy of morning in early summer when, in a ravishing flowered dressing-gown in red and white, she tripped down in the morning for her second cup of tea and, with bewitching audacity, entertained us in broad Yorkshire with titbits from home. We enjoyed many happy talks together, from which I gathered that she had in her much of her father's sane outlook, of her mother's quiet confidence, but ever lurking in her mind were thoughts of Gerald, her sailor man of the RNR, who on the return journey was to escort her home and formally ask Papa's consent to their engagement. And by this morning's post she writes to say that she has 'a simply beautiful ring with twin diamonds and everything is so thrilling and exciting'. Well, our blessings on their happy beginning.

November 16th

ON THE 9TH INST. MY OLD FRIEND AND COLLEAGUE FRED Walker suddenly passed over and was cremated today, thus terminating a private friendship of 46 years and an official association of 30. He died on his way home from the office after a sudden and acute cerebral haemorrhage, being discovered by two ladies who in the dark of evening stumbled over his body. To be informed by the police of his death, in the circumstances, was a great shock to his family, and with no men at home to help them, a telephone SOS at 11 p.m. enabled me to fill the breach and put in train such arrangements as called for immediate attention.

November 18th

A CAPTAIN IN THE RAC FROM HOLLAND IN WEDNESDAY'S *DT* writes, 'The Allied soldier is living today in the afterglow of his wonderful receptions in France, Belgium, and part of Holland. The memory of these receptions will help to cheer and inspire him through the rather cheerless days ahead . . . Crossing the German frontier, the days of bouquets are over, we are now entering the rotten egg stage.'

Our people at home are only geographically a step behind the men at the front in drawing cheer from such events as the liberation of N. Africa, Italy, France and the Low Countries, not to mention all that part of Russia so recently in German occupation. But as the captain says, in respect of personal dreams, 'And so, to all at home with a clear conscience, may I pass on this recipe for getting through a cheerless winter! Conjure up the joy on countless people's faces; feel the rough embrace of the peasant who runs across the stubble to greet you. Watch them dancing on the streets of Belgian villages; see the tears on the old men's faces as they raise their hats and mumble, "Merci"; listen to the church bells pealing in the hamlet behind you as you pass through on the heel of the enemy, and know you share in it. For in reality, there is on God's earth no tonic like it.' Yes, those of us not at the Front to witness these moving events know in our hearts that we are not unrelated to them, and in thought and spirit share with the liberated the joys of their liberation as we shared the despair of their former bondage. The ecstatic joy of the liberated may fairly be taken as some measure of their past sufferings, but what of the unnumbered tortured and dead? All the more reason, then, that we at home should beware of the specious arguments of the would-be forgiving peacemakers. Atonement must come first.

November 22nd

CELEBRATING HER 84TH BIRTHDAY THIS EVENING, WE PAID fireside homage to our charming old neighbour Mrs McDonald who, with her son, spent an agreeable couple of hours with us at Shieling, entertaining us with lively talk of earlier days. Declaring that she was in the direct line of descent from King Bruce of Scotland we felt that nothing less than the best of Shieling's vintage would be acceptable for a toast of royal dimensions.

November 26th

READING THE DEAN OF CANTERBURY'S BOOK *THE SOCIALIST Sixth of the World*, I find that Hewlett Johnson presents a vivid and absorbingly interesting picture of Russian social, economic and political development during the Stalin regime. In its relation of national minorities to the Soviet general plan, a place has been found for the Jews, that spare bit of our earth's surface to which I referred in my notes of 26/11/43 – a year ago today – in which they are free to achieve, without let or hindrance, national identity and independence. Starting from scratch 'where raw marshes awaited conquest, men and horses foundered in bog and mire tormented by midges and poisonous mosquitoes'. Many gave up the struggle, the majority however remained. Now mills hum and roads pierce the forest. The quartz rocks yield their gold, the mines their coal, the quarries their marble. Within ten years an electric power station, a furniture factory, a saw mill and lime works have been sectioned. The 42,000 acres under cultivation in 1929 reached 100,000 in 1939. The Siberian province of Birobyan is now a Jewish republic about twice as large as Palestine. Jewish settlers till the soil and cultural activity keeps pace with modern advances. One hundred and four Jewish schools and four technical colleges have been opened. The state allotments for the construction of municipal and cultural institutions have increased forty-fold. A new theatre, a new children's music and ballet school, a new park of rest and culture stands where yesterday wild marsh birds flew and beasts roamed. Nationalities mingle and dwell as freely in Birobyan as in any land on earth, for Russians, Ukrainians, Chinese and Cossacks no longer shun the Jew, nor he them. Surely in light of all this, it is not too much to hope that this is the beginning of better and happier days for them, as well as for us.

November 30th

A MODERN CHIRON, THAT GRAND OLD WARHORSE WINSTON Churchill, our Prime Minister, is 70 today and 'is still a young man with a bright future'. That, says Lawrence Hunt of the New York Bar in today's *DT*, is what Americans believe and, I might add, so do we in England. It is a belief partly based on a sure conviction that, of all the statesmen of the United Nations, he can best lead the way to a more decent world.

December 7th

FRANK'S LETTER THE OTHER DAY WAS FULL OF LONGING AND lovely things, exciting and interesting. Anyway, it is not of words that I intended to write but rather to refer to the effect of his letter, which I read over three times during my early-morning tea-drinking. Soon I found myself rummaging for my record of our Sussex tramp, which in turn brought to light 'October in Lakeland' and Nab Cottage, Thomas de Quincy, and dear old Clifford, now at rest somewhere in Flanders, sprinting the last half-mile or so of the twenty for that day to the pub at Ambleside that some restoring drink should be at hand for immediate consumption by the old 'uns on arrival. All day, after reading Frank's letter, my thoughts had a lyrical quality, finding expression, in the evening before a cosy fire in the big room, in Matthew Arnold's 'The Scholar Gypsy'.

Even now this dreary and dark night when, within, the fire glows agreeably and warm, I fancy, so easily, that once more I am away, somewhere, anywhere, walking easily with a friend, reliving those quiet joys. It all seems so real. So as I write I absently turn the pages of *Sweet Thames Run Softly,* here and there pausing to admire Robt Gibbings' beautiful engravings, which adorn his book, the fringed water-lily, the kingfisher, and Newbridge with its mediaeval arches. So I stoke the fires of my longing, and the past, living in the present, gives substance to the future. I doubt not that we shall find the scholar gypsy at the Meeting Place.

December 23rd

OUR FRIENDS ARRIVE FROM YORKSHIRE, RATHER EARLIER THAN expected, but all the more welcome for that. So for Christmas and until the end of December we shall have with us Maureen and her mother and for the period of his Christmas leave her father who, at Shieling, represents the Royal Navy. With the turkey already hanging indigently by its legs from the garage roof, the puddings actually made and partly cooked, the briny ham in soak, the beer made and bottled, and the wine nicely matured, some authentic Curaçao for liqueur, a bottle of whisky, which has travelled from Huddersfield, and something to smoke, Shieling is well equipped for the festive day. Already adorning the walls' plaques and pictures, and especially the shrine, is the well-berried holly and from the ceiling lights in the hall drapes the mystic mistletoe. On the polished mahogany dining-room table stands a fine primula in bloom, supplied by the greenhouse where some twenty more are coming along nicely. The reorientation of sleeping arrangements is completed and room made in the cloak cupboard for the hanging of extra garments. Christmas logs, matured and reserved for the occasion, sawn from the limbs of my neighbour's grand old weeping silver birch, blown down in the autumn gales, await their turn of duty. Our ration of oranges gleams golden in the twilight, where the unaccustomed sight of two lemons makes the mouth water. In the garden basket repose leeks, sprouts, artichokes, carrots, celery and a fat savoy; a couple of tins of Carnation milk brought by our guests supplement most usefully our abbreviated milk ration. On a dish nearby sits the results of a whole morning devoted to shelling the acceptable fruits of our fine almond tree planted eight years ago and under the wardrobe in my cold bedroom – hidden for security reasons – is what remains of our pear harvest in a tray. A last sortie to the shops supplied same-day items such as bread and a spare fruit cake. Our modest silver gleams and the piano is newly tuned. Truly the harvest is at hand to enjoy, and we humbly thank God and our fighting lads.

December 25th

CHRISTMAS DAY. MORNING DAWNS KEEN AND COLD TO REVEAL A heavy frost, which shines everything in sight. Inside, the bedroom windows are coated with ice fronds and exhaled breath becomes an instant vapour. Truly it is a white Christmas. A quietly happy day of joyful celebration and thanksgiving rounded off in the evening by a telephone talk with Frank.

December 31st

AS I SIT BY THE QUIET FIRESIDE MY THOUGHTS DRIFT PLEASANTLY across my active life and I find myself reviewing in retrospect the progression of men and events which, then but little realized, did so much to give direction to those of my interests that have meant so much to the happy and agreeable occupation of my retirement. And if this were not enough, the smiling faces of the seven happy youngsters at Shieling's Christmas Children's Party on Wednesday, in honour of Maureen, our guest now turned hostess, supplied confirmation as authentic as their youthful bloom. It was altogether a delightful event. Here was displayed much unexpected talent in songs at the piano, recitations and dialogue, and classical dancing. Animated by a spirit of friendly rivalry the visitors all put up a good show, which earned for them the admiration of their elders, an equally satisfying tea and the book gifts, which the young hostess graciously presented to each of her guests when, after the usual Christmas games, carriages were announced at 9 p.m.

And I'm not sure that the old 'uns didn't vie with the young 'uns for sheer youthfulness and high spirits and nobody seemed to worry unduly about the freezing night air or the iciness of the flagstones to the garden gate on this wonderful white night of the dying year as they trooped past under the full moon.

1945

January 5th

READING FOR THE SECOND TIME IN QUICK SUCCESSION HORACE Rissin's *New Year Gift Book*, I am more than ever delighted with 'This Plot of Earth – A Gardener's Chronicle' by Massingham, recently published. The author, aiming as I do to make his garden – and home – a self-sufficient unit of production, is appreciably further along the road and I find that much of what he has to say, in both the technical and philosophical sense, is informative and stimulating. In his philosophical, social and moral championship of the rights of man to his land – his plot of earth – he stresses also the spiritual value of its ownership. To keep the land in good heart is his slogan, then 'a garden is many things, a piece of man but also of nature, a textbook of economics, a stronghold of liberty, a means of safeguarding the principle of person, a vent for craftsmanship, a muse of character, a condition of health and philosophical maintenance, a poem and a prayer; in brief a way of keeping body and soul together'.

January 21st

LAST NIGHT AS I PEEPED FROM THE FRONT DOOR BEFORE GOING to bed, a quarter-moon, flooded with mystery, lit our snow-clad village. The ice fronds on the glass of the greenhouse elaborated themselves in shadowy relief on its walls. The plants were strangely erect and very still in their sleep and, standing there in the cold radiance, I felt that I was in some other, weirdly beautiful world.

This morning at dawn the constant drone overhead of heavy aeroplanes flying east reached down to the frozen earth invading my kitchen as I record these notes and I thought of the fine lads within them.

January 22nd

WITH THE GOOD NEWS OF RUSSIA'S ADVANCES ON THE EASTERN Front and the falling back of the enemy in the west after its recent thrust through our lines, and in Asia the creeping paralysis of the Japanese perimeter forces flung back across the Pacific by the Allies, comes in this morning's *DT* the report of President Roosevelt's fourth address from the White House in which he emphasizes the facts of life that have come home to us through this war: 'We have learned that we cannot live alone at peace, that our own well-being is dependent on the well-being of other nations far away. We have learned that we must live as men, not as ostriches, nor as dogs in the manger. We have learned the simple truth: as Emerson said, the only way to have a friend is to be one.' Friendliness is the only salve for mankind's troubles.

January 28th

A LITTLE LATE IS 5 P.M. TO GO WALKING THESE FROZEN DAYS, BUT a week of domestic chores, on account of Bobby's bronchitis, had kept me indoors more than usual and a longing to be abroad admitted of no denial, so out I must go. For some five miles I wandered at the river at Hampton Court. Much of it I had to myself and I enjoyed to the full all that it had to offer. A fisherman told me that, in spite of a blank and frozen day, he felt all the better for the rest and quiet away from his inspection job in a clattering machine shop where speed rather than ability mattered! And later, as I neared the confluence of the Mole with the Thames, 93 million miles away, at eye level, behind an array of stark trees silhouetted against the snow, moving pace for pace with me, was a cherry red sun, big as a harvest moon, sinking slowly below the horizon while a skein of five swans in formation overhead made mellow music with the rhythmic beating of their pinions.

February 18th

ALMOST WITHIN HOURS OF WRITING MY LAST ENTRY THE weather suddenly changed. The snow disappeared overnight and I awoke to a cold drizzle and presently a gale of wind which persisted the best part of a week. I've just come in from a short after-dinner walk with Bobby. In the 'dim out', the countryside is at last coming to life; peace we hope is getting nearer. Perhaps the owls are telling us this in their hooting.

March 28th

YESTERDAY WAS MY 66TH BIRTHDAY. IN THE LIFE OF A MAN THIS tally of years, as written, begins to assume sizeable proportions. But that is not how I feel. Today completes my first twelve months of retirement and I audit the accounts, so what of the balance sheet? Without any degradation of the regular standard of living at Shieling and anything in the nature of a wholly catastrophic misfortune, I may reasonably expect to preserve an economic solvency to the end of my days, whether soon or late. I may look forward to opportunity for the Voltairean cultivation of my own garden, achieving in the process not a few quiet delights twice enjoyed by the sharing.

April 15th

MY DEAR FRANK, WITH THE MUCH INTERRUPTED MORNING NOW over I've been looking over acres of correspondence and, as not infrequently happens, instead of getting down to the job of replying, I have dallied over two or three of your letters, and because of my browsing, I have missed the afternoon post, so this will have to await the morning collection. But I just cannot be hustled, these days. The golden sunshine and genial warmth, drowsy hum of bees invading the open lounge, the sight of massed red tulips towering over the riot of wallflowers set in the midst of my truly velvety lawn, now littered with the confetti of apple-blossom petals, makes of this a dreamy somnolent hour rich in enjoyment. Spoiled only slightly by the tearing, rending noise of planes as they race home low across the sky almost, it seems, at roof height. At least they are friendly. Thank God. And at this moment I would not change the scene for all the Thames or any other delights in the kingdom.

I am still attending the Kingston School of Art, of course, and get a good deal of fun out of it as well as instruction. Only yesterday two of its weaving students turned up at Shieling to see what I am doing here, 'just a two-minute look around, you know', but the Ancient Mariner, it seems, fixed 'em with his eye and they must have been late home for lunch. Anyway, I enjoyed having them. And now two other afternoon-tea visitors have just gone, not a little intrigued by these activities of mine. As I write, the shadows are lengthening on the lawn; the terracotta and green of the old 'forty thieves' jar glows softly in the light of the setting sun.

Soon it will be 9 p.m. and with it will come the BBC news bulletin, and my thoughts turn to that great heart, Franklin D. Roosevelt, now still, for whom surely all the world of friends and foes alike must mourn. Of that great triumvirate, to whose leadership in this global war all free men the world over look for the preservation of their freedom, the American President was perhaps the greatest Democrat and, with Abe Lincoln, the greatest Democrat of all time. A great statesman, wise and kind, perhaps no more simple or fitting epitaph could be inscribed on his homely tomb than that written of a great naturalist, now dead, 'Kindest of hearts, gentlest of gentlemen'. Truly it might be written of him that he was the greatest naturalist of them all. And of his successor, Harry Truman, 'We shall not falter either as a government or as a people in the accomplishment of the ends for which Franklin gave his life.' Brave words for brave days, and brave hopes for a new beginning. But we all must help. Yes, I seem almost to hear, at the twilight hour, the solemn notes of the bugle's sounding 'The Last Post' in his garden of peace in faraway America. Thine, Walter.*

* Roosevelt had died just three days previously, on April 12th, 1945.

May 1st

BOBBY'S 71ST BIRTHDAY SO WE CELEBRATE WITH A VISIT TO THE cinema to see Walt Disney's new picture *Fantasia* in Technicolor. Announced as a strictly scientific conception, to me it seemed the very essence of art. True, every resource of science was used in its production, but surely the inspiring mind was that of the artist, an artist in the living of life, which I imagine is the highest art. Unique in conception and the finest of the author's many wonderful pictures, it presented in a fantasmagorium of subtly co-ordinated music, colour, form and motion the story of life. Omitting entirely the conventional forms of expression, the salacious, and the rest of the crude film technique with which one is so sickeningly familiar, it portrayed through a series of vividly reflected impressions the beginning of earth from a boiling solar chaos to a steaming terrestrial globe and by way of the amoeba in the Paleolithic slime, through the stages of fish, to the beginnings of folklore and pagan mythology. Continuing by way of classical Greece and early culture to the Christian era and, finally to emphasize the ascendancy of good over evil, it throws into relief in a flame-like story the dual nature of man which, throughout, is so skilfully presented as to appear less a sermon than an entertainment.

Not without humour, too, there was something of the comic in the releasing of the waters by Donald Duck, of Bacchus drunkenly revelling in the torrent of wine, which overflowed down the mountain forge in the graceful ballet of the ostrich Pavlova, and the exhausted hippo with his attendant crocodile, or Pegasus on the lofty nest with her young. For the rest, and to the many for whom its symbolism was too subtle, it was magical entertainment and if placed a little above their heads, it could not fail to impress with its colourful mystery and suggestion.

May 8th

LAST EVENING MY NEIGHBOURS THE EGOUNOFFS FETCHED US for a quiet preliminary celebration of the unconditional surrender of Germany on the western front. With just the four of us sitting in their spacious conservatory we enjoyed pleasant, stimulating conversation until well after midnight. Some excellent pre-war Marsala made gladder hearts already glad and the tea *à la Russe* served later was most refreshing. Friendly neighbours always with something interesting to talk about, it is good to have them so handy.

It is 7 a.m. I have just hoisted the Union Jack over Shieling and decorated the front with a string of bunting. The rising sun peeps over the tree tops, shedding a golden light over the village. A thrush perched on a nearby sycamore fills the air with his triumphant song. So I look around my little house standing in its pleasant garden and in a mood of chastened contemplation regard the much that has been spared to me through the war years. In a surge of gratitude for this great dawning of peace over the earth I offer my thanks to God.

For this is VE Day, announcing as complete the formal surrender of the enemy on all European fronts. The day for which so many like my splendid nephew Clifford and many more died, and without whom London itself might have joined Carthage. It is a miraculous culmination to D Day for the success of which we then put our trust in Providence and the valiant efforts of our crusading legions.

I have the impression from a newsreel picture that our Prime Minister looks very tired. It is no small wonder. At 70 years of age to be still carrying with vigour the masterly direction of the Nation's affairs in the greatest and most terrific events of its long history is nothing short of superhuman. As the managing director of the biggest firm in the world his

A surge of gratitude for this great dawning.

services are beyond price. God bless and preserve him for a few quiet years of repose when at last his task is done. In the annals of the human race, no man so richly deserved immortality.

It is late evening. The King has spoken and, after a last stand to in reverent toast of my neighbour guests, I sit quietly to reflect on the day's happenings. And so we slip with the ease of well-conditioned gearing into normal running and the daily routines, secure from enemy disturbance and at night safe in our beds. Our private lives are once more our own. Yes, tomorrow I shall be glad to get back to the chores.

Acknowledgements

Love and thanks to 'those who served'.

To Annette Crossland for her enthusiasm, vision and support to secure for Walter what probably was his goal over all those years of writing these diaries: to be published at last.

To Peggy Gibbard, Mary Covers, Sarah and Stephen Musto and Lynne Woodgate for all the information and time that they gave us.

To Art McCulloch for a vision and supreme conviction that is rare among mortals.

To Lorraine, Ruby May and Matilda Musto for all their love.

CM

With much love and many thanks to the following:

To Chris Musto for trusting me with the discretion of his family.

To Jason Mayall for his encouragement, to Bruno Tilley for all his support and, finally, to M & P and the Harper family, for everything.

AMcC

[illegible]

[illegible] of the [illegible]

[illegible] for which so many

[illegible] bravely died [illegible]

[illegible] [illegible]

and without whom [illegible]

[illegible] and [illegible]

It is a [illegible]

[illegible] of which we [illegible]

and the [illegible]

[illegible]

[illegible]

[illegible]